CRICKET
MILESTONES

THE CRICKETER BOOK OF
CRICKET MILESTONES

ROBERT BROOKE

FOREWORD BY CHRISTOPHER MARTIN-JENKINS

St Michael

This edition published for
Marks and Spencer plc in 1987
by Century Benham Ltd, Brookmount House,
62-65 Chandos Place, London WC2N 4NW

ISBN 0 7126 2663 8
Produced by Lennard Books Ltd
Mackerye End, Harpenden, Herts AL5 5DR

Editor Michael Leitch
Designed by Pocknell & Co
Production Reynolds Clark Associates Ltd
Printed and bound in Yugoslavia

COVER PHOTOGRAPHS

FRONT
Top left Dennis Lillee
Top right Richard Hadlee
Centre W.G. Grace
Bottom left Ian Botham
Bottom right Viv Richards

BACK
Rodney Ontong

CONTENTS

PREFACE
——— 7 ———

FOREWORD
——— 9 ———

1980
——— 12 ———

1981
——— 22 ———

1982
——— 40 ———

1983
——— 64 ———

1984
——— 86 ———

1985
——— 114 ———

1986
——— 148 ———

1987
——— 184 ———

ACKNOWLEDGMENTS
——— 191 ———

PREFACE

In 1979 Reg Hayter, then editor of *The Cricketer,* agreed to publish some short articles by me, which touched upon some recently passed cricket 'milestones'. He declined to give me a contract but suggested I submit monthly offerings and matters would be reviewed at a later date. Time went by, 'Milestones' continued its monthly appearances, Hayter was succeeded by Christopher Martin-Jenkins, there was no further talk of either reviews or contracts and more than eight years later 'Milestones' retains its monthly slot; the one fixed point in an ever changing *Cricketer* format.

It was, however, a pleasant surprise when it was suggested that a 'Milestones' book might be of some interest to cricket buffs. The idea was that I update (and correct) many of the items which have appeared over the years in *The Cricketer* and that I also seek out and research new 'milestones' which have either been passed or have some relevance to recent feats. The result, after several months of pleasurable meandering along the highways and byways of cricket facts and feats is this volume and I hope it gives readers just a fraction of the pleasure its compilation has afforded me, also that it may settle a few arguments and start some more (but friendly ones, please!).

Some words of warning. I make no claims to have produced a comprehensive record book; I am neither sufficiently single-minded nor methodical to produce pages of cold statistics. A feat has to grab my imagination; I lack the self-discipline to embark upon the hard slog of researching something of no great interest to me. In any event, Frindall has compiled as comprehensive a record book as most people are likely to require. I have limited myself to what is 'not in Frindall' — the unusual, the whimsical, even, at times, the

faintly ludicrous.

Allowing for these riders, the reasons for some inclusions may seem somewhat elusive. If some players seem slightly over-exposed, I would not argue. My cricket heroes are, I suppose, J.E. Shilton, Dennis Amiss, Ranji Goel and Steve 'Piggy' Malone. I offer no excuse that the much underrated Amiss is well featured in these pages, nor for the deserved appearances of Goel and 'Piggy'. Even I, however, could find no valid excuse to include Jack Shilton, whose main claims to cricketing 'fame' are that he took another identity to secure an instant birth qualification for Warwickshire, and in 1895 achieved another unique cricketing feat. He is *surely* the only cricketer who had to be bought out of a debtors' prison to play in his own benefit match! I would reluctantly agree that Jack's 'milestones' have no place, even here!

I have deliberately attempted to avoid any controversy; this I am happy to leave to the officers and committee of The Association of Cricket Statisticians. A large amount of important and relevant work has been done by this body, but when we see attempts to alter history, that is where I feel a line should be drawn, and where our paths diverge. I have used traditional figures for W.G. Grace, among others; I see no good reason to change them.

Cricket to me has several facets. The battles of wit and skill, both individual and corporate, and the differing personalities of the participants are sources of infinite satisfaction and great enjoyment. Also to be savoured is the social side; cricket spectatorship or

reporting seems to bring the best out of so many. The company, be it 'exalted' or 'humble', almost always seems to be good. Finally the history of cricket, and its records and statistics; the latter are a vital part of the game but should not be treated too seriously. Certainly the passing of a 'milestone' seems to interest most cricket spectators, whether of the actual or armchair variety, while figures are manifestly important to a game which depends for its results on one team's achieving superior figures to another. But — the figures should be kept in their proper context. The game also abounds in stories of human triumphs and tragedies — behind every figure is at least one human being, and I try to keep all this in mind.

Over the 'Milestones' years I have built up a circle of regular correspondents who advise of my mistakes or suggest new lines of research. Notable among these friends are Mahinda Wijesinghe, Brian Croudy, Phil Bailey, Andrew Hignell and John Mace. I have also received much succour from regular habitués of Edgbaston, my home ground. Fellow cricket lovers such as scoreboard operator Roger Fisher, whose cheery greeting 'Hey, mate' is invariably the prelude to a wickedly difficult or utterly unanswerable cricket query, the Revd. Alan Power — an expert on two Bibles, cricket's and the Other One; John Mayo; Glenys Cunnington, and others whose chance remarks are often sufficient stimulus to plunge me into hours of sometimes fruitless and pointless research. They surely have their equivalents in every county; such people I hope will find something to interest them in this book.

Robert Brooke
June 1987

Robert Brooke has not yet been elected Pope and he is not infallible; but, with the possible exception of Irving Rosenwater or Bill Frindall, he is the least fallible, most painstaking and assiduous cricket researcher in the world, like an Alec Bedser or a Brian Statham renowned equally for his industry and his accuracy.

The 'Milestones' feature in *The Cricketer* was started by my predecessor as Editor, Reg Hayter, and eagerly adopted by me. Statisticians are a notoriously critical breed by nature, but Robert Brooke has been something of a pioneer amongst his fellow-men and in nearly a decade of his statistical features being published in the magazine, his errors or omissions have been countable on one hand.

Robert may not have the imagination of his poetical namesake, but he has, nevertheless, an admirable ability to dig like a mole down some by-way, or even main path, of cricketing achievement and emerge with facts which fascinate the follower of the game.

This unusual book is filled with examples. Each apparently straightforward item rewards a more careful look. How odd, for example, that when the 19-year-old Warwickshire bowler, Chris Lethbridge, got Geoff Boycott out with his first ball in first-class cricket he was, by some unwritten law of precedent, enabling sages like Robert Brooke to write him off as a long-term prospect in cricket of high class. The reason? It emerges from the list of those who have also taken a wicket with their very first ball that the vast majority swiftly disappeared into obscurity. Sure enough, Lethbridge is now a Minor County player, the brightness of that dawn having perhaps dazzled him.

FOREWORD

To show that no rule is without exceptions, there are four first-ball wicket-takers who went on to play Test cricket. If you wish to see who they are you must look to the item concerned. You will then discover that when S.C. Adams got a wicket with his first ball for Northants against Dublin University in 1926 (he took 6 for 32 and also made 87) his victim was a household name: the playwright Samuel Beckett. S.C. Adams himself swiftly faded into obscurity.

Robert Brooke is a patriot who claims to wear a red rose on 23 April despite chronic hay fever, and to abhor the waving of union jacks at cricket matches involving England, not because they might incite violence but because they ought to be replaced by the flag of St George. How he feels when the likes of Mike Denness and Tony Lewis play under the English banner he does not reveal. But he does admit that when Australia just failed to come back from the dead to beat England at Melbourne in 1982-83 he was deprived of recording the fact that their last-wicket pair would have broken the record for the 'most runs added after the fall of the ninth wicket for a one-wicket victory'. Thus his fascination for figures overcomes even his patriotism. Anyone who even begins to agree with him that cricket would not be the same game without its statistics will find the 'milestones' which lie ahead both absorbing and illuminating.

One other appetizer for you. We all know Mark Twain's aphorism about 'damned' statistics, but, generally speaking, figures don't tell lies. Good batsmen score runs; good bowlers take wickets. Therefore I find particularly interesting the list of leading run-scorers and wicket-takers in each decade since 1920. Who would have thought that the three leading bowlers of the 1970s were all spinners, with Bishen Bedi way ahead of Derek Underwood and Intikhab Alam. In the decade before, when English cricket in particular was supposed to be a slave to the medium-paced seamers, Derek Shackleton, the arch apostle of that type, lies second to the off-spinner, Fred Titmus, with a genuine fast bowler, F.S. Trueman, third. Shackleton also came second in the 1950s but the only other non-spinner in the top three of the six decades under review was Maurice Tate.

Is it not extraordinary that Intikhab, a leg-spinner, should have flourished so much as to lie third in the first-class wicket-takers of the world in the first decade to be dominated by limited-overs cricket? Had Abdul Qadir played in county cricket, no doubt he would have fared equally well in the 1980s, despite the modern prejudice against the leg-spinner. The top three over the 60 years were filled by six left-arm spinners, five leg-spinners (including Freeman twice) three off-spinners (Goddard twice) and only four (including Shackleton twice) of medium pace or above.

As for the batsmen, in the 1930s not even Don Bradman could get into the top three, who were Hammond, Sutcliffe and Ames. The first overseas player to make the list is the leading scorer of the 1970s, with another from outside England in second place (though both, of course, got many of their runs in county cricket). An Englishman was third. I shall not spoil all your fun so early in this book by naming them.

Christophre Martin-Jenkins

1980

Majid Khan on his way to more runs in Pakistan, this time during the one-day international at Sialkot in December, 1980.

TWO CENTURIES ON PAKISTANI'S FIRST-CLASS DÉBUT

Aamer Malik, who became the first Pakistani to score two centuries on his first-class début when obtaining 132 and 110★ for Lahore A against Railways at Lahore during the 1979–80 season, was reputedly born on January 4, 1963. He was thus only 17 years 10 days old when he completed the feat, and he became the third and youngest player to achieve it.

N.J. Contractor and A.R. Morris were 18 years 259 days and 18 years 342 days respectively on the first day of their début matches when they also scored a hundred in each innings. Interestingly,

Aamer Malik is not the youngest to score a début hundred, in a country renowned for cricketing precocity; Majid Khan's début 111★ for Lahore B v Khairpur at Lahore in 1961–62 was achieved at the age of 15 years 47 days. It has to be pointed out that Pakistani births are not registered, as is the law in Great Britain. However, there seems little reason to doubt the veracity of the claim on Majid's behalf.

The Indian record for the youngest player to score a hundred on his début seems to be held by R.S. Modi, who was 17 years 35 days when scoring 144 for Parsees v Europeans at Bombay in 1941–42. In New Zealand W.J. Mitchell scored 127★ for Northern Districts v Pakistan at Hamilton in 1964–65 when aged

17 years 66 days.

South Africa's best appears to be T.A. Harris, who was 17 years 112 days when scoring 114★ on his début for Griqualand West v OFS at Kimberley in 1933–34. In Australia B.K. Shepherd's début 103★ for West Australia v Queensland at Perth in 1955–56 was scored at the age of 17 years 241 days, while Sri Lanka's youngest is B.R. Jurangpathy who was 17 years 322 days when he scored 102 for Sri Lanka U23 v Pakistan U23 at Kandy during the 1984–85 season.

The record in England is believed to be 17 years 245 days. The player was G.J. Bryan, who scored 124 for Kent against Nottinghamshire at Trent Bridge in 1920.

Glenn Turner, a great accumulator through the 1970s for both New Zealand and Worcestershire.

A daunting sight for bowlers – Patsy Hendren on his way to the wicket.

Derek Shackleton, a consistent wicket taker for two decades.

GLENN TURNER: THE MOST PROLIFIC BATSMAN OF THE '70s

The 1970s finished on the last day of 1980, though in some quarters this has been 'celebrated' – erroneously – at the end of 1979. A decade runs from the years 1–10 just as the year 2,000 will be the last of the 20th century.

The heaviest scorer in first-class cricket during the decade was Glenn Turner, who scored 23,932 runs at an average of 53.30. Narrowly second was Zaheer Abbas with 23,690 runs (av 49.15) and these two were comfortably ahead of the rest. Heaviest English scorer was Dennis Amiss, with 20,064 runs, the only Englishman with more than 20,000. Turner's total is the third highest for any post-war decade. Tom Graveney's 24,744 (av 45.91) during the 1950s leads the field, and in the 1960s John Edrich scored 23,942 runs (av 47.41).

The most prolific scorer in any specific decade was Patsy Hendren, who totalled 29,601 runs in the 1920s for an average of 60.41. In the following decade Walter Hammond scored 28,663 (61.91) and there can be little doubt that, but for the start of the war, he would have overtaken Hendren. Third on the all-time list is Andy Sandham, who scored 26,855 first-class runs, average 51.94, in the 1920s, a decade in which Herbert Sutcliffe made 25,842 runs and Frank Woolley 25,422.

The only other batsmen to have exceeded Turner's figure in the 1970s are Tom Hayward, 24,398 (av 44.77) in the 1900s and Jack Hobbs, 24,447 (av 60.07) and Phil Mead 24,119 (av 56.35), both in the 1920s. Turner and Zaheer are, therefore numbers 11 and 12 on the all-time list.

BOWLERS

No bowler took 1,000 first-class wickets during the 1970s. The best total for a decade is the 2,230 Tich Freeman took in the 1920s. In post-war cricket Tony Lock holds the record with 1,857 in the 1950s. The best total for the 1960s was Fred Titmus's 1,267. Derek Shackleton's feat of taking 1,546 in the 1950s and again exceeding 1,000 in the 1960s is also noteworthy.

Allan Jones, an itinerant professional.

ALLAN JONES JOINS GLAMORGAN

When Allan Jones joined Glamorgan in 1980 he established a new record of playing first-class cricket for four counties. In 1982 Jim Cumbes equalled the record when he appeared for Warwickshire. With the increased, though not invariably upward, mobility of present-day county cricketers it is perhaps probable that Jones and Cumbes will be equalled before long; even five or more counties for one player is not beyond the realms of possibility. I have compiled a list of players who have appeared for three or more counties in first-class cricket; I date the list from 1873 when it was laid down that no player should play for more than one county in the same season. This rule has been broken on a number of occasions but it certainly made it more difficult for players to adopt the itinerant life – at least until recent years.

Personally one can only deplore any form of a county cricket 'transfer' system; on the other hand, reasonably free movement extended the county careers of Jim Cumbes and 'Piggy' Malone whose early demise would have been a great loss to county cricket.

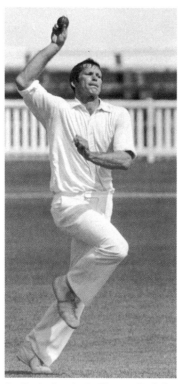

Jim Cumbes in action for Worcestershire before his final move to Warwickshire.

'Piggy' Malone – three counties in ten years of first-class cricket.

FIRST-CLASS CRICKETERS PLAYING FOR THREE OR MORE COUNTIES

Player	Counties/Seasons
FOUR COUNTIES	
A.A. Jones	Sussex 1966–69; Somerset 1970–75; Middlesex 1976–79; Glamorgan 1980–81
J. Cumbes	Lancs 1963–71; Surrey 1968–69; Worcs 1972–81; Warwicks 1982
THREE COUNTIES	
R. Berry	Lancs 1948–54; Worcs 1955–58; Derbys 1959–62
J. Birkenshaw	Yorks 1958–60; Leics 1961–80; Worcs 1981
A. Blackman	Surrey 1878; Kent 1879–80; Sussex 1881–87
J.B. Bolus	Yorks 1956–62; Notts 1963–72; Derbys 1973–75
T.W. Cartwright	Warwicks 1952–69; Somerset 1970–76; Glamorgan 1977
T.G.O. Cole	Lancs 1904; Derbys 1913; Somerset 1922
G.B. Cuthbertson	Sussex 1920; Middlesex 1921–27; Northants 1935–38
W.R. Genders	Derbys 1946; Worcs 1947–48; Somerset 1949
J.S.B. Gentry	Hants 1919; Surrey 1922–23; Essex 1925
S.S. Harris	Gloucs 1902; Surrey 1904; Sussex 1919
W.C. Hedley	Kent 1888; Somerset 1892–1904; Hants 1905
M. Hill	Notts 1953–65; Derbys 1966–67; Somerset 1970–71
R.D.V. Knight	Surrey 1968–70 & 1978–84; Gloucs 1971–75; Sussex 1976–77
A.P. Lucas	Surrey 1874–82; Middlesex 1883–88; Essex 1894–1907
L.L. MacFarlane	Northants 1979; Lancs 1982–84; Glamorgan 1985
S.J. Malone	Essex 1975–78; Hants 1980–84; Glamorgan 1985
C.R.N. Maxwell	Notts 1936–39; Middlesex 1946; Worcs 1948–51
J. Mercer	Sussex 1919–22; Glamorgan 1923–39; Northants 1947
W.T. Nevell	Middlesex 1936–38; Surrey 1939; Northants 1946–47
R.M. Prideaux	Kent 1960–61; Northants 1962–70; Sussex 1971–73
F.E. Rumsey	Worcs 1960–62; Somerset 1963–68; Derbys 1970
W.G.M. Sarel	Surrey 1904–09; Kent 1912–14; Sussex 1919–21
M.W.W. Selvey	Surrey 1968–71; Middlesex 1972–82; Glamorgan 1983–84
A.C. Shirreff	Hants 1946–47; Kent 1950–56; Somerset 1958
F.H. Sugg	Yorks 1883; Derbys 1884–86; Lancs 1887–99
R. Swetman	Surrey 1954–61; Notts 1966–67; Gloucs 1972–74
N.S. Taylor	Yorks 1982–83; Surrey 1984–85; Somerset 1986
I.R. Watson	Middlesex 1969; Northants 1971; Hants 1973
W.C. Wheeler	Middlesex 1873; Surrey 1875; Hants 1878–80
B. Wood	Yorkshire 1964; Lancs 1966–79; Derbys 1980–83
G.N. Wyatt	Gloucs 1873–76; Surrey 1877–79; Sussex 1883–86
Younis Ahmed	Surrey 1965–78; Worcs 1979–83; Glamorgan 1984–86

EIGHT LBWs IN OXFORD INNINGS

Two new records were set up in the Oxford University v Warwickshire match at Oxford in 1980. The total of eight lbw dismissals in the Oxford second innings beats the previous record of seven in an innings, held jointly by four teams: Patiala v Delhi at Patiala, 1953–54; Sussex v Glamorgan, Swansea, 1954; Sussex v Glamorgan, Hove, 1967, and Northamptonshire v Essex at Northampton, 1979.

Oxford suffered 12 lbws in the match. This beats the previous record for one side in a first-class match: 11, held jointly by Patiala in 1953–54 and Northamptonshire in 1979 in the matches mentioned above.

J.W. Hearne, second only to W.G. Grace.

PROCTER REACHES PERSONAL MILESTONE

During the match between Gloucestershire and Essex at Gloucester M.J. Procter reached a total of 20,000 runs and 1,000 wickets in first-class cricket. Procter is the 20th player to reach this all-round milestone but the 353 games he took were the third fewest. Only W.G. Grace (262 games) and J.W. Hearne (326 games) were quicker to the target in the number of games played. G.S. Sobers (363 games) is fourth on the list.

Mike Procter – a place among the great all–rounders.

15

Alan Jones of Glamorgan obtained the first and only double century of his first-class career against Hampshire at Basingstoke in 1980. It was Jones's 1022nd first-class innings and 564th match. This first beat the record of Yorkshire's David Denton whose first double century, in 1912, came in his 947th innings (and he obtained another a couple of weeks later). Denton still holds the record for the number of

LONG AWAITED DOUBLE CENTURY FOR ALAN JONES

matches – 602.

Although challenging no–one, Clive Radley of Middlesex achieved note when scoring his first double century in

1985 in his 514th match and 819th innings. A small number of recognized batsmen have played more innings than Jones without a double century, D.B. Close's 1,223 being the highest number. Jones was 42 years 232 days old, Radley 41 years 73 days. The oldest player to achieve a maiden double century was Joe Vine of Sussex, who scored 202 in 1920 aged 45 years 93 days.

Brian Close, 52 centuries but never passed the 200 runs mark.

Alan Jones on his way to a single century against Cambridge Univ. in 1982.

TITMUS RECALLED FOR MIDDLESEX

When F.J. Titmus played for Middlesex against Yorkshire at Scarborough he equalled the record of W. Rhodes in playing County Championship cricket in five decades – taking a decade as running from the years 0–9. Rhodes played in every decade from the 1890s to the 1930s, Titmus from the 1940s to the 1980s. Titmus also became the 17th player to play in any form of first-class cricket in five decades since the end of the 18th century, though until the 1850s it was difficult to decide which matches should count as first-class.

Only one player has appeared in first-class cricket in six decades. C.K. Nayudu made his first-class début for Hindus v Europeans in the 1916 Bombay Quadrangular Tournament and made his last appearance for a Governor's XI against a Chief Minister's XI in an Indian Defence Fund match at Nagpur in November 1963. This was classed as a first-class friendly match even though several players previously retired from normal cricket, such as G.S. Ramchand, N.B. Amarnath and M.H. Mankad, appeared, while there was also a case of father and son – the Mankads – playing on opposite sides, but the figures are included in first-class records, so Nayudu's feat must stand.

In Test cricket Rhodes is the only player to have played in five decades – a record likely to remain for all time. It may be worth noting that, technically, a decade runs from 1–10. If this were to be adhered to, a number of players would lose their five-decade record of appearances, and there would be a number of additions. Although Titmus himself ensured classification either way when he came out of retirement again in 1982 to play for Middlesex against Surrey.

F.J. Titmus, whose County Championship appearances in 29 seasons was already a Middlesex record, took the total to 30 seasons and his 31 seasons in first-class county cricket (for more than one county) took him into second place ahead of W.G. Quaife, W.G. Grace and W.E. Astill. A.N. Hornby, 33 seasons for Lancashire (1867–99), holds this record, although Titmus closed the gap with his re-appearance in 1982.

F.J. Titmus finished the season having bowled 172,364 balls in his first-class career. This places him second behind W. Rhodes, who holds the record with 184,890 balls. C.W.L. Parker lies third and J.T. Hearne fourth. Titmus has bowled 9,086 six-ball maiden overs during his first-class career, placing him first on the all-time list. W. Rhodes lies second.

Fred Titmus, right, whose appearance for Middlesex in 1980 extended his first-class career ahead of the legendary W.G. Grace.

BOYCOTT TOPS HOBBS FOR CONSISTENCY

The record for averaging more than 50 in consecutive seasons is held by G. Boycott of Yorkshire who achieved this feat in 11 consecutive seasons, 1970–80. Boycott's total in 1980 saw him overtake Jack Hobbs (10 between 1924–33). Boycott's fellow Yorkshireman, Herbert Sutcliffe, is third on the list with eight (1925–32), one ahead of Len Hutton and W.G. Grace.

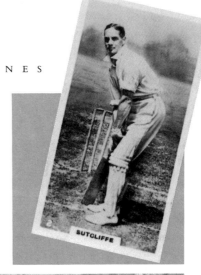

Geoff Boycott's consistency was the result of hours of practice in his spare moments. Here he is seen on a concrete strip during the West Indies tour of 1981.

RECORD SCORE FOR WESSELS

K.C. Wessels's 254 for Sussex v Middlesex at Hove in 1980 is the highest score by a South African in English first-class cricket, beating the 251 made by D.P.B. Morkel for Sir Julien Cahn's team v South America at West Bridgford in 1932. The previous best in county cricket by a South African was 246 by C.E.B. Rice for Notts v Sussex at Hove in 1976. Wessels's innings was also the highest score for Sussex for 47 years and the highest score at Hove in any first-class cricket since 1937.

Kepler Wessels during his record-breaking innings for Sussex against Middlesex. Paul Downton is the wicket-keeper.

D.P.B. Morkel, a South African Test cricketer between the wars.

19

1981

JACKMAN AND ATHEY CALLED UP FOR DUTY IN THE WEST INDIES

The selection of Robin Jackman and Bill Athey as replacements for Bob Willis and Brian Rose on the West Indies tour repeated a process which has become commonplace on English Test tours, and in fact utilization of players not originally in the tour party has been a feature of English tours throughout history. There follows a list of the chief instances.

A HISTORY OF REPLACEMENTS

Season	Tour of	Player/Achievements
1886–87	Australia	R. Wood (Victoria, ex-Lancs) deputized for W. Barnes. One Test: 6 runs (6.00).
1907–08	Australia	G. Gunn (Notts) brought in for A.O. Jones (taken ill). All Tests: 462 runs (51.33).
1922–23	S. Africa	G.B. Street (Sussex) replaced W.H. Livsey (Hants) (injured). One Test: 11 runs (11.00).
1929–30	W. Indies	W.F.F. Price (Middlesex) for R.T. Stanyforth (injured). No Tests.
1930–31	S. Africa	H.W. Lee (Middlesex) – coaching in South Africa – deputized for A. Sandham (injured in motor accident). One Test: 19 runs (9.50).
1936–37	Australia	T.H. Wade (Essex) – on holiday – deputized in several matches. Awarded tour colours but no Tests.
1947–48	W. Indies	L. Hutton (Yorks) – first to fly out. Two Tests: 171 runs (av. 42.75). Topped first-class averages: 578 runs (64.22).
1950–51	Australasia	R. Tattersall and J.B. Statham (Lancs) flew out late in tour. Tattersall three Tests: 8 wkts (19.50). Statham, one Test: 1 wkt.
1951–52	India	E. Leadbeater (Yorks) replace A.E.G. Rhodes (injured). Two Tests: 40 runs (20.00) 2 wkts (109.00).
1958–59	Australasia	E.R. Dexter (Sussex), J.B. Mortimore (Gloucs). Dexter, four Tests: 160 runs (26.67), 3 wkts (8.67). Mortimore, three Tests: 75 runs (25.00), 3 wkts (44.00)
1959–60	W. Indies	J.M. Parks (Sussex). Two matches: two centuries; one Test: 144 runs (144.00), 1 ct, 2 st.
1961–62	India & Pakistan	J.G. Binks (Yorks) for J.T. Murray (injured). No Tests.
1963–64	India	P.H. Parfitt (Middlesex) and M.C. Cowdrey (Kent). Parfitt, three Tests: 192 runs (64.00). Cowdrey, three Tests: 309 runs (103.00).
1964–65	S. Africa	K.E. Palmer (Somerset) was coaching in S. Africa. One Test: 10 runs (10.00), 1 wkt (189.00). No other matches.
1965–66	Australasia	B.R. Knight (Essex) for J.D.F. Larter (injured). Four Tests: 64 runs (16.00), 11 wkts (32.27).
1967–68	W. Indies	G.A.R. Lock (W. Australia). Two Tests: 94 runs (31.33), 4 wkts (53.00).
1968–69	Pakistan	C. Milburn (Northants). One Test: 139 runs (139.00). No other match.
1970–71	Australia	R.G.D. Willis (Surrey) for A. Ward (injured). Four Tests: 12 wkts (27.42).
1974–75	Australasia	M.C. Cowdrey (Kent) and B. Wood (Lancs) for D. Lloyd (injured). Cowdrey, five Tests: 165 runs (18.33). Wood: One Test: 33 runs (16.50).
1977–78	Pakistan & New Zealand	C.T. Radley (Middlesex) for J.M. Brearley (injured). Two Tests: 173 runs (86.50).
1978–79	Australia	D.L. Bairstow (Yorks) for R.W. Tolchard (injured). No first-class matches.
1980–81	W. Indies	R.D. Jackman (Surrey) and C.W.J. Athey (Yorks) for R.G.D. Willis and B.C. Rose (both injured). Jackman two Tests: 14 runs (4.66) 6 wickets (33.00). Athey two Tests: 7 runs (1.75).
1983–84	New Zealand	A.C.S. Pigott (Sussex) – playing and coaching in Wellington – replaced G.R. Dilley (injured). One Test.
1984–85	India	J.P. Agnew (Leics) went as general replacement. No Tests.
1985–86	W. Indies	W.N. Slack (Middlesex) for M.W. Gatting (injured). Two Tests: 62 runs (15.50).

Jim Parks and Colin Cowdrey (top) both of whom were remarkably successful after receiving a late call to join the England party in the West Indies and India respectively.

Robin Jackman (above right) in action during the West Indies tour of 1981 and Bill Athey (above left) who spent more time in the nets on that tour than he did in the middle.

MIDDLESEX FIELD ALL TEST TEAM

In their first county match of the 1981 season, against Essex, Middlesex fielded a team consisting of 11 Test players. It was the first time this had happened in the 104-year history of Test cricket. The history-making players were J.M. Brearley, G.D. Barlow, R.O. Butcher, P.R. Downton, P.H. Edmonds, J.E. Emburey, M.W. Gatting, C.T. Radley and M.W.W. Selvey (all England), W.W. Daniel (West Indies) and J.R. Thomson (Australia).

This particular record has had a slow and somewhat erratic progression as we shall now see.

When Yorkshire opened their 1877 first-class programme against Middlesex at Lord's their England players, having only just returned from Australia, were absent. For the next game, against Surrey at Sheffield, two of the five, Alan Hill and Andrew Greenwood, were still absent for

various reasons. However, the following week against Notts at Trent Bridge all five were in the team and a new record was created. The players were: T. Armitage, T. Emmett, A. Greenwood, A. Hill, G. Ulyett. Interestingly, Yorkshire lost the match.

They played in subsequent matches together but not until 1883 did Middlesex and Notts equal their record, and it was another two years before Notts beat it.

In the winter 1884–85 W. Attewell and W. Flowers had made their Test débuts and in the opening game of the 1885 season, v Sussex at Trent Bridge they joined four other Test players to achieve a new record of six. The players were: W. Attewell, W. Barnes, W. Flowers, J. Selby, W.H. Scotton, A. Shaw.

They helped to ensure a comfortable win, and in the next game, v Surrey, England's touring skipper Arthur Shrewsbury joined the team to bring the Notts Test representation up to a new record

of seven – yet they could only ensure a draw. They did, however, appear together successfully in subsequent matches.

Notts were very strong in the 1880s and they commenced the 1887 season with nine Test players among their probables, so it was no surprise that they achieved a new record when eight of them appeared together against Middlesex at Lord's. The players were W. Attewell, W. Barnes, W. Flowers, W. Gunn, W.H. Scotton, J. Selby, M. Sherwin, A. Shrewsbury. It was also no surprise when they won overwhelmingly. In the following match the record was equalled, A. Shaw replacing Selby.

Surrey were the next county to equal the record, employing eight Test men against Notts in 1895, and Yorkshire came into the picture in 1899, but there was then a gap of 25 years before Lancashire brought a new element into things when their eight Test players against Yorkshire at Old Trafford in 1924 included the Australian E.A. Macdonald. Lancs again achieved eight in 1925 while Middlesex and Yorkshire did so on occasions in the 1930s. Then at last, in 1939, after several near misses, Yorkshire took the field against Notts at Trent Bridge with nine Test players – all English, naturally – and had much the better of a rain-ruined draw. The nine were: W. Barber, W. Bowes, L. Hutton, M. Leyland, A. Mitchell, H. Sutcliffe, H. Verity, A. Wood, N.W.D. Yardley.

The same players played together several times in 1939 but it was not until 1953 that the record was equalled, Lancashire using nine Test players in two late matches. Yorkshire themselves equalled the record on a number of occasions in the 1960s, but it was finally beaten in 1972 – the new record-holders being the champions-elect, Warwickshire. For better or worse they took the field against Leics at Leicester in August with the following ten Test players: D.L. Amiss, D.J. Brown, J.A. Jameson, A.C. Smith, M.J.K. Smith, R.G.D. Willis (all England) and L.R. Gibbs, A.I. Kallicharran, R. Kanhai, D.L. Murray (West Indies). Ironically they had much the worse of a draw and their one non-Test player, N.M. McVicker, was the most successful bowler!

The general increase in overseas players in county cricket seemed to make an all-Test-player side inevitable but to the start of 1981 even Warwickshire's score had not been equalled. The imminent reduction in overseas players makes it most unlikely that any other county will, in the future, be in a position to equal Middlesex, who repeated the feat in several matches during the 1981 season, but never subsequently.

The 1981 Middlesex squad at the beginning of the season. Wayne Daniel is the only Test player missing from this team photo.

A Yorkshire team from 1938, minus Bill Bowes but containing seven of those Test players who took the field at Trent Bridge the following year. Standing, left to right: W. Barber, W. Ringrose (scorer), E.P. Robinson, T.F. Smailes, H.S. Hargreaves, H. Verity, L. Hutton, B. Heyhirst (masseur), C. Turner. Seated: A. Wood, H. Sutcliffe, A.B. Sellers (captain), M. Leyland, A. Mitchell.

BOYCOTT IS FIRST-BALL VICTIM FOR NEW WARWICKS ALL-ROUNDER

When Christopher Lethbridge, Warwickshire's 19-year-old Wakefield-born all-rounder, took the wicket of Geoff Boycott with his first ball on his first-class début in 1981 he became the first player to perform the feat for the county. H.J. Roberts actually took two wickets in his début over, against Middlesex at Edgbaston in 1932, but they came with his third and fourth balls.

Lethbridge joined a not-very-long list of players who have performed this feat. An interesting feature of the list is the unarguable fact that few of the first-ball bowlers enjoyed a 'career' in county cricket, though notable exceptions were Dick Barlow, Colin Blythe, Bill Copson and 'Sam' Cook. Another peculiar feature is that the 'victims' are by a considerable degree a far more accomplished group of players, to which Boycott is a fairly typical addition.

A final interesting point is the slightly eccentric look of the list. Sidney Adams's victim in 1926 played little cricket, finding that writing such plays as *Waiting for Godot* was far more rewarding, while Joe O'Gorman, conqueror in 1925 of the Glamorgan 'dandy' William Edric Bates, had a successful music-hall act with his brother Dave. Then there was A.E. Waters, who dismissed T.R. Morgan in 1923, and who was himself victim of R.H. Sharp two years later. Waters played only 16 games in all. Finally – why are Yorkshire players so susceptible to first balls, Boycott being the fifth out of 25?

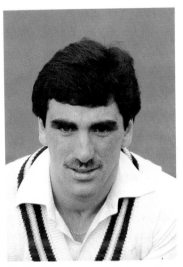

Chris Lethbridge – a memorable first ball in first-class cricket.

FIRST-BALL WICKET-TAKING DÉBUTANTS IN ENGLISH FIRST-CLASS CRICKET

Bowler/Victim	Match/Venue	Season
H. Stubberfield/W. Mortlock	Sussex v Surrey, Brighton	1857
G.P. Greenfield/E. Willsher	Gents v Players of South, The Oval	1866
R.G. Barlow/J. West	Lancs v Yorks, Sheffield	1871
G. McCanlis/A. Freeman	Kent v Surrey, The Oval	1873
[1]J.J.A. Parfitt/G. Ulyett	Surrey v Yorks, The Oval	1881
A.H. Grace/W. Newham	Gloucs v Sussex, Hove	1886
G. Waller/E.J. Lock	Yorks v Somerset, Sheffield	1893
M. Berkley/E. Wainwright	Essex v Yorks, Halifax	1894
[2]T. Lancaster/C.W. Wright	Lancs v Notts, Manchester	1894
H.G. Curgenven/F.L. Fane	Derbys v Essex, Leyton	1896
C. Blythe/F. Mitchell	Kent v Yorks, Tonbridge	1899
J.H.S. Hunt/P.R. Johnson	Middlesex v Somerset, Lord's	1902
L. Cook/C.P. McGahey	Lancs v Essex, Old Trafford	1907
C. Thorneycroft/A.P. Day	Northants v Kent, Catford	1907
[3]G. de L. Hough/J. G. Dixon	Kent v Essex, Leyton	1919
T.H. Collins/J.H. King	Notts v Leics, Trent Bridge	1921
[4]J. John/A.E.S. Rippon	Glamorgan v Somerset, Cardiff	1922
A.E. Waters/T.R. Morgan	Gloucs v Glamorgan, Cheltenham	1923
R.H. Sharp/A.E. Waters	Essex v Gloucs, Leyton	1925
[5]S.C. Adams/S.B. Beckett	Northants v Dublin U., Northampton	1926
J.G. O'Gorman/W.E. Bates	Surrey v Glamorgan, The Oval	1927
W.H. Copson/A. Sandham	Derby v Surrey, The Oval	1932
C. Cook/J.O. Newton-Thompson	Gloucs v Oxford U., Oxford	1946
E.W. Tilley/A.E. Alderman	Leics v Derbys, Derby	1946
[6]J. Lee/A.H. Dyson	Leics v Glamorgan, Cardiff	1947
G.A. Robertson/N.H. Rogers	Cambridge U. v Hants, Cambridge	1950
[7]F.C. Brailsford/E.R. Dexter	Derbys v Sussex, Derby	1958
[8]C. Lethbridge/G. Boycott	Warwicks v Yorks, Edgbaston	1981

WILLS'S CIGARETTES.

C. BLYTHE (KENT).

Notes

[1] His first three wickets were Test players: G. Ulyett, T. Emmett, E. Peate.

[2] Figures of 7–54 included the wickets of W. Gunn, W. Flowers, W. Attewell, A. O. Jones.

[3] This was Hough's only first-class wicket. He also scored 87 not out.

[4] His only first-class match.

[5] Took 6–32 and scored 87. The match was only marginally first-class.

[6] His only wicket in his only first-class match.

[7] His only wicket and only bowling spell in first-class cricket. Figures were 2 overs, 1 maiden, 2 runs, 1 wicket.

[8] Scored 69 in his only innings – the third highest début score for 'first ballers'. Also, at 19 years old, he is the youngest in the list. R.G. Barlow and C. Blythe were aged 20.

FIRST CENTURY FOR BOB TAYLOR AFTER 22 SEASONS

In 1981 Bob Taylor obtained his maiden first-class century for Derbyshire against Yorkshire at Dore (Abbeydale Park) which is uniquely a ground used for home matches at some time by both participants. Apart from the personal satisfaction which scoring his maiden hundred in his 40th year must have afforded Taylor, the innings contained several interesting and peculiar, if somewhat esoteric, statistical features.

Taylor passed his first milestone long before completing his century. When 19 he passed Tony Lock's career total of 10,342 runs, so becoming the highest-scoring first-class cricketer not to record a century. 'Unfortunately', on completing his hundred Taylor returned the record to Lock, who seems certain to retain his lead for a considerable time. The leaders are now as follows.

Player	Runs	Best Score
G.A.R. Lock (Surrey, Leics, W. Australia)	10342	89
D. Shackleton (Hants)	9574	87*
R.T.D. Perks (Worcs)	8956	75
C.W.L. Parker (Gloucs)	7951	82

Another record Taylor beat on passing Lock's career total was the highest number of runs without a hundred in a full or part career. Taylor finally reached 10,423 runs without a century and is therefore 81 ahead of Lock. Third on the list is A.C. Smith, who scored two hundreds against Hants in 1959 but for the remainder of his career never scored another century while making a further 9,599 runs. Derek Shackleton and Reg Perks, with career totals of 9,574 and 8,956 runs respectively follow Smith, while next comes Geoff Miller with 8,610 runs before he reached his first century in 1984. He is followed by George Reuben Cox, whose 122 for Sussex against Cambridge in 1911 was the second and last hundred of a career which stretched until 1928 and involved 8,449 further runs.

Taylor gained two records on completing his century. His

The end of another Tony Lock innings. Wicket-keeper Deryck Murray and skipper Gary Sobers celebrate his departure on the fourth day's play of the Fourth Test Match at the Queen's Park Oval in 1968.

Bob Taylor in aggressive mood against Yorkshire in 1980; he had to wait another year for his first century.

hundredth run was the 10,424th of his career, thus passing A.H.H. Gilligan, whose first and only century was the 7,064th of his career. The leaders in this list are:

Player	Runs before first 100	Year
R.W. Taylor (Derbys)	10423	1981
G. Miller (Derbys)	8610	1984
A.H.H. Gilligan (Sussex)	7063	1929
W. Attewell (Notts)	6918	1897
G.S. Boyes (Hants)	6097	1936
A.S. Brown (Gloucs)	5889	1965

Secondly, though many have had longer careers without even one century, Taylor, in waiting 22 seasons before recording his first, shattered every previous record. J.T. Rawlin of Middlesex in 1899, and William Attewell, both achieved their maiden century in their 17th season and they are far ahead of anyone else.

W. Attewell and J.T. Rawlin (top), previous joint holders of the record captured by Bob Taylor.

Geoff Miller who came so near to a first century during the Second Test match against India in 1982.

HUMPAGE JOINS THE ELITE

Geoff Humpage's fine season in 1981 was, perhaps, even better than generally realized. Averaging 50.03 for his 1,701 runs, he is only the fourth recognized wicket-keeper ever to average more than 50 for a full English first-class season.

FOREMOST KEEPER-BATSMEN

Player	Runs	Av'ge	Season
L.E.G. Ames (Kent)	2482	(57.72)	1932
L.E.G. Ames (Kent)	3058	(58.80)	1933
L.E.G. Ames (Kent)	2113	(57.10)	1934
C.L. Walcott (W Indies)	1674	(55.80)	1950
J.M. Parks (Sussex)	2313	(51.40)	1959
G.W. Humpage (Warwicks)	1701	(50.03)	1981

Les Ames, still the most successful wicket-keeper/batsman.

More runs for Geoff Humpage during 1981.

RICE'S RARITY

When Clive Rice scored 105★ for Nottinghamshire in 1981 against Hampshire at Bournemouth, the Notts total of 143 broke the record for the lowest all-out score to contain a century in first-class cricket. It is in fact extremely rare for a total of 160 or less to include a century, and there follows a list of all instances traced.

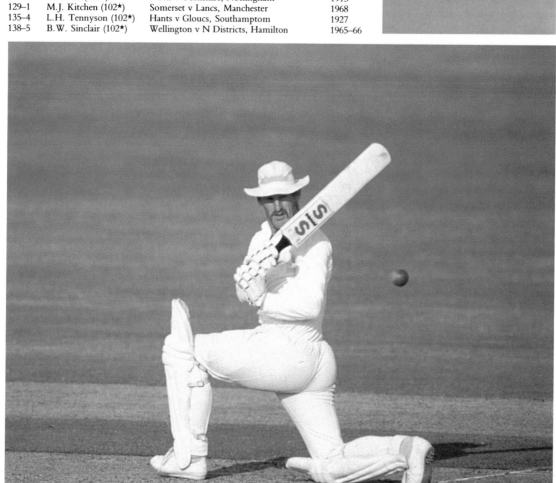

LOWEST ALL-OUT SCORES TO CONTAIN A CENTURY

Total	Player	Match/Venue	Season
143	C.E.B. Rice (105★)	Notts v Kent, Bournemouth	1981
144	F.E. Woolley (103★)	Kent v Warwicks, Folkestone	1931
148	R.P. Meherhomji (100)	Parsees v Europeans, Bombay	1907–08
153	T.W. Graveney (100)	Gloucs v Essex, Romford	1956
156	G.M. Emmett (104★)	Gloucs v Oxford U, Oxford	1948
157	S. Jayasinghe (106)	Leics v Northants, Northampton	1964
157	J.E. Timms (100)	Northants v Kent, Dover	1934
158	T.G. Evans (101)	Kent v Leics, Leicester	1951
159	W.G. Grace (126)	South v North, Hull	1876
159	T.W. Graveney (107★)	Worcs v Leics, Leicester	1968
159	J.R. Reid (100)	Wellington v Auckland, Auckland	1951–52
160	J.R. Reid (100)	New Zealand v England, Christchurch	1962–63

NB: F.H.B. Champain (97) last out for Gloucs. (137) v Lancs. 1897.
Next are the leading instances of a batsman obtaining 100 in an uncompleted innings of less than 143.

129–3	G. Gunn (109★)	Notts v Yorkshire, Nottingham	1913
129–1	M.J. Kitchen (102★)	Somerset v Lancs, Manchester	1968
135–4	L.H. Tennyson (102★)	Hants v Gloucs, Southampton	1927
138–5	B.W. Sinclair (102★)	Wellington v N Districts, Hamilton	1965–66

The defiant Clive Rice.

16-YEAR OLD PLAYS FOR YORKSHIRE

When Yorkshire's pace bowler Paul Jarvis made his first-class début against Sussex at Hove in September 1981 he became the youngest-ever Yorkshire player in first-class cricket. At 16 years 75 days he easily beat the previous record held by Doug Padgett, who made his Yorkshire début in 1951 aged 16 years 320 days. At the time I decided to compile a list of each county's youngest performer and with a couple of amendments I reproduce this list now. In the light of information contained in the George Newnes *Cricketers' Who's Who* I now accept that Glamorgan's youngest cricketer was A.R. Gabe-Jones and not J.S. Pressdee (16–59 in 1949), though Pressdee is the youngest cricketer not to hold his county's record.

My own investigations confirm that Charles Robertson Young is almost certainly the youngest player ever in English first-class cricket. Young was born at Dharwar, near Bombay, on February 2, 1852 and played for Hants against Kent at Gravesend

Paul Jarvis, only just 16 when he made his Yorkshire début.

in 1867 aged 15 years 131 days on the opening day. Young was an interesting, if mysterious, character. An inspection of birth records in the India Office confirmed the date of birth and that he was a son of David Young, Assistant Superintendent Revenue Surveyor for Southern Marathee County. A younger brother was also born there but he does not appear to have been a cricketer. Young played, with mixed success, for Hampshire until 1890. In 1891 he was granted a benefit match at Southampton and at the time he is believed to have lived in the Fremantle area of the town, working as a clerk. There is a possibility that he then became an umpire but I feel that he has never been positively identified since 1891. His name does not appear in the national death registers for England or Scotland, nor is there a will lodged at Somerset House. It is as if he disappeared from the face of the earth.

As regards young county cricketers in general, I feel that the raised school-leaving age, shortage of cricket in state schools and general lack of proper encouragement will make the very young (under-18) county cricketer a very rare bird indeed, and most of the present county records could remain for all time.

YOUNGEST PLAYER FOR EACH COUNTY

County	Player	Age (Yrs–days)	Season
Derbys	F.W. Swarbrook	16–196	1967
*Essex	B. Taylor	16–322	1949
Glamorgan	A.R.Gabe-Jones	15–274	1922
*Gloucs	W.W.F. Pullen	15–346	1882
*Hants	C.R. Young	15–131	1867
Kent	H.T.W. Hardinge	16–111	1902
Lancs	P.T. Marner	16–149	1952
Leics	N.E. Briers	16–103	1971
Middlesex	F.J. Titmus	16–213	1949
Northants	T.B.G. Welch	16–12	1922
Notts	R.C. Tinley	16–288	1847
*Somerset	C.E. Winter	15–288	1882
Surrey	G.A.R. Lock	17–8	1946
*Sussex	J.M. Mare	16–177	1870
*Warwicks	F.R. Santall	16–23	1919
Worcs	M.E.W. Passey	16–63	1953
Yorks	P.W. Jarvis	16–75	1981

*The asterisks indicate that all first-class matches involving the county have been taken into consideration but that the record for an official County Championship match (i.e. since the 1889 meeting of county secretaries which officially recognized the Championship from the following season) is different. The Championship records are as follows.

County	Player	Age (Yrs–days)	Season
Essex	S.J. Cray	17–3	1938
Gloucs	D.F. Pope	16–242	1925
Hants	A.S. Kennedy	16–168	1907
Notts	P. Johnson	17–77	1982
Somerset	J.H. Harris	16–101	1952
Sussex	J.R.T. Barclay	16–209	1970
Warwicks	R.G. Thompson	16–227	1949

Ages given are for first day of début match.

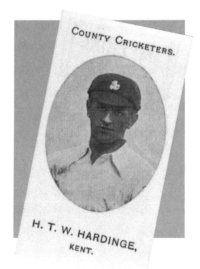

COUNTY CRICKETERS.

H.T.W. HARDINGE, KENT.

OLDEST PLAYERS FOR EACH COUNTY

County	Player	Age (Yrs–days)	Season
Derbys	H. Elliott	55–276	1947
Essex	P.A. Perrin	52–101	1928
Glamorgan	J.C. Clay	51–164	1949
Gloucs	E.M. Grace	54–236	1896
*Hants	J. Small, Sr	61–106	1798
*Kent	Lord Harris	60–151	1911
Lancs	A.N. Hornby	52–152	1899
Leics	C.E. De Trafford	56–24	1920
*Middlesex	J.T. Hearne	56–90	1923
Northants	J. Mercer	52–49	1947
*Notts	W. Clarke, Sr	56–237	1855
Somerset	E. Robson	53–73	1923
*Surrey	J. Shuter	54–141	1909
*Sussex	F.W. Lillywhite	61–44	1853
Warwicks	W.G. Quaife	56–143	1928
Worcs	R.H. Moss	57–91	1925
*Yorks	G.H. Hirst	58–6	1929

*The records for official County Championship matches are different for these counties, and are as follows:

Hants	H.B. Bethune	52–188	1897
Kent	F.E. Woolley	51–97	1938
Middlesex	J.T. Rawlin	52–210	1909
Notts	R. Daft	55–300	1891
Surrey	J.B. Hobbs	51–258	1934
Sussex	G.R. Cox	54–203	1928
Yorks	W. Rhodes	52–297	1930

The above list was compiled to 'complete the record'. It is 38 years since the last new entry and it seems unlikely that there will be any further additions in the future.
Ages given are for last day of final match.

E.M. Grace, who played Championship cricket to an older age than his more illustrious brother.

Willie Quaife among Warwickshire colleagues during his final season in 1928. Left to right: E.J. Smith, W.G. Quaife, F.S.G. Calthorpe, J.H. Parsons, L.A. Bates, H. Howell.

YOUNGEST COUNTY CHAMPIONSHIP CENTURIES FOR EACH COUNTY

County	Player	Age (Yrs–days)	Match/Venue		Season
Derbys	I.W. Hall	19–226	113	v Hants, Derby	1959
Essex	A.J. Turner	19–43	111	v Yorks, Huddersfield	1897
Glamorgan	M.P. Maynard	19–159	102	v Yorks, Swansea	1985
Gloucs	M.W. Alleyne	18–55	116★	v Sussex, Bristol	1986
Hants	G.N. Bignell	18–256	102	v Kent, Portsmouth	1905
Kent	G.J. Bryan	17–247	124	v Notts, Trent Bridge	1920
Lancs	C. Washbrook	18–188	152	v Surrey, Old Trafford	1934
Leics	D.I. Gower	19–112	102★	v Middlesex, Lord's	1976
Middlesex	D.C.S. Compton	18–27	100★	v Northants, No'ton	1936
Northants	H.F. Bagnall	18–188	103	v Sussex, No'ton	1922
Notts	P. Johnson	18–128	‡25	v Gloucs, Bristol	1983
Somerset	A.T.M. Jones	18–104	106	v Leics, Leicester	1938
Surrey	J.N. Crawford	18–257	119★	v Derbys, Derby	1905
Sussex	D.J. Semmence	18–85	108	v Notts, Trent Bridge	1956
Warwicks	R. Sale	19–266	101	v Sussex, Edgbaston	1939
Worcs	D.N. Patel	17–270	107	v Surrey, Worcester	1976
Yorks	L. Hutton	18–33	196	v Worcs, Worcester	1934

It is emphasized that the above records apply only to the County Championship. For first-class county matches against non-county teams – in other words non-competitive matches, largely unaffected by qualification rules current at the time – the following additions can be made.

Glamorgan	M.J. Llewellyn	18–215	112★	v Camb U, Swansea	1972
Worcs	D.N. Patel	17–215	100★	v Oxford U, Oxford Parks	1976

A photograph of 18-year old David Gower from his first pre-season photocall for Leicestershire.

An interesting postscript to cricketers' age records may be a list of the youngest players to have appeared in first-class cricket in each major cricket-playing country. Although lack of data precludes my including Sri Lanka, the youngest players in each of the other countries, according to my records, are as in the following list.

YOUNGEST FIRST-CLASS CRICKETERS BY COUNTRY

Player/Country	Age (Yrs–days)	Match/Venue	Season
[1]Alim-ud-din (I)	12–73	Rajputna v Baroda, Baroda	1942–43
[1]Iqbal Qasim (P)	12–363	Bahawalpur v Karachi Whites, Bahawalpur	1970–71
C.R. Young (E)	15–131	Hants v Kent, Gravesend	1867
C.C. Dacre (NZ)	15–224	Auckland v Wellington, Auckland	1914–15
L.J. Junor (A)	15–265	Victoria v W Australia, Melbourne	1929–30
R.E. Marshall (WI)	15–276	Barbados v Trinidad, Port of Spain	1945–46
J.E. Waddington (SA)	15–324	Griqualand W v E Province, Kimberley	1934–35

[1] It must be mentioned that the first two on the list are only 'claimed' ages; no documentry proof has been produced.

RECORD YEAR FOR DENNIS LILLEE

It is generally known that the 1,811 runs scored in Tests during 1976 by West Indian batsman Vivian Richards is the most for a calendar year. Perhaps less widely known is the Test wickets record for a calendar year, the 85 taken for Australia by Dennis Lillee in 1981. The former achievement is covered annually in *Wisden:* that august publication lists players who have exceeded 1,000 runs in a calendar year, and for the record I give in the second table the leaders in the list. The bowling record is not so well publicized and so in the fourth table I give all those who have taken more than 70 Test wickets in a calendar year. It will be noted that neither record has been seriously challenged since being set – a great tribute to the two holders.

I felt it might also be of interest to list those players who have scored most runs and taken most wickets in Test cricket during *any* period of twelve months. In the first and third tables I have listed the first batsman to score 1,000 runs in twelve months and the first bowler to take 50 wickets. It is not without interest that both were Australians and both set their record during the same period. Tables are on pages 35 and 36.

Dennis Lillee, who claimed the record for most Test wickets during 1981.

Viv Richards – a record total in Test matches during 1976.

The scoreboard records Clem Hill's massive innings for South Australia against New South Wales, made in the season before his record Test haul.

MOST TEST RUNS BY ONE PLAYER DURING ANY TWELVE-MONTH PERIOD: THE PROGRESS OF THE RECORD

Player	Dates	Inns	N.O.	Runs	Av'ge
C. Hill (A)	13.12.1901–11.11.1902	23	2	1106	52.66
W.R. Hammond (E)	23.6.1928–18.6.1929	14	2	1172	97.66
W.R. Hammond (E)	30.11.1928–20.8.1929	17	3	1257	89.78
D.G. Bradman (A)	13.6.1930–4.3.1931	13	0	1421	109.30
R.B. Simpson (A)	6.12.1963–5.12.1964	27	3	1426	59.41
R.B. Simpson (A)	4.6.1964–17.5.1965	27	3	1465	61.04
I.V.A.Richards (WI)	28.11.1975–17.8.1976	24	0	1181	75.45
S.M. Gavaskar (I)	16.10.1978–14.10.1979	27	2	1984	79.36
Note also the following:					
D.L. Amiss (E)	2.2.1974–30.1.1975	26	2	1428	59.50
(best for England)					
Zaheer Abbas (P)	22.3.1982–4.2.1983	15	1	1184	84.57
(best for Pakistan)					
A.R. Border (A)	13.6.1985–17.3.1986	27	4	1464	63.65
(missed equalling Australian record by 1 run)					

C. HILL

1,000 TEST RUNS IN CALENDAR YEAR

Wisden 1987 contains a list of batsmen scoring 1,000 Test runs in a calendar year (Jan–Dec).
The leaders in the list are:

Player	Inns	N.O.	Runs	Av'ge	Year
I.V.A Richards (WI)	19	0	1710	90.00	1976
S.M. Gavaskar (I)	27	1	1555	59.80	1979
G.R. Viswanath (I)	26	3	1388	60.34	1979
R.B. Simpson (A)	26	3	1381	60.04	1964
D.L. Amiss (E)	22	2	1379	68.95	1974

Another big innings for Bob Simpson. He is applauded by Jim Parks and Colin Cowdrey after reaching 200 off the bowling of David Allen at Adelaide in 1966.

MOST TEST WICKETS BY ONE PLAYER DURING ANY TWELVE-MONTH PERIOD: THE PROGRESS OF THE RECORD

Player	Dates	Runs	Wkts	Av'ge
H. Trumble (A)	13.12.1901–14.10.1902	1059	54	19.61
S.F. Barnes (E)	15.12.1911–22.8.1912	1182	73	16.19
G.D. McKenzie (A)	4.6.1964–17.5.1965	1816	74	24.54
I.T. Botham (E)	12.2.1978–11.2.1979	1397	75	18.62
Kapil Dev (I)	24.1.1979–20.1.1980	1761	78	22.57
Kapil Dev (I)	12.7.1979–19.2.1980	1771	79	22.41
D.K. Lillee (A)	30.11.1980–29.11.1981	1708	85	20.09
Imran Khan (P)	22.3.1982–4.2.1983	1235	88	14.03
Note also the following:				
M.D. Marshall (WI)	14.6.1984–9.5.1985	1477	79	18.69
(best of W. Indies)				
Kapil Dev (I)	23.12.1982–14.12.1983	1786	77	23.19
(best 12-month total not to include an England tour)				

BEST TEST BOWLING IN CALENDAR YEAR

Player	Runs	Wkts	Av'ge	Year
D.K. Lillee (A)	1781	85	20.95	1981
Kapil Dev (I)	1720	74	23.24	1979
M.D. Marshall (WI)	1360	73	18.63	1984
J. Garner (WI)	1425	72	19.79	1984
G.D. McKenzie (A)	1737	71	24.46	1964

The records for Marshall and Garner do not include runs conceded on the last two days of
the year. Australia batted during both these days, neither bowler took a wicket and their
figures at the close of the year are not available. It is estimated that about 1 run per wicket
would be added to their average.

H. Trumble, whose 54 wickets were an Australian record for 62 years.

1982

KANHAI'S RETURN

Rohan Kanhai's return to first-class cricket in 1981–82 with the International XI in Pakistan enabled him to set up a new record among West Indian cricketers for length of first-class career. Only three West Indians have a first-class career spanning more than 26 years, and they are as follows:

Player	Début	Last Appearance	Span (Yrs–days)
R. Kanhai	5.2.1955	13.10.1982	26–250
R.E. Marshall	26.1.1946	12.9.1972	26–229
G.A. Headley	9.2.1928	10.9.1954	26–214

In each case the length of time is measured from the first day of the début match to the last day of the final match.

Rohan Kanhai on his Test début at Edgbaston in 1957 after being selected as a wicket-keeper/batsman.

Rohan Kanhai's last appearance at The Oval in September 1982, when he played for an Old World XI against Old England.

WARWICKSHIRE'S EXPENSIVE RECORD

There was an interesting letter in a 1982 issue of *The Cricketer* from a reader inquiring whether a county had ever done worse than Warwickshire, whose wickets in the 1981 County Championship, excluding extras and run-outs, cost 45.13 runs each. The answer – depressing for all Warwickshire followers – is no. I list all counties I have found who took their wickets in a County Championship season for more than 38 runs apiece. Again, all extras and run-outs are ignored.

Warwickshire also achieved third place for their performance in 1982, while in 1986 Somerset and Glamorgan crept into the list.

MOST EXPENSIVE COUNTIES

County	Season	Runs	Wkts	Av'ge	Final Position
Warwicks	1981	9793	217	45.13	Last
Derbys	1901	8493	200	42.47	Last
Warwicks	1982	9773	232	42.12	Last
Notts	1951	10948	267	41.00	Last
Warwicks	1979	8504	211	40.30	15th
Worcs	1920	6480	161	40.25	15th*
Somerset	1986	9224	235	39.25	16th
Notts	1949	12612	322	39.17	Last
Glamorgan	1986	8087	208	38.88	Last
Essex	1928	12230	317	38.58	16th
Worcs	1933	12480	326	38.28	15th

*Of 16.

WARWICKSHIRE AVERAGES 1981: FIRST CLASS MATCHES
BOWLING

Bowler	Overs	Mdns	Runs	Wts	Av'ge	5/ Inns.	10/ Mch.	B/B Inns.	Mch.	BD	Ct	LBW	St
R. G. D. Willis	138.3	29	371	13	28.54	1	—	5/61	5/61	3	9	1	
W. Hogg	521.2	102	1794	50	35.88	1	—	4/46	8/111	15	29	6	
G. C. Small	395.3	52	1590	42	37.86	1	—	6/76	7/133	9	28	5	
D. R. Doshi	669.3	163	1949	45	43.31	1	—	5/73	5/73	6	19	8	9
S. P. Perryman	305.4	64	1046	24	43.58	—	—	5/52	6/65	6	17	1	
A. M. Ferreira	436.3	83	1542	32	48.19	—	—	4/73	4/134	3	3	1	1
C. Lethbridge	113	12	501	7	71.57	—	—	2/26	2/30	3	3	1	
Asif Din	70	8	371	5	74.20	—	—	1/11	1/11	4	1	—	
S. P. Sutcliffe	124.3	17	485	6	80.83	—	—	2/68	4/140	4	1	1	—
Also bowled:													
A.I.Kallicharran	35.5	3	133	2	66.50	—	—	1/14	1/14		2		
S. J. Rouse	42.3	8	169	2	84.50	—	—	2/46	2/46	1	1	—	
D. M. Smith	23	3	98	1		—	—	1/55	1/98		1		
T. A. Lloyd	24	2	106	0									
D. C. Hopkins	13	2	35	0							1		
S. H. Wootton	1	0	7	0									
Extras			718	5									
TOTALS			10915	234	46.65	4	—	6/76	8/111				

Sad reading from the 1982 Warwickshire CCC handbook.

DAVID STEELE REJOINS NORTHANTS

When David Steele returned to Northants in 1982 after a spell with Derbyshire, he joined the small band of players who have returned to play first-class cricket for a county they had previously appeared for and then left to play first-class cricket for another county. Only examples since 1873, when a rules change made it harder for players to change counties, are listed.

Player	Counties/Seasons
D. Bottom	Derbys 1894–98; Notts 1899; Derbys 1901
L.D. Brownlee	Gloucs 1901; Somerset 1902; Gloucs 1902–09
H.B. Chinnery	Surrey 1897; Middlesex 1899–1902; Surrey 1904
L.L. Cranfield	Gloucs 1903; Somerset 1906; Gloucs 1910–22
J. Cumbes	Lancs 1963–67; Surrey 1968–70; Lancs 1971
[1]W.G. Grace	Gloucs 1873–77; Kent 1877; Gloucs 1877–99
F.H. Guttridge	Notts 1889–90; Sussex 1892–94; Notts 1896–1900
J.K. Hall	Surrey 1958–59; Sussex 1960; Surrey 1962
[2]T.A. Higson	Derbys 1899 Lancs 1905–09; Derbys 1910; Lancs 1923
M.L. Hill	Somerset 1921–22; Glamorgan 1923; Somerset 1924–32
R. Illingworth	Yorks 1951–68; Leics 1969–78; Yorks 1982–83
[3]M.F.S. Jewell	Worcs 1909–13; Sussex 1914–19; Worcs (1) 1919; Sussex (1) 1919; Worcs (1) 1919; Sussex (1) 1919; Worcs (3) 1919; Sussex (1) 1919; Worcs 1919–33
R.D.V. Knight	Surrey 1968–70; Gloucs 1971–75; Sussex 1976–77; Surrey 1978–84
[4]A.F. Lane	Worcs 1914; Warwicks 1919–25; Worcs 1927–32
A.J.H. Luard	Gloucs 1892–96; Hants 1897; Gloucs 1907
S. Oldham	Yorks 1974–79; Derbys 1980–83; Yorks 1984–85
C.H. Palmer	Hants 1899–1901; Worcs (1) 1904; Hants 1904–07
[5]A.W. Ridley	Hants 1875–77; Kent 1877; Hants 1878
D.C. Robinson	Gloucs 1905–06; Essex 1908; Gloucs 1910–26
D.J. Semmence	Sussex 1956–59; Essex 1962; Sussex 1967–68
F.J. Shacklock	Notts 1883; Derbys 1884–85; Notts 1886–93
A. Shaw	Notts 1873–87; Sussex 1894–95; Notts 1897
D.M. Smith	Surrey 1973–83; Worcs 1984–86; Surrey 1987
D.S. Steele	Northants 1963–78; Derbys 1979–81; Northants 1982–84
F.J. Titmus	Middlesex 1949–76; Surrey 1978; Middlesex 1979–82
[6]F.T. Welman	Middlesex 1880; Somerset 1882–85; Middlesex 1887–88; Somerset 1895–1901
A.H. Wilkins	Glamorgan 1976–79; Gloucs 1980–81; Glamorgan 1983

The great 'W.G.' who made a guest appearance for a Kent XI in 1877.

[1,5] Grace and Ridley both had a single appearance for 'A Kent XI' in the 1877 Canterbury Festival. This not being a *bona fide* county team perhaps they do not qualify for the list.

[2,6] Higson and Welman are alone in performing a 'double' feat – if one excludes M.F.S. Jewell's freakish peripateticisms in 1919.

[3] M.F.S. Jewell's itinerant behaviour in 1919 is without parallel. Worcs did not compete in the Championship in 1919, but their games against first-class opposition were all ranked first-class so he broke Rule 1 of the Rules of County Cricket then current. Since Jewell had a birth qualification for neither county, other rules may also have been ignored.

[4] A.F. ('Spinny') Lane played for Worcs as a professional in 1914 but afterwards was an amateur.

David Steele, back again at Northants.

DIFFERENT DECADES

In a letter to *The Cricketer*, in 1982 a reader referred to the 'Leading aggregates of five decades' compiled by Irving Rosenwater in the Jubilee issue (April 1971). He felt that it would be interesting to give the same statistics for the period 1970 to 1979–80 as were given in this article for the five previous decades of the existence of *The Cricketer*. The qualifications were 10,000 runs or 1,000 wickets for the decades 1920 to 1929–30, 1930 to 1939–40; 1950 to 1959–60 and 1960 to 1969–70. For the period 1940 to 1949–50, when a part of the decade was taken up with the war, 500 wickets was used as a qualification.

It was felt that for a realistic comparison to be made the same qualifications should be used for the 1970s as were used in the previous full decades, and the results, given in the table, are extremely interesting. Naturally these figures differ from those given on page 13 which were based on a 1–10 decade.

Previous totals for 1,000 runs were 43 in the 1920s, 51 in the 1930s, 61 in the 1950s and 63 in the 1960s. Therefore it would appear that the 1970s figure of 54 holds up fairly well, though the comparative shortage of Englishmen must make somewhat depressing reading for the 'home' market. However, the collapse in the wicket-taking ability of bowlers during the 1970s is nothing short of catastrophic, and is only partly explicable by the reduced number of matches in England. Are there not, after all, more overseas tours available for the best English players, while some 'overseas' players played first-class cricket for all twelve months of several years in the 1970s?

ALL QUALIFIERS

1970 to 1979–80: (10,000 runs)

G.M. Turner	24,562
Zaheer Abbas	21,855
G. Boycott	21,411
D.L. Amiss	20,171
B.A. Richards	19,653
C.H. Lloyd	17,879
B.F. Davison	17,345
C.G. Greenidge	17,312
A.I. Kallicharran	17,304
Majid Khan	17,243
S.M. Gavaskar	16,718
Sadiq Mohammed	16,561
K.W.R. Fletcher	16,360
M.J. Procter	16,278
Mushtaq Mohammed	16,089
G.S. Chappell	14,916
I.V.A. Richards	14,865
Asif Iqbal	14,745
M.H. Denness	14,380
J.H. Edrich	14,184
G.R.J. Roope	14,117
M.J. Harris	14,081
A. Jones	14,055
M.J. Smith	13,668
Younis Ahmed	13,601
C.T. Radley	13,396
D.S. Steele	12,946
G.R. Viswanath	12,799
J.M. Brearley	12,714
R.C. Fredericks	12,553
J.H. Hampshire	12,480
R. Kanhai	12,203
D. Lloyd	12,103
A.W. Greig	12,102
B. Dudleston	12,048
K.S. McEwan	12,008
B. Wood	11,731
J.A. Ormrod	11,412
J.A. Jameson	11,234
R.D.V. Knight	11,215
R.A. Woolmer	11,092
J.F. Steele	11,047
I.M. Chappell	11,009
D.W. Randall	10,964
G.P. Howarth	10,923
R.T. Virgin	10,705
M.J. Smedley	10,638
N.G. Featherstone	10,620
C.E.B. Rice	10,364
Javed Miandad	10,337
F.C. Hayes	10,313
B. Luckhurst	10,190
D.R. Turner	10,116
B.L. D'Oliveira	10,075

(1,000 wickets)

B.S. Bedi	1,231

TOP THREE

1920 to 1929–30	
E.H. Hendren	30,476 runs
A. Sandham	26,647 runs
F.E. Woolley	25,502 runs
A.P. Freeman	2,058 wkts
C.W.L. Parker	1,843 wkts
M.W. Tate	1,764 wkts

1930 to 1939–40	
W.R. Hammond	31,165 runs
H. Sutcliffe	23,708 runs
L.E.G. Ames	21,350 runs
H. Verity	1,956 wkts
T.W.J. Goddard	1,723 wkts
A.P. Freeman	1,628 wkts

1940 to 1949–50	
D.C.S. Compton	15,947 runs
L. Hutton	14,324 runs
W.J. Edrich	11,710 runs
T.W.J. Goddard	700 wkts
D.V.P. Wright	636 wkts
W.E. Hollies	619 wkts

1950 to 1959–60	
T.W. Graveney	24,834 runs
P.B.H. May	23,951 runs
D. Kenyon	22,365 runs
G.A.R. Lock	1,639 wkts
D. Shackleton	1,497 wkts
J.H. Wardle	1,497 wkts

1960 to 1969–70	
J.H. Edrich	23,553 runs
K.F. Barrington	20,860 runs
P.H. Parfitt	19,814 runs
F.J. Titmus	1,279 wkts
D. Shackleton	1,239 wkts
F.S. Trueman	1,191 wkts

1970 to 1979–80	
G.M. Turner	24,562 runs
Zaheer Abbas	21,855 runs
G. Boycott	21,411 runs
B.S. Bedi	1,231 wkts
D.L. Underwood	989 wkts
Intikhab Alam	966 wkts

Glenn Turner who was best known during the early part of his career for his sound defence.

Bishen Bedi, who added only two more wickets to his total for the decade
during the Second Test at Lord's in 1979.

Wally Hammond (above), the leading run accumulator of the 1930s
and (left) Hedley Verity who took the most wickets during that same
decade.

UNIVERSITY CAPTAIN'S GREAT START

Good weather and an early start saw several splendid innings during April 1982 and perhaps the most noteworthy feat came from Cambridge University captain Derek Pringle. He became only the fifth batsman ever to score 300 first-class runs in the April of an English season. Mark Benson and Ken McEwan have subsequently joined Pringle in this achievement.

Player	Inns	N.O.	Runs	H.S.	Av'ge	Season
D.L. Amiss (Warwicks)	4	0	407	164	101.75	1976
G.A. Gooch (Essex)	5	1	405	220	101.25	1984
D.R. Pringle (Cambridge U.)	6	2	361	127	90.25	1982
M.R. Benson (Kent)	4	0	360	122	90.00	1987
G.M. Turner (NZ)	3	1	335	151★	167.50	1973
K.S. McEwan (Essex)	6	0	327	110	54.50	1985
J.M. Brearley (Middlesex)	4	1	322	153	107.33	1976
G.A. Gooch (Essex)	6	0	312	99	52.00	1985
G.A. Gooch (Essex)	4	0	300	205	75.00	1980

Pringle's early successes in 1982 brought him a Test place in the series against India.

Amiss currently holds the English record for runs in April but is well short of the worldwide best. While on tour in the West Indies in April 1972, Glenn Turner had the following records:

Inns	N.O.	Runs	H.S.	Av'ge
5	0	639	259	127.70

The previous holder of the record was Sunil Gavaskar, who in April of the previous year, also in the West Indies, had scored 488 runs at an average of 97.60. The only others to score 400 runs in April are Mushtaq Mohammad in Pakistan in 1963, Majid Khan in Pakistan in 1966, and Clive Lloyd in the West Indies in 1973.

Bill Frindall, in his *Wisden Book of Cricket Records*, covers the 'Most Runs in a Month' record quite adequately. The best figures for each of the other months of the English season are listed below.

MOST RUNS IN CALENDAR MONTH

Month	Player	Runs	Season
May	W.R. Hammond (Gloucs)	1042	1927
June	L. Hutton (Yorks)	1294	1949
July	M.J.K. Smith (Warwicks)	1209	1959
August	W.R. Hammond (Gloucs)	1281	1936

STEVENSON'S LAST STAND

Not surprisingly, the last-wicket stand of 149 between G. Boycott and G.B. Stevenson for Yorkshire against Warwickshire at Edgbaston in 1982 contained a number of statistically significant points. That it was a new Yorkshire record for the last wicket, beating the 148 of Lord Hawke and D. Hunter against Kent which had stood since 1898, was widely commented upon; perhaps not so well known are the facts that it was the highest 10th-wicket stand involving either side and the best-ever at Edgbaston.

The stand was the highest 10th-wicket partnership involving an opening batsman. The previous best was 144, between Shakoor Ahmed (opener) and Pervez Sajjad for Lahore Greens v Karachi Blues, at Karachi in 1965–66. The previous best in England was 136, involving G. Challenor (opener) and G.N. Francis for West Indies v Surrey at The Oval in 1923.

The latest stand is the only time the No.11 has out-scored the opener. Stevenson's century was the eighth by a No.11 in all first-class cricket, the third in the County Championship and the first since T.P.B. Smith scored 163 for Essex v Derbyshire at Chesterfield in 1947. Stevenson's 115 not out is the highest *undefeated* innings by a No.11 in all first-class cricket and the fourth highest score from that position.

W. R. HAMMOND, Gloucestershire

Graham Stevenson, who outscored Geoff Boycott in their record-breaking 10th-wicket stand.

TURNER'S HUNDRED – THE HIDDEN STATISTICS

Glenn Turner's 100th hundred, against Warwickshire in May 1982, was celebrated appropriately in the July issue with Brian Brain's excellent article. There are, however, many statistical aspects to the feat which have not been covered. Though the 19th batsman to achieve 100 first-class hundreds, Turner is only the second non-Englishman, and the first New Zealander, to reach this milestone. At the age of 35 years and three days, he is also the third youngest in the list and the first to go on to a triple century in the same innings.

It was not generally noticed that during his historic innings Turner scored more than 100 runs in both the morning and afternoon sessions of play. Although I feel that it is impossible to obtain *all* instances of this feat, since some have almost certainly never been recorded in either press or scorebook, I am reasonably confident that the list on page 51 is accurate and complete for first-class innings played in England since the first war.

Glenn Turner celebrates his 100th hundred with a well-earned gin and tonic before proceeding to an undefeated 311.

100 FIRST-CLASS HUNDREDS

Player	Début season	Date of 100th 100	Age	Final Score/Match/Venue	1st-class careers record Inns	Runs	Av'ge
W.G. Grace (Gloucs)	1865	18. 5.1895	46	288 Gloucs v Somerset, Bristol	1113	41863	40.68
T.W. Hayward (Surrey)	1893	27. 6.1913	42	139 Surrey v Lancs, Oval	1076	41534	24.34
J.B. Hobbs (Surrey)	1905	8. 5.1923	40	116★ Surrey v Somerset, Bath	821	34929	45.96
C.P. Mead (Hants)	1905	19. 7.1927	40	100★ Hants v Northants, Kettering	892	37216	47.53
E.H. Hendren (Middlesex)	1907	3.11.1928	39	100 MCC v Victoria, Melbourne	740	32946	51.64
F.E. Woolley (Kent)	1906	28. 8.1929	42	176 Kent v Middlesex, Lord's	031	39967	41.42
H. Sutcliffe (Yorks)	1919	7. 7.1932	37	132 Yorks v Gloucs, Bradford	700	33530	54.70
G.E. Tyldesley (Lancs)	1909	7. 7.1934	45	122 Lancs v. Northants, Peterborough	919	37105	45.25
W.R. Hammond (Gloucs)	1920	13. 6.1935	32	116 Gloucs v Somerset, Bristol	680	32081	52.94
A. Sandham (Surrey)	1911	26. 6.1935	44	103 Surrey v Hants, Basingstoke	871	37809	47.56
D.G. Bradman (NSW/S Aust)	1927–28	15.11.1947	39	172 Australian XI v India, Sydney	295	24495	95.31
L.E.G. Ames (Kent)	1926	11. 8.1950	44	131 Kent v Middlesex, Canterbury	915	36340	44.05
L. Hutton (Yorks)	1934	15. 7.1951	35	151 Yorks v Surrey, Oval	619	30647	56.23
D.C.S. Compton (Middlesex)	1936	11. 6.1952	34	107 Middlesex v Northants, Lord's	552	28264	58.88
T.W. Graveney (Gloucs/Worcs)	1948	5. 8.1964	37	132 Worcs v Northants, Worcester	940	37307	44.89
M.C. Cowdrey (Kent)	1950	5. 7.1973	40	100★ Kent v. Surrey, Maidstone	1035	39934	43.64
J.H. Edrich (Surrey)	1956	12. 7.1977	40	101★ Surrey v. Derby, Oval	945	38783	45.84
G. Boycott (Yorks)	1962	11. 8.1977	36	191 England v Australia, Leeds	645	31318	57.36
G.M. Turner (Otago/Worcs)	1964–65	29. 5.1982	35	311★ Worcs v Warwicks, Worcester	779	33426	49.23
Zaheer Abbas (Gloucs, etc.)	1965–66	10.12.1982	35	215 Pakistan v India, Lahore	658	31005	53.55
D.L. Amiss (Warwicks)	1960	29. 7.1986	43	101★ Warwicks v Lancs, Edgbaston	1081	41866	43.61

Len Hutton is congratulated on his 100th hundred by Norman Yardley in the dressing-room at The Oval. Looking on are Don Brennan, left, and Willie Watson, right.

Above One hundred hundreds at last for Dennis Amiss. John Abrahams, left, and Geoff Humpage are the first with their congratulations and Lancashire wicket-keeper Graeme Fowler moves in to add a few words of his own.

Left Tom Hayward, left, the second man after W.G. Grace to reach 100 hundreds, takes the field with Jack Hobbs who was to become the third to this same 'milestone' ten years later.

100 RUNS IN BOTH MORNING AND AFTERNOON SESSIONS

Player	Score	Match/Venue	Year
[1] J.R. Hobbs	215	Surrey v Warwicks, Edgbaston	1925
[2] K.S. Duleepsinhji	254★	Cambridge U. v Middlesex, Cambridge	1927
D.G. Bradman	334	Australia v England, Leeds	1930
E. Paynter	322	Lancs v Sussex, Hove	1937
A.E. Fagg	244	Kent v Essex, Colchester	1938
A.R. Morris	290	Australians v Gloucs, Bristol	1948
L. Hutton	241	Players v Gents, Scarborough	1953
C.G. Greenidge	273★	D.H. Robins' XI v Pakistanis, Eastbourne	1974
K.S. McEwan	218	Essex v Sussex, Chelmsford	1977
G.M. Turner	311★	Worcs v Warwicks, Worcester	1982
K.R. Rutherford	317	N Zealanders v D.B. Close's XI, Scarborough	1986

[1] Out before tea.
[2] Went from 30★ to 143★ before lunch, and to 254★ in the afternoon.

No attempt has been made to collect overseas examples, but one may note that Bradman achieved the feat twice in Australia, in his 452★ in 1929–30 and his 369 in 1935–36, while Trumper did so in his 292★ in 1898–99.

Turner is the 15th batsman to score more than 300 runs in a day's play. No. 16 was I.V.A. Richards, whose 322 for Somerset v Warwicks at Taunton in 1985 is the best by any officially designated 'overseas' player in county cricket.

Arthur Morris, a century either side of lunch in 1948.

ILLINGWORTH CAPTAINS YORKSHIRE

The return to county cricket of Ray Illingworth prompted much discussion as to whether records had been beaten, and I have set out to examine some of the possibilities.

Illingworth was appointed captain of Yorkshire in March 1982, two weeks after his 50th birthday, and made his début as captain the following three days against Essex. The only other instance of a 50-year-old being officially appointed captain of a first-class county side occurred in 1897, A.N. Hornby being chosen to lead Lancashire. However, Hornby, also club president, only captained the side in A.C. MacLaren's absence, whereas Illingworth was first-choice skipper. His appointment was therefore unarguably the more remarkable. Here is a list of players appointed captain aged 45 or more.

Age	Player
50	A.N. Hornby (Lancs), 1897; had previously captained the side for many years
50	R. Illingworth (Yorks), 1982
48	J.C. Clay (Glamorgan), 1946; appointed for the third time; previous skipper, M.J.L. Turnbull, killed in action
48	R.E.S. Wyatt (Worcs), 1950; had been joint captain with A.F.T. White in 1949; captained Warwicks 1930–37
47	W.E. Astill (Leics)
46	A.W. Lupton (Yorks)
45	J. Sharp (Lancs)
45	N. Gifford (Warwicks)

The above details refer to age at the time of appointment. The following players remained as official county captains into their fifties.

Age	Player
51	A.N. Hornby (Lancs), 1898; was 51 years, 196 days at the start of his last Championship match as officially appointed captain for Lancs v Derbys, Old Trafford
51	R. Illingworth (Yorks), 1983; was 51 years, 94 days on the first day of his last Championship match as official Yorkshire captain v Essex, Chelmsford
50	W.G. Grace (Gloucs), 1899
50	R.E.S. Wyatt (Worcs), 1951

Oldest current skipper is Norman 'Babe' Gifford, 47 years old at the start of Warwickshire's 1987 season.

A.N. Hornby, Lancashire captain at the age of 50.

Ray Illingworth, in conversation with Geoff Boycott, shortly after he had taken over the captaincy of Yorkshire.

CENTURY IN EACH INNINGS FOR UNCAPPED LLOYDS

Jeremy Lloyds's feat of scoring hundreds in both innings of Somerset's game with Northants in 1982 while still uncapped provoked the query as to whether it had been done before. Proper investigation of the feat is impossible since full lists of capped players do not exist, except for the period since the last war. In that time, however, the feat has been performed as follows:

TWO HUNDREDS IN A MATCH FOR UNCAPPED BATSMAN

Player	Scores	Match/Venue	Season
E.I. Lester	126 & 142	Yorks v Northants, Northampton	1947
J.M. Allan	121★ & 105	Kent v Northants, Northampton	1955
J.H. Edrich	112 & 124	Surrey v Notts, Nottingham	1959
N.W. Hill	101 & 102	Notts v Lancashire, Nottingham	1959
B.A. Richardson	126 & 105	Warwicks v Cambridge U., Edgbaston	1967
B.A. Richards	130 & 104★	Hants v Northants, Northampton	1968
R.G. Williams	109 & 151★	Northants v Warwicks, Northampton	1979
J.W. Lloyds	132★ & 102★	Somerset v Northants, Northampton	1982
D.G. Aslett	168 & 119	Kent v Derbys, Chesterfield	1983

Richardson is the only one of these players never to receive his cap. The above were his only first-class hundreds and he gave up county cricket before the next season.

VAIN GLORY FOR WARWICKSHIRE PAIR

The fourth-wicket stand of 470 by Alvin Kallicharran and Geoffrey Humpage for Warwickshire against Lancashire at Southport in 1982 was an English record for the wicket, the fourth best for any wicket in England and the ninth best in the world. The stand was the largest involving a wicket-keeper in English cricket and the second largest anywhere, after the unbroken 574 shared by C.L. Walcott and F.M.M. Worrell for Barbados against Trinidad at Port of Spain in 1945–46. Walcott kept wicket in this game. Humpage's 254 was the highest for any Warwickshire wicket-keeper and the highest for any player who kept wicket throughout a county match since J.R. Freeman's 286 for Essex v Northants at Northampton in 1921.

Jeremy Lloyds (top) and Derek Aslett (above), exceptional performances while still uncapped.

COUNTY CHAMPIONSHIP   LANCASHIRE versus WARWICKSHIRE
at Southport   Lancs won by 10 wkts   Wed 28th, Thurs 29th & Fri 30th JULY 1982

Wed & Thurs 11-6.30 (lunch 1.15 tea 4.10) Fri 11.00-5.30 or 6.00 (lunch 1.00 tea 3.40)

Umpires : H.D.BIRD & J.VAN GELOVEN   Warks won the toss & elected to bat   Price : 10p

LANCASHIRE

		First Innings		Second Innings	
1	G.FOWLER	b Asif Din	126	not out	128
2	D.LLOYD	c Humpage b Small	10	not out	88
3	I.COCKBAIN	c Amiss b Kallicharran	98	(Fowler was injured whilst	
4	C.H.LLOYD (capt)	c Humpage b Kallicharran	45	fielding and then batting with	
5	D.P.HUGHES	c Small b Kallicharran	14	the aid of a runner - scoring	
6	J.ABRAHAMS	not out	51	a century in each innings)	
7	S.J.O'SHAUGHNESSY	not out	26		
8	J.SIMMONS				
9	I.FOLLEY				
10	C.J.SCOTT (w/k)	lbw Brown (sub)	9		
11	L.L.McFARLANE				

Bonus Points   EXTRAS.. -b, 13-lb, 3-w, 19-nb. 35   EXTRAS.. -b, 2-lb, -w, 8-nb. 10
Lancs 4 Warks 2   TOTAL .... for 6 wkts dec 414   TOTAL 226

FALL OF WICKETS

First Innings									Second Innings								
1	2	3	4	5	6	7	8	9	1	2	3	4	5	6	7	8	9
34	109	194	305	327	333												

BOWLING ANALYSIS

	O	M	R	W	Wds	NBs	O	M	R	W	Wds	NBs
Small	15	4	38	1	..	4	11	2	30	..	..	.4
Hartley	14	..	66	..	2	11	9	1	38	..	..	3
Sutcliffe	38	9	103	..	..	..	19	5	60	..	..	..
Lethbridge	14	5	58	..	..	2	9	2	27	..	..	1
Kallicharran	13	3	32	3	..	..	6	..	35	..	..	..
Asif Din	6	1	35	1	1	..	5	..	25	..	..	..
Lloyd (T.A)	..	..	..	..	..	..	1	..	1	..	..	..
Brown (see note)	13	3	47	1	..	2	..	..	..	..	..	..

WARWICKSHIRE

		First Innings		Second Innings	
1	D.L.AMISS (capt)	c Abrahams b McFarlane	6	c Scott b McFarlane	24
2	T.A.LLOYD	c Scott b Folley	23	b McFarlane	5
3	A.I.KALLICHARRAN	not out	230	c Lloyd (D) b O'Shaughnessy	0
4	ASIF DIN			c Hughes b O'Shaughnessy	21
5	G.W.HUMPAGE (w/k)	b Lloyd (D)	254	c Abrahams b O'Shaughnessy	21
6	R.I.H.B.DYER	c Simmons b McFarlane	0	c Abrahams b McFarlane	0
7	S.H.WOOTTON			b McFarlane	0
8	C.LETHBRIDGE	(The stand of 470 was the highest		c Hughes b Folley	18
9	P.HARTLEY	4th wicket stand in England and		c Scott b McFarlane	16
10	G.C.SMALL	the record for any Warwickshire		lbw McFarlane	0
11	S.P.SUTCLIFFE	wicket).		not out	7

Bonus Points   EXTRAS.. 1-b, 6-lb, 1-w, 2-nb. 10   EXTRAS.. 1-b, 2-lb, 1-w, -nb. 4
Lancs 1 Warks 4   TOTAL ... for 4 wkts dec 523   TOTAL......................111

FALL OF WICKETS

First Innings									Second Innings								
1	2	3	4	5	6	7	8	9	1	2	3	4	5	6	7	8	9
5	6	53	523						1	1	47	47	47	47	76	81	99

BOWLING ANALYSIS

	O	M	R	W	Wds	NBs	O	M	R	W	Wds	NBs
McFarlane	11	2	90	2	1	..	20	4	59	6	1	..
Folley	15	3	64	1	..	..	11	5	19	1	..	..
O'Shaughnessy	15	2	62	0	..	2	7.1	..	29	3	..	..
Simmons	20	2	97	0	..	..	1	1	..	..	..	..
Hughes	20	2	79	0	..	..	..	..	..	..	..	..
Abrahams	15	3	76	0	..	..	..	..	..	..	..	..
Lloyd (D)	10.1	1	45	1	..	..	..	..	..	..	..	..

* David Brown replaced Gladstone Small who was called into the Test Squad. Small later
rejoined the Warwickshire team having not been selected for the Test Team.

An historic scorecard.

The scoring of two double centuries in one Championship innings is a particularly unusual feat, as this table shows.

TWO DOUBLE CENTURIES IN ONE COUNTY CHAMPIONSHIP INNINGS

Players/Scores	Match/Venue	Season
J.T. Brown 300 & J. Tunnicliffe 243	Yorks v Derbys, Chesterfield	1898
R.M. Poore 304 & E.G. Wynyard 225	Hants v Somerset, Taunton	1899
C.B. Fry 209 & E.H. Killick 200	Sussex v Yorks, Hove	1901
J.B. Hobbs 205 & E.G. Hayes 276	Surrey v Hants, The Oval	1909
J.W. Hearne 218★ & E.H. Hendren 201	Middlesex v. Hants, Lord's	1919
E.H. Bowley 228 & M.W. Tate 203	Sussex v Northants, Hove	1921
H. Sutcliffe 313 & P. Holmes 224★	Yorks v Essex, Leyton	1932
W.H. Ashdown 332 & L.E.G. Ames 202★	Kent v Essex, Brentwood	1932
D.E. Davies 215 & W.E. Jones 212★	Glamorgan v Essex, Brentwood	1948
D. Brookes 204★ & D.W. Barrick 211	Northants v Essex, Northampton	1952
J.A. Jameson 240★ & R.B. Kanhai 213★	Warwicks v Gloucs, Edgbaston	1974
A.I. Kallicharran 230★ & G.W. Humpage 254	Warwicks v Lancs, Southport	1982

J.T. Brown (below) and J. Tunnicliffe (right) who shared 543 runs in Yorkshire's total of 662 in 1898.

A further four such performances have been recorded in other first-class cricket in England while the feat, though still rare, is comparatively more common abroad. Where the latest performance is *unique* is that Kallicharran and Humpage finished on the losing side.

Humpage's 254 for a losing side set me wondering about higher losing individual scores. There have been very few, as the next table shows.

HIGHEST INDIVIDUAL SCORES ON A LOSING SIDE

Score	Player	Match Details	Season
343*	P.A. Perrin	Essex (597 & 97) v Derbys (548 & 149 for 1), Chesterfield	1904
309	V.S. Hazare	The Rest (133 & 387) v Hindus (581 for 5 dec.) Bombay	1943–44
280*	C.P. Mead	Hants (190 & 507) v Notts (412 & 286 for 8), Southampton	1921
270	F.E. Woolley	Kent (445 & 159) v Middlesex (457 & 148 for 3), Canterbury	1923
257*	L.C. Braund	Somerset (388 & 120) v Worcs (344 & 166 for 2), Worcester	1913
254	G.W. Humpage	Warwicks (523 for 4 dec & 111) v Lancs (414 for 6 dec & 226 for 0), Southport	1982

As for the highest stand for a team eventually to lose, the Kallicharran-Humpage partnership was a new record for all first-class cricket by a considerable margin. In 1972 Alan Jones and Roy Fredericks added 330 for the Glamorgan first wicket against Northants at Swansea in a game eventually lost by 29 runs. Even more remarkable perhaps was the game between Hindus and The Rest at Bombay in 1943–44. Vijay and Vivek Hazare (The Rest) produced a sixth-wicket partnership of 300 in a game later lost by an innings (see table). Vijay's personal contribution was an amazing 309 out of 387.

A further point for discussion was whether Warwickshire's 523 for four declared was the largest on record for a losing side. The answer here is that it is nowhere near. In English first-class cricket this dubious record is held by Essex, whose nine-wickets defeat by Derbyshire at Chesterfield in 1904 came after a first innings of 597. Worldwide the record appears to be held by Maharashtra. Their second-innings 604 against Bombay at Pune in the 1948–49 Ranji Trophy semi-final was not sufficient to enable them to avoid defeat by a massive 354 runs.

Warwickshire's change of fortune can perhaps be compared with what happened against Hampshire at Edgbaston in 1922 – the visitors winning by 155 runs after following on and losing their 6th second innings wicket when still 22 runs behind, and the India match of 1971, when after a first innings of 377 for three declared, with Jameson scoring 231, they lost by an innings.

HEMMINGS CLAIMS ALL TEN

September is a traditionally barren month for cricketing milestones but one particularly notable feat was performed in 1982 by Eddie Hemmings, the Notts and England off-spinner taking all 10 wickets in an innings for an International XI v West Indian XI at Kingston, Jamaica. This was a non-competitive, four-day but undoubtedly first-class game.

Hemmings was the first

Eddie Hemmings – a purple patch in 1982–83.

to achieve the feat for many years. Shahid Mahmood being the last to take all 10 in a first-class match when playing for Karachi Whites v Khairpur at Karachi's National

Stadium in the 1969–70 season; strangely enough, this also took place in September! The only subsequent instance was Pradeep Sunderam (10 for 78 for Rajasthan v Vidarbha, Jodhpur, 1985–86 – the second instance in the Ranji Trophy).

The last Englishman to perform the feat before Hemmings was N.I. Thomson (10 for 49 for Sussex v Warwicks, 1964), and the last England Test player was J.C. Laker (10 for 53 for England v Australia, Old Trafford, 1956). Eddie is also the first Englishman touring abroad to perform such a feat, and the first tourist of any sort since Clarrie Grimmett's 10 for 37 for Australia v Yorkshire at Bramall Lane, Sheffield in 1930.

With regard to the West Indies it would appear to be the first instance of the feat in what is unarguably a first-class match. A.E. Hinds took 10 for 36 in the first innings for A.B. St Hill's team v Trinidad at Port of Spain in January 1901, but though almost certainly first-class it was a 12-a-side game; H.P. Simmons took the 11th wicket.

Costing 175 runs, Hemmings's 10 wickets are the most expensive in one innings ever. In fact the following are the only instances of more than 100 runs being conceded.

Ian Thomson, still the last man to take all ten wickets in English first-class cricket.

EXPENSIVE TENNERS

Analysis	Player	Match/Venue	Season
10–175	E.E. Hemmings	International XI v West Indian XI, Kingston	1982–83
10–131	A.P. Freeman	Kent v Lancs, Maidstone	1929
10–129	James Lillywhite	South v North, Canterbury	1872
10–127	V.W.C. Jupp	Northants v Kent, Tunbridge Wells	1932
10–113	T.W.J. Goddard	Gloucs v Worcs, Cheltenham	1937
10–104	V.E. Walker	Middlesex v Lancs, Old Trafford	1865
10–102	R. Berry	Lancs v Worcs, Blackpool	1953

Hemmings's all-10 feat came in an innings total of 419 by the West Indies XI. This is the highest-ever score in which a bowler has taken all 10 wickets. The previous best was 360 totalled by Kent v Northants at Tunbridge Wells when V.W.C. Jupp took 10 for 127 in 1932. A.P. Freeman took 10 for 131 when Lancashire totalled 347 v Kent at Maidstone in 1929, while T.E. Bailey's 10 for 90 for Essex at Clacton in 1949 came in a Lancashire score of 331.

Readers may be interested that the first known instance of a bowler taking all 10 wickets in an innings in the equivalent of a modern 'first-class' match was when Edmund Hinkly performed the feat for Kent against England at Lord's in July 1848. Hinkly, a 29-year-old fast left-arm outswing bowler took all 10 wickets in the second innings after obtaining six in the first. On this, his first appearance at Lord's, Hinkly bowled unchanged with W.R. Hillyer to skittle England for 120 and 74, but England's bowlers, including all-time 'greats' in John Wisden, William Lillywhite and William Clark made even better use of a dubious wicket and Kent were finally beaten by 55 runs.

V.W.C.JUPP

Right A scorecard that Robin Hobbs was no doubt delighted to sign.

FAST HOOKES

History was made at Adelaide in October 1982 when South Australian captain David Hookes scored 107 in 55 minutes against Victoria, reaching his century in 43 minutes. This is the fastest time recorded for a first-class 100 in Australia and, coming from 34 balls, it is almost certainly the fastest in this respect in all first-class cricket.

R.N.S. Hobbs and B.L. Cairns have both reached centuries in 45 balls but even Fender's historic effort in 1920 took at least 40 balls, while none of the old-time fast scorers ever seems to have taken fewer than 50 balls.

Hookes's 100 was only the fifth in Australia to have been reached inside one hour; details of all five are listed below.

FASTEST CENTURIES IN AUSTRALIA

Player	Mins to 100	Final Score	Match/Venue	Season
V.T. Trumper	57	101	NSW v Vict, Sydney	1905–06
J.N. Crawford	53	114	MCC v S Aus, Adelaide	1907–08
D.R.A. Gehrs	50	119	S Aus v W Aus, Adelaide	1912–13
L.N. Constantine	52	100	W Indies v Tas, Launceston	1930–31
D.W. Hookes	43	107	S Aus v Vict, Adelaide	1982–83

ESSEX COUNTY CRICKET CLUB

ESSEX v. AUSTRALIA

HOURS OF PLAY .... at ...CHELMSFORD ON 23rd, 25th and 26th AUGUST, 1975.

1st DAY 11.30 - 6.30 ..... 2nd DAY 11.30 - 6.30 ..... 3rd DAY 11.30 - 6.00 at 6.30

LUNCH INTERVAL 1.30 to 2.10 ...... TEA INTERVAL 4.15 ......

TOSS WON BY AUSTRALIA WHO BATTED

Best wishes

Rick Auld

AUSTRALIA WON BY 98 RUNS.

ESSEX

		1st INNINGS		2nd INNINGS	
1	D.E.A. EDMEADES	lbw b WALKER	15	ABSENT SICK	—
2	B.R. HARDIE	A. THOMSON		b NOT OUT	—
3	K.S. McEWAN	B. WALKER	0	NOT OUT	—
4	* K.W.R. FLETCHER	RETIRED HURT	71	HIT WKT b THOMSON	88
5	G.A. GOOCH	st ROBINSON b HALLETT	24	ABSENT HURT	—
6	K.D. BOYCE	RUN OUT	60	lbw b WALKER	—
7	S.R. TURNER	b WALKER	79	c ROBINSON b WALKER	11
8	N. SMITH	st ROBINSON b HALLETT	46	c TURNER b WALKER	11
9	R.E.S. HOBBS	c GILMORE b HIGGS	46	c HIGGS b THOMSON	24
10	J.K. LEVER	NOT OUT	5	c LAIRD b HIGGS	100
11	D. ACFIELD	DID NOT BAT		c THOMSON b HIGGS	0
				st ROBINSON b HALLETT	10
EXTRAS		b - 2 lb - w 10 nb 12		b - 4 lb 1 w 2 nb 7	

TOTAL for 8 dec. 330   TOTAL 254

FALL OF WICKETS

1st INNS.	1	2	3	4	5	6	7	8	9	
	15	23	150	194	212	279	324	330		
2nd INNS.	1	2	3	4	5	6	7	8	9	
	42	50	65	95	109	242	243	254		

BOWLING ANALYSIS

	O	M	R	W	Nb	Wd		O	M	R	W	Nb	Wd
A. THOMSON	12	1	64	1				7		35	2		
R. WALKER	15	3	103	2				12	2	35	3		
J. HIGGS	2							13		21	2		
G. GILMORE	18	2	89	2				7.1		76	1		
A. HALLETT													

AUSTRALIA

		1st INNINGS		2nd INNINGS	
1	A. TURNER	lbw b HOBBS	33	c ACFIELD b TURNER	110
2	B.M. LAIRD	c EDMEADES b LEVER	127	c SMITH b TURNER	72
3	R. EDWARDS	RUN OUT		c b ACFIELD	
4	* R.W. MARSH	lbw b ACFIELD	101	c b ACFIELD	19
5	G.J. GILMORE	NOT OUT	30	NOT OUT	39
6	D. ROBINSON	NOT OUT	2	DID NOT BAT	
7	J.R. THOMSON	DID NOT BAT	39	DID NOT BAT	
8	M.H.N. WALKER	DID NOT BAT		DID NOT BAT	
9	J.D. HIGGS	NOT OUT		c HARDIE b HOBBS	1
10	K.D. WALTERS	DID NOT BAT		lbw b LEVER	4
11	A.A. HALLETT	DID NOT BAT	10	NOT OUT	
EXTRAS		b 2 lb 11 w - nb 19		DID NOT BAT	

TOTAL for 6 dec. 365   TOTAL for 4 dec. 325

FALL OF WICKETS

1st INNS.	1	2	3	4	5	6	7	8	9	
	103	162	243	247	259	350				
2nd INNS.	1	2	3	4	5	6	7	8	9	
	105	192	202	257						

BOWLING ANALYSIS

	O	M	R	W	Nb	Wd		O	M	R	W
K. BOYCE											
J. LEVER		6	39	1							
D. ACFIELD	12	2									

UMPIRES

David Hookes in aggressive mood, watched by Derek Randall with Bob Taylor behind the stumps.

1983

BEST OF ZAHEER

Zaheer Abbas enjoyed a record-breaking season in Pakistan in 1982–83. The most publicized of his records was his becoming the first Asian, and 20th batsman in all, to reach a total of 100 first-class centuries.

Zaheer's 215 for Pakistan v India at Lahore was achieved in his 658th first-class innings. The only batsmen to have reached the hundred in fewer innings are:

D.G. Bradman	295
D.C.S. Compton	552
L. Hutton	619
G. Boycott	645

The hundredth run of his 100th century was the 30,890th of his career. Only Bradman (24,495), Compton (28,264) and Hutton (30,647) had scored fewer runs when they achieved their 100th hundred.

Earlier in the season Zaheer placed himself on another pedestal when he scored 125 and 101 for Pakistan International Airways v Karachi at Karachi, thus obtaining a century in each innings of a match for a record eighth time. He had previously shared the record of seven with W.R. Hammond. All Zaheer's double feats had been achieved in the space of 6½ years, as the list shows.

Scores	Match/Venue	Season	Result
216★ & 156★	Gloucs v Surrey, The Oval	1976	Drawn
230★ & 104★	Gloucs v Kent, Canterbury	1976	Won
205★ & 108★	Gloucs v Sussex, Cheltenham	1977	Won
100★ & 100★	PIA v Railways, Lahore	1980–81	Won
215★ & 150★	Gloucs v Somerset, Bath	1981	Drawn
133★ & 128	Gloucs v Northants, Northampton	1981	Drawn
162★ & 107	Gloucs v Lancs, Gloucester	1982	Drawn
125 & 101	PIA v Karachi, Karachi	1982–83	Drawn

It will be seen that on no fewer than six occasions, the feat came in a County Championship match. This too is a record, J.B. Hobbs coming second with five, and represents an answer to those doubters who feel Zaheer scored many cheap runs against sub-standard Pakistani opposition. It is also of interest that Zaheer has finished on the winning side on three of the eight occasions, and never on the losing side. If this sounds unimpressive one can examine the efficacy of the other leaders with regard to match-winning abilities.

No. Times	Player	Results
7	W.R. Hammond	won 3, lost 1
6	J.B. Hobbs	won 2, lost 1
	G.M. Turner	won 3, lost 0
5	C.B. Fry	won 0, lost 1

Despite the limitations in scope of the figures, Zaheer certainly does not suffer by comparison. Even Bradman's four such performances were only match-winners on two occasions, while none of Jessop's four 'doubles' were for a winning side.

An examination of those batsmen who have scored 200 and 100 in the same match is also of interest. Two of Zaheer's four were for the winning side, and both of Maurice Hallam's also; most of the others, including Arthur Fagg's two double centuries in the match for Kent v Essex in 1938, were match-drawing performances. Hallam is virtually the only batsman in the list who was not a habitual high-scorer. Was the Leicestershire stalwart the only one to adapt his methods to the needs of his side, whereas the others piled up runs as of habit?

BATSMEN SCORING 200 AND 100 IN SAME MATCH

No. Times	Player	Results
4	Zaheer Abbas	won 2, drawn 2
2	M. R. Hallam	won 2
1	W.M. Armstrong	won
	K.D. Walters	won
	K.S. Duleepsinhji	won
	L. Baichan	drawn
	G.S. Chappell	drawn
	A.E. Fagg	drawn
	S.M. Gavaskar	drawn
	Hanumant Sigh	drawn
	H.T.W. Hardinge	drawn
	C.P. Mead	drawn
	Qasim Omar	drawn
	D.W. Randall	drawn
	L.G. Rowe	drawn
	Salahuddin	drawn
	Shafiq Ahmed	drawn
	B. Sutcliffe	drawn
	Talat Ali	drawn
	D.G. Bradman	lost

Zaheer enjoying more applause from an enthusiastic Pakistan crowd.

GREAT SCORING ON THE SUB-CONTINENT

Amidst the world-wide concentration on Tests and limited-overs internationals in 1982-83, ordinary first-class cricket – at least that found on the Indian sub-continent – remained alive and flourishing. Milestones were being passed and records broken.

Qasim Omar was not a name instantly recognizable to the cricket world at that time. Yet in the closing weeks of 1982 he set several run-scoring records and no-one, bar the writer, noticed.

Omar opened his 1982–83 first-class season in October with 47 and 7 not out for the Muslim Commercial Bank v Rawalpindi at Faisalabad in the Qaid-I-Azam Competition. He then scored an unbeaten 203 against Railways at the Bagh-I-Jinnah ground, following this with 89 v Allied Bank at the Gaddafi Stadium, Gulberg, and then a double of 210★ and 110 v Lahore at the Association ground there.

By the end of October he had 686 runs. A couple of quiet games followed but another superb double of 174 and 110★ against Karachi at the National Stadium there took him past 1,000 runs for the season, the first time any batsman had exceeded 1,000 runs for a season before the turn of the year. Omar reached four figures on November 24, the earliest date for reaching such an aggregate for any non-English season, beating Andrew Sandham who reached 1,000 runs in India in the 1926–27 season on December 10. Purely domestically, Omar had by then become the first batsman to score 1,000 runs in a season in the 25 years of the Qaid-I-Azam Competition, the previous record of 853 having been obtained by Agha Zahid for Habib Bank in 1981–82.

Omar then left the MCB side to play two matches against the Indian tourists, in which he increased his tally for the 1982 part of the 1982–83 season to 1,275, taking him past Sandham's total of 1,227 for the 1926 part of the 1926–27 Indian tour, and

establishing a new record. Although well placed at the turn of the year to set a new record for a Pakistan season, for a variety of reasons Qasim Omar did not play another first-class innings during the season. He nevertheless finished second in the batting averages, with 1,275 runs at 91.07. In a high-scoring season Zaheer Abbas topped the averages with 1,371 runs at 97.92.

There follows a list of batsmen to have completed 1,000 runs before the end of December during a season in one country outside England.

Zaheer's own record for the season – 1,597 runs in 1973–74 – remained intact, but another milestone was passed: during the final game of the season Abdul Qadir took eight United Bank wickets to ensure the PACC

Trophy for his team, Habib Bank. His fifth wicket, that of Test player Sikander Bakht, was his 100th of the season – a milestone never before passed in Pakistan. The previous record was 90 wickets (13.23) by Abdur Raqib in 1977–78.

While Qasim Omar and Zaheer Abbas were completing 1,000 runs in the Pakistani season before the turn of the year, David Hookes was also achieving this milestone in Australia. What is more, in scoring his 1,000th run on December 19 he set a new record for Australia. Hookes proceeded to another Australian record by scoring, 1,163 runs by the end of December, beating Ponsford's 1,146 in the first half of the 1927–28 season in the only five innings he played.

1000 RUNS BEFORE END OF DECEMBER IN A NON-ENGLISH SEASON

Player	Country	Season	Inns	N.O.	Runs	H.S.	Av'ge	100s
Qasim Omar	Pakistan	1982–83	18	4	1275	210★	91.07	6
A. Sandham	India	1926–27	19	2	1227	150	72.18	6
A.R. Border	Australia	1985–86	17	2	1172	194	78.13	5
D.W. Hookes	Australia	1982–83	18	1	1163	146	68.41	3
W.H. Ponsford	Australia	1927–28	5	0	1146	437	229.20	4
Zaheer Abbas	Pakistan	1982–83	11	0	1122	215	102.00	6
G.M. Yallop	Australia	1983–84	10	1	1102	268	122.44	5
R.B. Simpson	Australia	1963–64	12	1	1078	359	98.00	4
The Nawab of Pataudi	India	1964–65	19	3	1063	154	66.44	5
R.B. Simpson	Australia	1962–63	15	1	1052	205	75.14	5
G. Boycott	Australia	1970–71	16	3	1051	173	80.85	4
D.C.S. Compton	S Africa	1948–49	11	2	1048	300	116.44	5
H. Sutcliffe	Australia	1923–33	10	1	1004	194	111.56	5

Andy Sandham, still the fastest to 1,000 runs in India.

1,000 RUNS IN AUSTRALIAN SEASON BEFORE END OF DECEMBER

Player	Season	Date Achieved	Total Runs by Year End	Av'ge
D.W. Hookes	1982–83	December 19	1163	68.51
R.B. Simpson	1962–63	December 22	1052	75.14
A.R. Border	1985–86	December 26	1172	78.13
R.B. Simpson	1963–64	December 26	1078	98.00
G. Boycott	1970–71	Decmber 27	1051	80.85
G.M. Yallop	1983–84	December 28	1102	122.44
W.H. Ponsford	1927–28	December 30	1146	229.20
H. Sutcliffe	1932–33	Decmber 31	1004	111.56

NARROW MISS FOR AUSTRALIA

The last day of the Melbourne Test of the 1982–83 series was understandably lauded for its excitement; England finally scraped victory to keep the Ashes temporarily alive. Yet this writer confesses he was glued to his radio hoping Australia would level the scores and then achieve victory with a six.

Overwhelming reasons are needed for one's nationalistic fervour to be so transcended – one hopes the motives *were* sufficiently strong. The fact is that had Australia performed the feat outlined above, finishing the match victorious after an unbroken last-wicket stand of 79, they would have established a new record for first-class cricket for most runs added after the fall of the 9th wicket to achieve a one-wicket victory.

The first 'first-class' or 'Great' match for which a reasonably full scorecard survives took place in 1744 when a 10th-wicket stand of about 10 between Messrs Cutbush and Hadswell

enabled Kent to defeat an All-England XI by one wicket. The game was played at Bunhill Fields, now the ground of the Honourable Artillery Company and still used for cricket in 1987. The ground is situated just north of Chiswell Street, between City Road and Bunhill Row, EC1, and *not*, as claimed by some authorities, further north near Finsbury Park. Since 1744 one-wicket victories have averaged little more than one per year and the highest stand to bring such a win is only 77.

This occurred in February 1936. The venue was Madras, and the match involved the Maharaja of Patiala's Australian team and the Madras Presidency. The tourists began their second innings needing 261 for victory – a target which must have seemed remote when the Australian No. 11, Victorian pace bowler Tom Leather, joined Queensland Test player Ron Oxenham with the score 185 for nine. However, defying all the odds, they actually added 77 to win the match.

LAST-WICKET WINNERS

Runs in Stand	Players	Match/Venue	Season
77	R.K. Oxenham & T.W. Leather	Australian XI v Madras Pres., Madras	1935–36
66	P.I. Bedford & M.O.C. Sturt	Middlesex v Gloucs, Gloucester	1961
64	G.W. Humpage & R.G.D. Willis	Warwicks v Yorks, Edgbaston	1983
57	J.B. Mortimore & J. Davey	Gloucs v Glamorgan, Bristol	1973
54	J.M. Gregory & E.J. Long	A.I.F. v Yorks, Sheffield	1919
53	A. Stone & J. Newman	Hants v Kent, Canterbury	1908
53	Abdur Rahim & Wahid Khan	Peshawar v Lahore, Sialkot	1983–84
51	A. Geringer & E.O. Simons	Transvaal B v OFS, Pretoria	1983–84
49	K.J. McCarthy & M. Hendricks	S Australia v New South Wales, Sydney	1971–72
48	A.W. Nourse & P.W. Sherwell	S Africa v England, Johannesburg	1905–06
48	A. Edwards & P. Dunn	W Australia v W Indians, Perth	1951–52
47	A. Woodcock & J.P. Whiteside	Leics v Warwicks, Leicester	1896
46	G.F. Grace v W.S. Patterson	Gents v Players, Lord's	1877
43	W.H. Livsey & G.S. Boyes	Hants v Surrey, Soiuthampton	1924
42	R. Roopnaraine & S.G. Russell	Cambridge U v Scotland, Cambridge	1966

SMITH BROTHERS OPEN FOR HAMPSHIRE

When Robin and Christopher Smith opened the batting for Natal in the 1982–83 season, a South African reader asked whether any brothers in the past had built reputations as opening partners. The short answer is no, but I felt it might be interesting to examine some of these pairs.

Starting with cricket's greatest brotherhood, E.M. and W.G. Grace opened the Gloucestshire innings regularly for more than 20 years from 1870, but although initially they averaged more than 50 together, their final average opening stand for their county career was only 28. However, their record matches that of any other pair of brothers and they did have seven century opening stands. A third Grace, G. F., also opened for Gloucestershire occasionally, but never with W.G. and apparently only three times with E.M.

One of the most famous county *batting* brotherhoods was the Fosters. There were seven of them, with several often playing in the same Worcestershire team; yet rarely did two of them open an innings together and only one century opening stand has been traced. The Palairets, Lionel and Richard, are another renowned batting brotherhood, and one easily imagined them, around the turn of the century, regularly looking after the opening bowlers in their own stylish manner, paving the way for Sammy Woods, and seasoned pros like Len Braund and Ernest Robson. Nothing of the sort! Despite continual problems with their early batting, Somerset rarely used the Palairets in harness and I can trace no significant opening stand between them.

The early Middlesex sides were strong in brotherhoods. Neither the Walkers nor the Douglases managed to create a formidable opening pair from their many permutations, but A.J. and H.R. Webbe showed promise

before the latter's early death.

In the last two decades of Victoria's reign Kent often included George, Frank and Alec Hearne – professionals and gritty batsmen ideally equipped to seeing off the likes of Tom Richardson and Bill Lockwood. All three Hearne combinations were used as opening pairs on occasion, but all were singular failures, with only one stand of 50 traced.

The three Bryan brothers often frequented the Kent teams of the 1920s and 1930s, embellishing August of most seasons with their stylish skills. J.L. opened on many occasions, but with one of his brothers? Not on your life, not with Wally Hardinge around!

The most regular and prolific opening pair of brothers seems to have been Somerset's Lees, Frank and Jack. Between 1931 and 1934 they took part in eight century first-wicket stands, on two occasions exceeding 200, and in one match adding more than 100 in each innings. Even they lacked real consistency however, and their career average

The Smith brothers, Robin (left) and Chris (right).

is less than 30. Staying with Somerset, the Rippon twins, A.D.E. and A.E.S., promised well in 1914 and 1919 but after adding 144 against Essex in 1919 they broke up, A.D.E. leaving the first-class game. J.S. and W.H. Denton were another pair of twins who promised much as openers. They obtained two century stands in 1913 and 1914 but did not re-emerge as a pair after the war. W.H. also opened with younger brother A.D. on a few occasions, with average success.

The Shuter brothers of Surrey opened once, in 1878, the Quaifes of Warwickshire several times in the 1890s, with little success. They hailed from Sussex, but this county, famed for its cricketing families, has never found an opening pair from one, though Jim and Harry Parks tried briefly in 1928.

Finally Worcestershire, in addition to the Fosters, had the Richardsons (who did not open together) and Fred and Eddie Cooper. The latter pair enjoyed two century opening stands in 1947 and 1948. Unfortunately Fred, after showing great promise, found difficult war experiences affecting him, and he decided on premature retirement and a less unnerving occupation.

The Natal Smiths, Chris and Robin, then re-emerged in 1983 as the Hampshire Smiths and both scored a century in the first

innings of their county's game with Lancashire, which provoked further interest. It will be seen from the table below that this is the first such feat for Hampshire, and in county cricket as a whole there have been few such cases of fraternal co-operation in the same innings. Indeed Denis Compton did his best to run big brother Leslie out before anything had a chance to develop, while the

Kentish Hearnes, in particular, rarely seemd to bat well together.

It may be noted that Robin Smith scored his century on his Championship début; only D.O. Baldry – 151 v Glamorgan at Portsmouth in 1959 – had previously done this for Hampshire. The Smiths no longer open the batting, but may well equal their centuries feat in the future.

BEST OPENING STANDS FOR BROTHERS IN COUNTY CRICKET

Runs	Players	Match/Venue	Season
234	J.W. & F.S. Lee	Somerset v Essex, Leyton	1932
213	J.W. & F.S. Lee	Somerset v Surrey, Weston	1934
168	J.S. & W.H. Denton	Northants v Leics, Leicester	1913
163	F. & E. Cooper	Worcs v Essex, Worcester	1947
156	E.M. & W.G. Grace	Gloucs v Surrey, The Oval	1873

CENTURIES BY BROTHERS IN SAME INNINGS IN FIRST-CLASS INTER-COUNTY CRICKET

Players/Scores	Match/Venue	Season
E.M. Grace 108 & G.F. Grace 115★	Gloucs v Notts, Clifton College	1872
L.C.H. Palairet 109 & R.C.N. Palairet 106	Somerset v Middlesex, Lord's	1895
L.C.H. Palairet 154 & R.C.N. Palairet 156	Somerset v Sussex, Taunton	1896
Walter Quaife 101 & William Quaife 117	Warwicks v Leics, Leicester	1899
W.L. Foster 140 & R.E. Foster 134	Worcs v Hants, Worcester (1st inns)	1899
W.L. Foster 172★ & R.E. Foster 101★	Worcs v Hants, Worcester (2nd inns)	1899
William Quaife 223★ & Walter Quaife 115	Warwicks v Essex, Leyton	1900
H.K. Foster 152 & R.E. Foster 111	Worcs v Derbys, Derby	1901
H.K. Foster 112 & R.E. Foster 109	Worcs v Derbys, Worcester	1902
G.W. Beldam 140 & E.A. Beldam 105	Middlesex v Somerset Lord's	1904
H.K. Foster 123 ret hurt & R.E. Foster 174	Worcs v Kent, Worcester	1907
George Gunn 143 & J.R. Gunn 160	Notts v Gloucs, Bristol	1911
J.T. Tyldesley 129 & G.E. Tyldesley 109	Lancs v Leics, Leicester	1913★
J.T. Tyldesley 210 & G.E. Tyldesley 110	Lancs v Surrey, The Oval	1913★
George Gunn 185★ & J.R. Gunn 111★	Notts v Surrey, Trent Bridge	1919
J.H. Parks 115 & H.W. Parks 123	Sussex v Lancs, Eastbourne	1930
J.W. Lee 109 & F.S. Lee 140	Somerset v Essex, Leyton	1932
J.G. Langridge 159 & J. Langridge 130	Sussex v Kent, Maidstone	1934
J.H. Parks 168 & H.W. Parks 155	Sussex v Hants, Portsmouth	1937
J.G. Langridge 110 & J. Langridge 119★	Sussex v Worcs, Worcester	1938
J.G. Langridge 100 & J. Langridge 103	Sussex v Gloucs, Bristol	1946
C.L. Smith 100 & R.A. Smith 100★	Hants v Lancs, Bournemouth	1983

★Consecutive matches

LANCASHIRE WHIRLWINDS

One of the most remarkable happenings of the 1983 English season was the astonishing batting by Steve O'Shaughnessy and Graeme Fowler for Lancashire against Leicestershire at Old Trafford. O'Shaughnessy's personal achievement has been well documented, but the statistics for the partnership have been less well covered.

On the third afternoon Leicestershire declared and Lancashire started their second innings at 3.05pm, O'Shaughnessy and Fowler facing the far from demonic bowling of David Gower and James Whitaker. Tea was taken 35 minutes later when the score had been taken to 190 for 0 in 17 overs. O'Shaughnessy had reached 101 not out in 35 minutes, which equalled the time for the fastest-ever first-class century, by P.G.H. Fender for Surrey v Northants at Northampton in 1920. The partnership reached 100 in 21 minutes, thus equalling the shortest known time for a century partnership by A. Sims and V.T.

Trumper for an Australian XI v Canterbury at Christchurch in 1913–14.

O'Shaughnessy's 101★ included 17 fours, five sixes and three singles, believed to be the least number of scoring strokes ever needed to reach a century, Oddly, his hundred could have been even faster! For several overs he and Fowler assiduously blocked the bowling of Gower and Whitaker.

Shortly after tea O'Shaughnessy, who had added four to his score, was dismissed for 105 in 43 minutes. The first-wicket partnership had added 201 in this time. This is the fastest-ever substantial partnership in first-class cricket. The only stands which come anywhere near to rivaling it are the 171 in 42 minutes by Fender and H.A. Peach when Fender obtained his own fast century and 152 in 29 minutes by J.D. Love and and P.E. Robinson for Yorkshire v Sussex at Hove in 1985.

Three minutes later Fowler, who had scored 83 in 65 minutes in the Lancashire first innings, reached his own century

in 46 minutes and was dismissed two minutes later without adding to his score. In an incredible burst of scoring before tea Fowler hit sixes from ten consecutive scoring strokes. This is most certainly a record, the previous best being six off consecutive scoring strokes (and successive balls) by G.S. Sobers for Notts v Glamorgan at Swansea in 1968 and by M.J. Procter for Gloucestershire v Somerset at Taunton in 1979. Fowler also hit two fours before his run of sixes and two immediately after and actually scored 76 from 14 scoring strokes.

Not only was this the first innings to produce two innings of 100 each in fewer than 50 minutes, but it was all the more significant in that they were the opening pair.

Steve O'Shaughnessy, always an aggressive batsman.

Percy Fender, whose record of 35 minutes still has not been bettered.

GIFFORD SIGNED BY WARWICKS

Warwickshire's signing from Worcestershire in 1983 of the middle-aged Norman Gifford on a two-year contract set one wondering whether any cricketer older than him had been transferred between two first-class counties on a playing contract. The answer, at least in the last 50 years, and probably in all time, is no. Warwickshire and Gifford had in fact achieved a new cricketing milestone, as the table shows. The list is limited to players aged 40 years or more at the start of the new season.

The dramatic increase in the rate of transfer of older players is apparent, and although it is not the brief of this writer to comment on the statistics one feels it could be seen as a damning indictment of the recent policy of some counties. One wonders whether in laying the blame for England's lack of success on overseas players, the arrows are being shot at the wrong target.

TRANSFERS OF PLAYERS OVER 40

Player	Counties	Season	Age
N. Gifford	Worcs-Warwicks	1983	43yrs 2mths
J.D. Bond	Lancs-Notts	1974	42yrs 0mths
T.W. Cartwright	Somerset-Glamorgan	1977	41yrs 9mths
D.S. Steele	Derbys-Northants	1982	41yrs 7mths
J.M. Parks	Sussex-Somerset	1973	41yrs 6mths
C.W. Grove	Warwicks-Worcs	1954	41yrs 5mths
J.A. Ormrod	Worcs-Lancs	1984	41yrs 4 mths
J.H. Hampshire	Yorks-Derbys	1982	41yrs 3mths
J. Birkenshaw	Leics-Worcs	1981	40yrs 6mths
D.B. Close	Yorks-Somerset	1971	40yrs 2mths

Notes
J.C. Laker, who played for Essex from 1962, is omitted since there was a two-season gap after his leaving Surrey. Also he was not a contracted player with Essex.
F.S. Trueman is omitted since there was a gap between his playing for Yorks and Derbys, and he then only played limited-overs matches. Similarly players such as J.A. Snow, H.J. Rhodes and R.G.A. Headley do not qualify.
Players such as F.J. Titmus, J. Mercer and G.E.E. Lambert are omitted since they did not move on a playing contract, likewise R. Illingworth, who transferred from Leics to Yorks as cricket manager.
Amateurs who changed counties are also omitted, since they were not contracted players: such players as R.E.S. Wyatt (Warwicks-Worcs), R.H. Moss (Lancs-Worcs) and W.C. Caesar (Surrey-Somerset) were older than Gifford.

Warwickshire skipper Norman Gifford welcomes the 1986 'new boys'. Left to right: Brian McMillan, Gordon Parsons and Robert Weir.

YOUNG BARNETT TO LEAD DERBYSHIRE

In recent seasons those responsible for appointing county captains have by and large tended to equate age with efficiency despite lack of supporting evidence, so it was both surprising and, to this writer, refreshing to hear that Kim Barnett had been chosen as official Derbyshire skipper. Barnett was 22 years 315 days on the first day of his first-class captaincy début match and I set out to compile a list of all those who were appointed official county captain before their 23rd birthday. Since in many cases it has not been possible to discover the actual date of appointment I have used the date of the first day of their first match. The position of the county at the end of the first season has been given for seasons since 1890, when the Championship was given official status.

Success for Kim Barnett after Derbyshire had won the Asda Trophy at Scarborough in 1985.

F.R. Foster, Championship-winning captain of Warwickshire in his first season.

YOUNGEST COUNTY CAPTAINS

Age (yrs–days)	Name/County	Date of Birth	Date of Captaincy	End Season Posn
21–174	G. Strachan (Surrey)	21.11.1850	13.5.1872	–
22–38	M.C. Bird (Surrey)	25.3.1888	2.5.1910	2nd
22–101	H.W.R.Bencraft (Hants)	4.3.1858	14.6.1880	–
22–101	F.R. Foster (Warwicks)	31.1.1889	11.5.1911	1st
22–160	A.C. MacLaren (Lancs)	1.12.1871	10.5.1894	5th
22–174	R.H. Moore (Hants)	14.11.1913	6.5.1936	10th
22–237	S.J. Symington (Leics)	16.9.1926	11.5.1949	17th
22–286	M.St.J. Packe (Leics)	21.8.1916	3.6.1939	17th
22–287	H. Morris (Glamorgan)	5.10.1963	19.7.1986	17th
22–315	K.J. Barnett (Derbys)	17.7.1960	28.5.1983	9th
22–320	Hon M.B. Hawke (Yorks)	16.8.1860	2.7.1883	–
22–322	W.G. Grace (Gloucs)	18.7.1848	5.6.1871	–
22–325	F.P. Miller (Surrey)	29.7.1828	19.6.1851	–

Notes
Record books name S.H. Akroyd, born 13.2.1849. Surrey captain for 1869. It seems likely that he first led Surrey on 14.6.1869, aged 20 years 121 days, which puts him top of the list. However, there seems some doubt whether he was official captain for the season so I have omitted him. Similarly it is probable that C.G. Taylor captained Sussex in 1839 aged 22 years 201 days, while J.M. Cotterill may have led Sussex in 1874, aged 22 years 239 days.

GREAT SECOND INNINGS TOTAL BY HANTS

To score more than 400 to win after a declaration is a very rare feat indeed, as the following list of all such instances traced in the Championship reveals. The list was compiled following Hampshire's victory over Essex.

Astonishingly, the feat was achieved again in the 1983 season by Warwickshire who made the remarkable winning score of 417 for two against Glamorgan. More Press speculation was aroused by the goings-on in the game between Essex and Middlesex at Chelmsford. Middlesex, 206 in arrears on first innings, proceeded to save the game by batting out the rest of the

match to score 634 for seven. The difference between their first and second innings totals was 551, a new record for all first-class cricket in England. It also equalled the record for first-class cricket anywhere.

Unlike some records, this was achieved against what were originally overwhelming odds; it was a genuine performance and one feels disappointed that one more run was not scored in the Middlesex second innings (or one fewer in the first). The four instances of the largest variations between a side's two innings totals in a match are as follows. Middlesex's score of 634 for seven was the highest in county cricket

HIGHEST WINNING SECOND INNINGS SCORES

Winning Score	Wkts Lost of Declaring Side/Match/Venue		Season
502–6	9	Middlesex v Notts, Trent Bridge	1925
428–5	6	Sussex v Northants, Kettering	1939
419–6	8	Notts v Leics, Trent Bridge	1926
417–2	0	Warwicks v Glamorgan, Edgbaston	1983
410–6	6	Hants v Essex, Southend	1983
404–5	9	Lancs v Hants, Southampton	1910

The clock and the scoreboard tell the story of Warwickshire's successful chase.

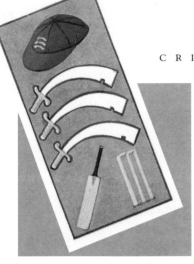

GREATEST DIFFERENCE BETWEEN FIRST AND SECOND INNINGS TOTALS

Runs Difference	Team/Scores	Opponents/Venue	Season
551	Barbados (175 & 726-7 dec)	Trinidad, Bridgetown	1926-27
551	Pakistan (106 & 657 8 dec)	West Indies, Bridgetown	1957-58
551	Middlesex (83 & 634-7)	Essex, Chelmsford	1983
543	Somerset (87 & 630)	Yorkshire, Headingley	1901

BEST-EVER SECOND-INNINGS SCORE

Runs	Match	Venue	Season
770	New South Wales v South Australia	Adelaide	1920-21

BEST EVER SECOND INNINGS SCORE IN ENGLISH FIRST-CLASS CRICKET

Runs	Match	Venue	Season
703-9 dec	Cambridge University v Sussex	Hove	1890

BEST FOUR IN COUNTY CHAMPIONSHIP

Runs	Match	Venue	Season
634-7	Middlesex v Essex	Chelmsford	1983
630	Somerset v Yorkshire	Headingley	1901
585-7	Warwickshire v Surrey	The Oval	1905
577-4	Glamorgan v Gloucs	Newport	1939

since 1947; what may not have been realized is that it is the highest-ever second-innings score in the County Championship, and the second highest in English first-class cricket.

BLAZING JUNE FOR EDMONDS

During the month of June 1983, Phil Edmonds took 54 first-class wickets for 700 runs and it was recognized by some people in cricket that the taking of 50 wickets in a calendar month is now a very rare feat. Before Edmonds the last player to do so was Essex's John Lever who took 53 wickets in June 1979; since Edmonds the feat has not been repeated.

It so happens that a fellow researcher, Darren Senior from Yorkshire, has done some 'digging' into the whole subject of wickets in a month, and with Senior's help I feel I can put the efforts of Edmonds and Lever into some sort of perspective. I have listed the best total for each full month of an English first-class season, and also every other instance of more than 80 wickets. It may be of interest that the holder of the record, C.L. Townsend, achieved it as an 18-year-old just out of Clifton College. The right-arm off-spinner never quite repeated his marvellous form of August 1895, though he became a fine all-rounder and won two England caps.

A curious theory has been propounded over the years that spin bowlers improve with age. Townsend was among the first of numerous spin bowling prodigies to expose the theory as the nonsense it certainly is. The 'Glad Seasons' of 'Ram & Val', and the fragile genius of India's Laxman Shivaramakrishman, are among the most notable of the post-war examples.

MOST WICKETS IN A MONTH

Month	Wkts	Player	County	Season
May	77	C.W.L. Parker	Gloucs	1931
June	91	A.P. Freeman	Kent	1930
July	93	A.P. Freeman	Kent	1929
	85	A.P. Freeman	Kent	1928
August	94	C.L. Townsend	Gloucs	1895
	86	A.P. Freeman	Kent	1933
	84	J. Southerton	Surrey, Sussex	1870

A record haul for Phil Edmonds in June 1983.

The young C.L. Townsend pictured in the summer of 1895.

SEVEN IN A ROW FOR WARWICKS

Warwickshire's run of victories in seven successive Championship games aroused speculation about a record. Although Warwickshire did win eight in succession spread over two seasons, 1911 and 1912, seven wins is a record for them in one season and the best since Surrey, the eventual champions, won eight in succession in June and July 1957. Warwickshire's run was obviously a commendable achievement, but the following list perhaps puts things into their proper perspective.

SUCCESSIVE WINS IN CHAMPIONSHIP

Wins	County	Season	Final Position
13	Yorkshire	1923	1st
12	Yorkshire	1925	1st
11	Kent	1906	1st
9	Surrey	1896	4th
	Middlesex	1920	1st
	Yorkshire	1932	1st
	Surrey	1955	1st

Eight successive wins have been achieved by Surrey (four times), Yorkshire (three times), Lancashire and Middlesex (twice), Kent and Sussex (once each). Yorkshire have four times had seven successive wins, Surrey three times, Middlesex twice and Kent and Warwickshire once each.

During 1920 and 1921 Middlesex achieved a record 17 wins in successive Championship games. Yorkshire won 16 in succession in 1932 and 1933 and Surrey 15 in 1954 and 1955.

A.B. Sellers, who was appointed captain of Yorkshire in 1933 in the middle of their run of 16 Championship victories. **Inset** The Middlesex team of 1921.

GIFFORD IN HIS PRIME

The form of Warwickshire's Norman Gifford was a feature of the 1983 season. His 104 wickets was the most ever for a bowler in his début season for Warwickshire, beating Dilip Doshi's 101 in 1980. It was the fourth time Gifford has taken 100 wickets, but the first since 1970. The gap of 13 years and seasons is unusually long, but not a record, as the table shows.

LONGEST INTERVAL BETWEEN 100 WICKET SEASONS

Bowler	County	Season	Wkts	Interval (Seasons)	Interval (Years)
P.J. Sainsbury	Hants	1955	102	16	16
	Hants	1971	107		
N. Gifford	Worcs	1970	105	13	13
	Warwicks	1983	104		
[1]F.R. Brown	Surrey	1932	120	11	17
	Northants	1949	111		

[1] Brown performed the double each time – there were no 1,000 run seasons between.

Gifford, aged 43, was unusually old to take 100 wickets, as the next table shows. Listed are bowlers who have taken 100 wickets aged 43 or more in post-war cricket. Where a bowler

Peter Sainsbury, a consistent wicket–taker but there were 16 years between his two most successful seasons.

performed the feat more than once, only the oldest age is given, with the number of times.

Gifford was also among the oldest players to take 100 wickets for his county for the first time, as this table indicates.

OLDEST BOWLERS TO TAKE 100 WICKETS FOR A COUNTY FOR THE FIRST TIME

Bowler	Season	Age at Start of Season
E. Robinson (Yorks)	1928	44
P.T. Mills (Gloucs)	1926	43
W.A. Humphreys (Sussex)	1893	43
A. Booth (Yorks)	1946	43
W.E. Alley (Somerset)	1962	43
N. Gifford (Warwicks)	1983	43
G.W. Brook (Worcs)	1930	41

G.W. Brook made his first-class début in 1930 after 'amending' his date of birth to make himself appear seven years younger than he was. T. Emmett and J. Southerton took 100 wickets for the first time in 1886 and 1870 respectively, when aged 44 and 42, but the cricket set-up was so different in those days that they have been excluded.

OLDEST BOWLERS TO TAKE 100 WICKETS IN A POSTWAR SEASON

Bowler	No Times	Season	Oldest age at start of season
T.W.J. Goddard (Gloucs)	5	1946–50	49
J.C. Clay (Glamorgan)	1	1946	48
J.M. Sims (Middlesex)	3	1947–49	45★
W.E. Hollies (Warwicks)	1	1957	44★
A.W. Wellard (Somerset)	1	1946	44
D. Shackleton (Hants)	1	1968	43★
R.T.D. Perks (Worcs)	1	1955	43
A. Booth (Yorks)	1	1946	43
W.E. Alley (Somerset)	1	1962	43
N. Gifford (Warwicks)	1	1983	43

The oldest bowler to take 100 wickets in a season was Charlie Parker of Gloucestershire who took 108 wickets in 1936 aged 52. Wilfrid Rhodes (Yorkshire) was 51 when he took 100 wickets in 1929.

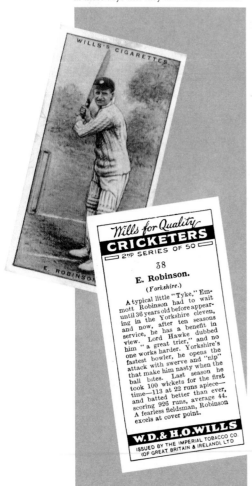

Tom Goddard, regular success throughout his forties.

ANOTHER 1,000 RUNS FOR ALAN JONES

During 1983, his last season, Alan Jones completed 1,000 runs for his county for the 23rd consecutive season; only Philip Mead, with at least 1,000 runs for Hampshire in 27 consecutive seasons (1906–36, war years excluded), has exceeded this total.

BATSMEN SCORING 1,000 RUNS FOR THEIR COUNTY IN 20 OR MORE SEASONS

No. Times	Player	Seasons
27	C.P. Mead (Hants)	1906–36
23	A. Jones (Glamorgan)	1961–83
21	H. Sutcliffe (Yorks)	1919–39
20	T.W. Hayward (Surrey)	1895–1914
20	Jas Langridge (Sussex)	1927–52

Alan Jones, second only in consistency to Philip Mead (top).

EIGHT BEFORE LUNCH FOR JEFFERIES

When Lancashire's South African left-arm seamer, Steve Jefferies, took eight Notts wickets on the first morning at Trent Bridge in June 1983 it was appreciated as a fine performance (though Lancs subsequently lost the match) but perhaps the feat is rarer than was supposed at the time. I have personally always equated 8 wickets before lunch in one innings with a century innings before lunch but it is in fact a good deal less common. Although the list below looks lengthy, it averages out at hardly more than one performance per season since the first, in 1862, while the last 20 English seasons have seen only six.

Regrettably I am forced to confine my list to Great Britain – too little data is available, even from contemporary reports, for a meaningful overseas list to be compiled. However, Bill Frindall has pointed out that Dennis Lillee achieved 8–29 before lunch for an Australian XI v World XI at Perth in 1971–72 – certainly a mighty achievement.

A vast amount of the information in this list has never been published. I have personally looked at contemporary newspaper reports of all the possible instances, but will accept that there may be a small number of omissions.

Bobby Peel – the destroyer of Notts in 1888.

Tom Richardson – eight wickets before lunch in three successive seasons.

EIGHT OR MORE WICKETS IN ONE INNINGS BEFORE LUNCH

Player	Analysis[1]	Match/Venue	Season
James Lillywhite	9–29	Sussex v MCC, Lord's	1862
R.C. Tinley	8–12	Notts v Cambridgeshire, Trent Bridge	1862
W.E. Maitland	8–58	Oxford U. v MCC, Lord's	1864
J. Grundy	9–19	Notts v Kent, Trent Bridge	1864
G. Wootton	8–15	England XI v Kent, Canterbury	1864
G. Wootton	9–37	MCC v Oxford U, Lord's	1865
G. Freeman	8–11	Yorks v Cambridgeshire, Holbeck	1868
G. Freeman	8–29	Yorks v Surrey, Sheffield	1869
J. Southerton	9–30	South v North, Lord's	1875
A.G. Steel	8–40	Cambridge U. v MCC, Cambridge	1878
W.G. Grace	9–23	MCC v Derbys, Lord's	1878
G. Nash	8–14	Lancs v Somerset, Old Trafford	1882
W.G. Grace	8–31	Gloucs v Somerset, Old Trafford	1882
E. Barratt	8–48	Surrey v Sussex, The Oval	1883
E. Peate	8–23	North v Australians, Old Trafford	1886
R. Peel	8–12	Yorks v Notts, Sheffield	1888
G.A. Lohmann	8–13	Surrey v Lancs, Old Trafford	1888
G. Bean	8–29	Sussex v MCC, Lord's	1889
A.W. Mold	9–41	Lancs v York, Huddersfield	1890
J.W. Sharpe	9–47	Surrey v Middlesex, The Oval	1891
E. Wainwright	8–49	Yorks v Middlesex, Sheffield	1891
J.T. Hearne	9–32	Middlesex v Notts, Trent Bridge	1891
T. Richardson	9–47	Surrey v Yorks, Sheffield	1893
J. Briggs	8–19	Lancs v Yorks, Headingley	1893
J.T. Rawlin	8–29	Middlesex v Gloucs, Clifton	1893
T. Richardson	10–45	Surrey v Essex, The Oval	1894
T. Richardson	9–49	Surrey v Sussex, The Oval	1895
A.W. Mold	8–33	Lancs v Surrey, Old Trafford	1896
R. Peel	8–27	Yorks v The South, Scarborough	1896
J. Briggs	8–39	Lancs v Hants, Old Trafford	1897
C.L. Townsend	9–48	Gloucs v Middlesex, Lord's	1898
G.L. Jessop	8–34	Cambridge U. v Hants, Cambridge	1898
S. Haigh	8–21	Yorks v Hants, Southampton	1898
F.W. Stocks	8–22	Oxford U. v A.J. Webbe's Team, Oxford	1899
S. Santall	8–23	Warwicks v Leics, Edgbaston	1900
J.H. Sinclair	8–32	London County v Derbys, Crystal Palace	1901

F.W. Tate	8–28	Sussex v Hants, Southampton	1902
W. Rhodes	8–26	Yorks v Kent, Catford	1902
F.M. Spry	8–80	Gloucs v Worcs, Worcester	1902
B. Cranfield	8–39	Somerset v Gloucs, Gloucester	1903
C. Blythe	9–30	Kent v Hants, Tonbridge	1904
C. Blythe	8–72	Kent v Essex, Leyton	1905
G.A. Wilson	8–30	Worcs v Somerset, Taunton	1905
W. Brearley	9–47	Lancs v Somerset, Old Trafford	1905
W. Huddleston	9–36	Lancs v Notts, Liverpool	1906
E.G. Dennett	10–40	Gloucs v Essex, Bristol	1906
H. Dean	8–43	Lancs v Oxford U., Oxford	1907
W. Mead	8–39	Essex v Notts, Leyton	1907
E.G. Dennett	8–9	Gloucs v Northants, Gloucester	1907
F.A. Tarrant	9–41	Middlesex v Gloucs, Bristol	1907
P.R. May	8–49	Gents of Sth v Players of Sth, Hastings	1907
T.G. Wass	8–29	Notts v Essex, Trent Bridge	1908
W. Brearley	8–61	Lancs v Essex, Old Trafford	1908
H. Dean	9–35	Lancs v Warwicks, Liverpool	1909
W.C. Smith	8–35	Surrey v Derbys, The Oval	1910
G.H. Hirst	8–80	Yorks v Somerset, Sheffield	1910
W. Huddleston	8–31	Lancs v Derbys, Glossop	1910
G.H. Hirst	9–41	Yorks v Worcs, Worcester	1911
C. Blythe	8–45	Kent v Gloucs, Cheltenham	1911
J.W. Hearne	9–82	Middlesex v Surrey, Lord's	1911
E.G. Hayes	8–22	Surrey v Gloucs, The Oval	1912
S.F. Barnes	8–29	England v South Africa, The Oval	1912
S.G. Smith	8–39	Northants v Somerset, Bath	1912
W.C. Smith	8–61	Surrey v Gloucs, Bristol	1913
H. Dean	8–27	Lancs v Hants, Liverpool	1914
W. Wells	8–35	Northants v Yorks, Sheffield	1919
J.W.H.T. Douglas	8–39	Essex v Derbys, Derby	1920
[2]W. Bestwick	10–40	Derbys v Glamorgan, Cardiff	1921
A.S. Kennedy	8–11	Hants v Glamorgan, Cardiff	1921
F.C.L. Matthews	9–39	Notts v Northants, Trent Bridge	1923
F.C.L. Matthews	8–33	Notts v Kent, Canterbury	1924
V.W.C. Jupp	8–18	Northants v Glamorgan, Swansea	1925
J. Mercer	8–39	Glamorgan v Gloucs, Swansea	1926
A.S. Kennedy	10–37	Players v Gentlemen, The Oval	1927
W.R. Hammond	9–23	Gloucs v Worcs, Cheltenham	1928
T.W.J. Goddard	9–21	Gloucs v Cambridge U., Cheltenham	1929
C.W.L. Parker	8–38	Gloucs v Surrey, Cheltenham	1930
G.S. Boyes	8–37	Hants v Leics, Leicester	1930
T.W.J. Goddard	8–44	Gloucs v Glamorgan, Swansea	1930
C.W.L. Parker	8–39	Gloucs v Notts, Bristol	1931
G.A.E. Paine	8–44	Warwicks v Northants, Peterborough	1931
A.P. Freeman	8–35	Kent v Somerset, Canterbury	1931
A.P. Freeman	8–38	Kent v Northants, Tunbridge Wells	1932
G.A.E. Paine	8–43	Warwicks v Worcs, Edgbaston	1934
W.E. Astill	8–50	Leics v Warwicks, Edgbaston	1934
H.A. Smith	8–44	Leics v Northants, Northampton	1935
W.E. Bowes	8–18	Yorks v Northants, Kettering	1935
M.S. Nichols	9–32	Essex v Notts, Trent Bridge	1936
W.H.R. Andrews	8–12	Somerset v Surrey, The Oval	1937
W.H. Copson	8–11	Derby v Warwicks, Derby	1937
J.M. Sims	8–32	Middlesex v Derbys, Lord's	1939
S.H. Martin	8–24	Worcs v Sussex, Worcester	1939
W.H.R. Andrews	8–25	Somerset v Hants, Portsmouth	1946
T.W.J. Goddard	8–70	Gloucs v Warwicks, Gloucester	1949
J.C. Laker	8–2	England v The Rest, Bradford	1950
C.W. Grove	9–39	Warwicks v Sussex, Edgbaston	1952
A.V. Bedser	8–18	Surrey v Warwicks, The Oval	1963
F.S. Trueman	8–28	Yorks v Kent, Dover	1954
D.J. Halfyard	9–39	Kent v Glamorgan, Neath	1957
D.B. Close	8–41	Yorks v Kent, Headingley	1959
K.E. Palmer	9–57	Somerset v Notts, Trent Bridge	1963
R. Harman	8–12	Surrey v Notts, Trent Bridge	1964
R.V. Webster	8–19	Warwicks v Cambridge U., Cambridge	1966
J. Cotton	9–29	Leics v Indians, Leicester	1967
A.G. Nicholson	8–22	Yorks v Kent, Canterbury	1968
Sarfraz Nawaz	8–27	Pakistanis v Notts, Trent Bridge	1974
G.B. Stevenson	8–65	Yorks v Lancs, Headingley	1978
S.T. Jefferies	8–46	Lancs v Notts, Trent Bridge	1983

[1] The figures quoted are the final analyses for the innings, the figures at lunch are hardly ever available, but in every instance 8 wickets or more were taken during the innings before lunch.

[2] All 10 wickets before lunch – a unique achievement.

Jim Laker, and Tony Nicholson (below), two successful bowlers in the pre-lunch period.

SIX GLOUCS BATSMEN PASS 1000 RUNS

A Gloucestershire life-member pointed out that six Gloucestershire batsmen exceeded 1,000 runs in the 1983 County Championship and asked for some details on the rarity of such a feat.

The fact is that since the reduction of the fixture list in 1969 it has become *very* rare for a county to have six batsmen scoring 1,000 runs in a Championship season. Prior to the Gloucs feat Nottinghamshire, in 1975, when they finished 13th, were the last county to have six such batsmen and before that Middlesex (16th) and Surrey (5th) both achieved the feat in 1970. Gloucestershire have to go back to 1953, when they were 6th, and

Tom Graveney, Jack Crapp, Arthur Milton, George Emmett, Andy Wilson and Martin Young all scored more than 1,000 runs.

It is interesting that only Glamorgan, Leicestershire and Somerset have never had six

batsmen scoring 1,000 runs in a Championship season and on only four occasions have seven batsmen scored 1,000 runs for one county in the same season. These four instances are listed below.

1928 Sussex (7th)	
E.H. Bowley	2130
James Langridge	1396
A.F. Wensley	1334
J.H. Parks	1241
H.W. Parks	1192
M.W. Tate	1174
K.S. Duleepsinhji	1082

1937 Sussex (5th)	
J.H. Parks	2578
J.G. Langridge	2364
James Langridge	1765
G. Cox	1729
T.E. Cook	1598
A.J. Holmes	1108
H.W. Parks	1093

1938 Gloucs (10th)	
W.R. Hammond	2180
J.F. Crapp	1671
B.O. Allen	1543
C.J. Barnett	1490
W.L. Neale	1337
A.E. Wilson	1131
G.M. Emmett	1050

1962 Warwicks (3rd)	
W.J. Stewart	2100
M.J.K. Smith	1988
K. Ibadulla	1863
A.C. Smith,	1101
T.W. Cartwright	1082
N.F. Horner	1060
R.E. Hitchcock	1058

The Gloucestershire squad of 1983, with six prolific batsmen (Broad, Stovold, Shepherd, Hignell, Romaines and Bainbridge) but still only 12th in the Championship.

James Langridge, part of a strong Sussex batting line-up between the wars.

1 9 8 4

GAVASKAR ENDS
THE SEQUENCE

An innings of 110 by S.M. Gavaskar for Bombay v Maharashtra in late January 1984 had a significance not noted, so far as I am aware, in any report. The century broke a run of six consecutive first-class hundreds by Gavaskar – all made in *Test* matches. The centuries were as follows:

Score	Match/Venue	Season
155	v Sri Lanka, Madras	1982–83
127★	v Pakistan, Faisalabad	1982–83
147★	v W. Indies, Georgetown	1982–83
103★	v Pakistan, Bangalore	1983–84
121	v W. Indies, Delhi	1983–84
236★	v W. Indies, Madras	1983–84

Researching back I found that Gavaskar had performed the same feat in 1978–79, when his two centuries against Pakistan and four against the West Indies came consecutively. The record, however, is held by West Indian C.L. Walcott. During the period 1953–54 to 1954–55 Walcott obtained eight Test hundreds, but none in any other first-class matches. Walcott's centuries were as follows:

Score	Match/Venue	Season
220	v England, Bridgetown	1953–54
124	v England, Port of Spain	1953–54
116	v England, Kingston	1953–54
108	v Australia, Kingston	1953–54
126&110	v Australia, Port of Spain	1954–55
155&110	v Australia, Kingston	1954–55

I find that K.D. Walters scored five consecutive first-class centuries in Tests for Australia in 1968–69, 1969–70. Several players have in fact scored four consecutive first-class hundreds in Tests. Perhaps the most startling was the performance of Australia's R.B. Simpson, whose last four centuries were spread over 10 years, 1967–68, 1977–78, and all in Tests.

Australian Test centurion Doug Walters.

Sunil Gavaskar, a consistent Test centurion.

HADLEE'S OUTSTANDING ALL-ROUND PERFORMANCE

One of the features of New Zealand's victory over England at Christchurch in February 1984 was the all-round display of Richard Hadlee. Hadlee was both the highest run-scorer and leading wicket-taker during the match, and joins a very short list of players who have performed this outstanding all-round feat in Test cricket. Only games not disrupted by bad weather are counted in the list. As will be seen, such a performance is usually a match-winning one, proving the value of a world-class all-rounder.

Hadlee also made his mark as a batsman alone during the match, his only innings of 99 exceeding the totals of the opposition in both their innings, England being all out for 82 and 96. This is the 34th time a player had performed this feat in Test cricket, but the first time by a New Zealander. Achieving the feat without scoring a century, as Hadlee did, has happened only once before, when W.A. Brown's innings of 62 for Australia v New Zealand at Wellington in 1945–46 exceeded both totals of the opposition, 42 and 54. Since this match was awarded Test status retrospectively, Hadlee's feat is, in a way, unique.

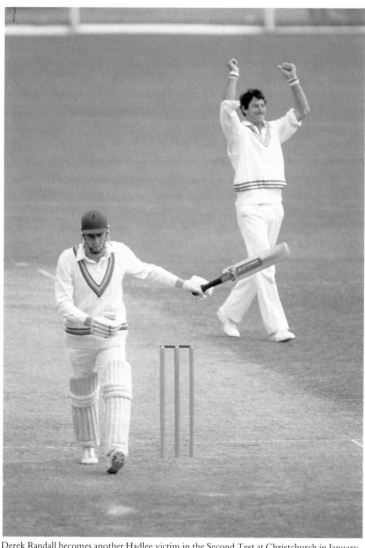

Derek Randall becomes another Hadlee victim in the Second Test at Christchurch in January 1984.

HIGHEST RUN-SCORER & LEADING WICKET-TAKER IN MATCH

Player	Runs/Wkts	Match/Season	Result
A.G. Steel	135, 21; 3–34, 3–49	E v A, Sydney 1882–83	Lost
W.J. Edrich	191, 22*; 4–95, 4–77	E v SA, Old Trafford 1947	Won
D.S. Atkinson	219, 20*; 2–108, 5–65	WI v A, Bridgetown 1954–55	Drawn
G.S. Sobers	174; 5–41, 3–39	WI v E, Headingley 1966	Won
Mushtaq Mohammad	121, 56; 5–28, 3–69	P v WI, Port of Spain 1976–77	Won
I.T. Botham	103, 30*; 5–73, 3–38	E v NZ, Christchurch 1977–78	Won
I.T. Botham	108; 0–17, 8–34	E v P, Lord's 1978	Won
I.T. Botham	114; 6–58, 7–48	E v I, Bombay 1979–80	Won
R.J. Hadlee	99; 3–16, 5–28	NZ v E, Christchurch 1983–84	Won

YALLOP'S RECORD GALLOP

In all countries bar England the first-class programme has been expanded in recent years, enabling a number of 'milestones' to be passed. This has lately applied especially to Australia, where the recent prolific scoring of Graham Yallop in 1983–84 saw one new record and a number of other worthy statistical feats.

Yallop's record concerns the number of runs he scored in Australian first-class cricket during the calendar year 1983; during his innings of 268 against Pakistan at Melbourne he exceeded the previous record held by Sir Donald Bradman. The list of batsmen with more than 1,500 runs is now as follows:

Bill Edrich, successful with both bat and ball against South Africa in 1947.

1,500 RUNS IN CALENDAR YEAR IN AUSTRALIA

Player	Year	Inns	N.O.	Runs	H.S.	Av'ge	100s
G.N. Yallop	1983	18	1	1834	268	107.88	8
D.G. Bradman	1929	20	3	1763	340	103.71	7
W.H. Ponsford	1927	11	0	1604	437	145.82	7
G.S. Chappell	1975	27	2	1601	144	64.04	7
D.G. Bradman	1937	19	2	1573	270	92.53	6
K.C. Wessels	1982	26	0	1527	220	58.73	7
D.G. Bradman	1931	16	0	1503	226	93.94	7
D.W. Hookes	1982	25	1	1501	146	62.54	3

Yallop also played first-class cricket in Sri Lanka during the year and passed another 'milestone' by becoming only the second batsman to exceed 2,000 runs during a calendar year without the aid of first-class cricket in England.

2000 RUNS IN A CALENDAR YEAR OUTSIDE ENGLAND

Player	Year	Inns	N.O.	Runs	H.S.	Av'ge	100s
W.M. Lawry	1965	30	4	2071	246	79.65	7
G.N. Yallop	1983	21	2	2005	268	105.53	8

Graham Yallop, whose record-breaking year of 1983 also included a visit to England for the Prudential World Cup.
Top Don Bradman, many of whose records still seem far beyond the reach of any current player.

NICK COOK'S IMPRESSIVE START TO TEST CRICKET

To the statistically-minded observer one of the more interesting features of England's Test exploits in 1983 and 1984 was the bowling of left-arm spinner, Nick Cook.

It was not generally noticed, or at least was not broadcast, that in taking 17 wickets in his first two Test matches in 1983 Cook made the best-ever start to a Test career by an England spin bowler, beating Robert Peel's 14 wickets in his first two Tests, in 1884–85. England's most successful spin bowler ever, Jim Laker, took 11 wickets in his first two Test matches. Cook's four wickets against New Zealand in the first Test of the winter tour took his total to 21 in three, six more than the previous record for an English spinner, shared by Peel, Laker and 'Tich' Freeman.

Cook was then dropped (in the light of this article, a decision in defiance of all logic) but with 11 wickets in the first Test against Pakistan on his return, he took his total to 32 in four Tests, which is a record for *any* English bowler in his first four Tests, beating Tom Richardson's 31 in 1894–95. England's previous best spinner was 'Tich' Freeman, with 19 for four. Despite taking only two wickets in his next Test, Cook's 34 in five kept him at the top of the English bowlers' list, one better than the start made by Richardson and Fred Trueman. The previous best for an England spinner was Laker's 22 in five. Though taking only one wicket in the last Test of the winter, Cook remains the leading English spinner after six Tests, his total of 35 exceeding by seven that of Roy Tattersall in his first six Tests. The tables show the leading bowlers after one, two, three, four, five and six Tests.

Nick Cook, whose successful run extended into the tour to Pakistan in 1983–84 with 11 wickets in the Karachi Test.

ONE TEST

Wkts	Bowler	Season(s)	Pace
12	F. Martin	1890	Med
11	C.S. Marriott	1933	Slow
	A.V. Bedser	1946	Med

Best for all countries:

16	R.A.L. Massie (A)	1972	Med

Best spin bowlers for all countries:

11	C.V. Grimmett (A)	1924–25
11	C.S. Marriott (E)	1933
11	A.L. Valentine (WI)	1950

TWO TESTS

Wkts	Bowler	Season(s)	Pace
22	A.V. Bedser	1946	Med
19	S.F. Barnes	1901–02	Med
17	N.G.B. Cook	1983	Slow

Bedser's total is best for all countries

Best spin bowlers are C.V. Grimmett (A) &
A.L. Valentine (WI) both 18

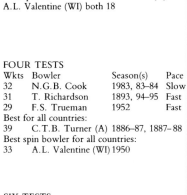

THREE TESTS

Wkts	Bowler	Season(s)	Pace
24	A.V. Bedser	1946	Med
	F.S. Trueman	1952	Fast
23	T. Richardson	1893, 94–95	Fast

Cook's 21 is best for an England slow bowler.

Best for all countries:

29	C.T.B. Turner (A)	1886, 87–88	

Best spin bowler for all countries:

26	H.V. Hordern (A)	1910–11, 11–12

FOUR TESTS

Wkts	Bowler	Season(s)	Pace
32	N.G.B. Cook	1983, 83–84	Slow
31	T. Richardson	1893, 94–95	Fast
29	F.S. Trueman	1952	Fast

Best for all countries:

39	C.T.B. Turner (A)	1886–87, 1887–88

Best spin bowler for all countries:

33	A.L. Valentine (WI)	1950

FIVE TESTS

Wkts	Bowler	Season(s)	Pace
34	N.G.B. Cook	1983, 83–84	Slow
33	T. Richardson	1893, 94–95	Fast
	F.S. Trueman	1952–53	Fast

Best for all countries:

45	C.T.B. Turner (A)	1886–87, 88

Best spin bowler for all countries:

39	A.L. Valentine (WI)	1950, 51–52

SIX TESTS

Wkts	Bowler	Season(s)	Pace
42	T. Richardson	1893, 94–95	Fast
40	F.R. Foster	1911–12, 13	Med
38	M.W. Tate	1924, 24–25	Med

Cook's 35 best for English slow bowler.

Best for all countries:

50	C.T.B. Turner (A)	1886–87, 88

Best spin bowler, all countries

43	A.L. Valentine (WI)	1950–51, 52

C.S. Marriott (above), S.F. Barnes (above right) and A.V. Bedser (top), all of whom enjoyed early success in Test cricket. While Bedser and Barnes went on to enjoy long and fruitful Test careers, the unfortunate C.S. Marriott was never asked to play a second Test.

Cook's Test career seems to have ended with his having played 9 Tests. Although he obviously did not retain his early strike rate (otherwise he would not have been discarded so quickly), his record of 40 wickets in his first 9 Tests places him top of the list among modern English spinners. The all-time list for leading English spinners after 9 Tests also shows Cook in a good light – specially in comparison with his successors, the older Middlesex pair of Emburey and Edmonds.

MOST WICKETS FOR A SPIN BOWLER AFTER NINE TESTS

Wkts	Player
55	R. Peel
44	A.P. Freeman
42	W. Rhodes
40	N.G.B. Cook
33	J.C. White
33	P.H. Edmonds
32	J.C. Laker
31	D.L. Underwood
30	C. Blythe

The qualification is 30 wickets, so J.E. Emburey (24) cannot be included.

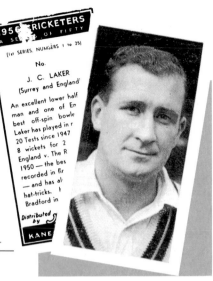

1956 CRICKETERS
A SERIES OF FIFTY
(1st SERIES. NUMBERS 1 to 25)
No.
J. C. LAKER
(Surrey and England)
An excellent lower half man and one of En best off-spin bowle Laker has played in r 20 Tests since 1947 8 wickets for 2 England v. The R 1950 — the bes recorded in fir — and has al hat-tricks. Bradford in
Distributed by
KANE

C.T.B. Turner had a successful start to his Test career for Australia but in the end played in only 17 Test matches.

UNDERWOOD'S MAIDEN CENTURY

The 1984 season was a goldmine for students of individual centuries; among the most notable was Derek Underwood's maiden century in his 618th innings. Only Bob Taylor needed more. The list of batsmen who needed most innings appears below.

MOST INNINGS BEFORE FIRST HUNDRED

Inns	Player	County	Season Achieved	Age
744	R.W. Taylor	Derbys	1981	39
618	D.L. Underwood	Kent	1984	39
569	G.S. Boyes	Hants	1936	37
564	W. Attewell	Notts	1897	36
483	F.S. Trueman	Yorks	1963	32
435	A.H.H. Gilligan	Sussex	1929	33
426	G.E.E. Lambert	Gloucs	1955	36
408	H.A. Smith	Leics	1937	36

As a matter of interest, the cricketers who played most first-class innings without *ever* recording a century are as listed below:

MOST INNINGS WITHOUT EVER SCORING A HUNDRED

Inns	Player	H.S.	County	Career Dates
954	C.W.L. Parker	82	Gloucs	1903–35
919	J.T. Hearne	71	Middlesex	1888–1923
884	R.T.D. Perks	75	Worcs	1930–55
852	D. Shackleton	87★	Hants	1948–69
837	D.J. Shepherd	73	Glamorgan	1950–72
835	H. Strudwick	93	Surrey	1902–27
812	G.A.R. Lock	89	Surrey, Leics, W Aus	1946–71

Among current players, Warwickshire's N. Gifford is the leader, having played 755 innings without a century; obviously he will now be aiming for 800, and inclusion in the list above.

Derek Underwood, who would no doubt claim that he was a much under-rated batsman, and Herbert Strudwick (above left), a brilliant wicket-keeper but whose long career as a batsman was mostly undistinguished.

DÉBUT HUNDREDS FOR SURREY PAIR

When Surrey players N.J. Falkner and K.T. Medlycott both obtained a century on their first-class débuts against Cambridge University at Banstead in 1984 it was the first time such a feat had been achieved in England; indeed it is such a rarity that I felt it worthwhile recording the few instances I have traced.

TWO PLAYERS MAKING DÉBUT CENTURIES IN SAME FIRST-CLASS MATCH

Players/Scores	Match/Venue	Season
N.L. Gooden (102), A.G. Moyes (104)	S. Australia v W. Australia, Melbourne	1912–13
O.W. Bill (115), L.R. Leabetter (128)	NSW v Tasmania, Sydney	1929–30
F.E. Fontaine (118), R.J. Lawson (119)	Victoria v Tasmania, Hobart	1930–31
K. Medlycott (117★), N.J. Falkner (101★)	Surrey v Cambridge U., Banstead	1984

SOME NEAR MISSES

R.G. Draper (114), W.D. Wilson (97)	E. Province v OFS, P Elizabeth	1945–46
J.A. Claughton (112), S.M. Clements (91)	Oxford U. v Gloucs, Oxford	1976
A. Du Toit (102), J. Kennedy (97)	Boland v Border, Stellenbosch	1980–81

I can find nothing in first-class inter-county cricket better than:

J.E. Hill (139★), A. Law (58)	Warwicks v Notts, Trent Bridge	1894

Nick Falkner (below) and Keith Medlycott (below left) both enjoying their debut match against Cambridge University.

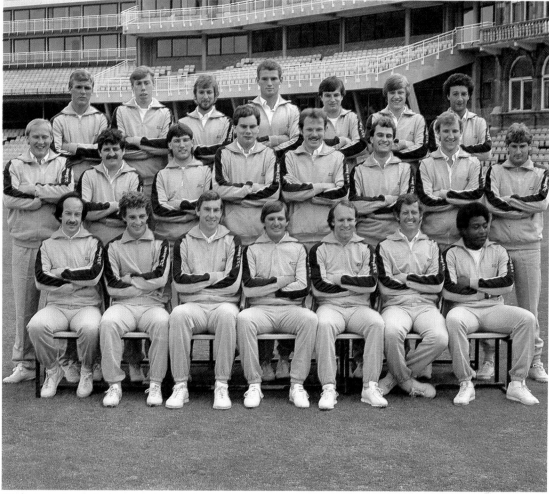

A host of centurions in the Surrey squad of 1984.

SURREY FIELD ELEVEN CENTURIONS

An interesting 'milestone' concerning hundreds was passed in 1984 by Surrey against Kent at Canterbury, and repeated in the following game v Gloucs at Cheltenham. Every Surrey player in these matches had scored a first-class century. These were the first occasions Surrey had fielded such a team, and my researches indicate it had only happened in county cricket on eight previous occasions, although Kent subsequently achieved the same feat in their match against Northants at Maidstone in 1985.

ALL-CENTURION TEAMS

Sussex v Northants, Hastings 1920: V.W.C. Jupp, J. Vine, E.H. Bowley, R.R. Relf, A.E. Relf, R.A. Young, H.L. Wilson, M.W. Tate, K.S. Ranjitsinhji, A.E.R. Gilligan, G.R. Cox.

Sussex v Leics, Horsham 1921: V.W.C. Jupp, E.H. Bowley, M.W. Tate, H.L. Wilson, K.A. Higgs, W.J. Malden, H.S. Malik, A.E. Relf, G.R. Cox, G.B. Street, A.E.R. Gilligan.

Notts v Gloucs, Bristol 1932: W.W. Keeton, W. Walker, A.W. Carr, A. Staples, G.V. Gunn, J. Hardstaff, F.W. Shipston, S.J. Staples, B. Lilley, H. Larwood, W. Voce.

Notts v Northants, Northamptom 1933: W.W. Keeton, C.B. Harris, W. Walker, A.W. Carr, A. Staples, F.W. Shipston, G.V. Gunn, B. Lilley, S.J. Staples, H. Larwood, W. Voce.

Yorks v Derbys, Chesterfield 1981: G. Boycott, R.G. Lumb, C.W.J. Athey, J.H. Hampshire, J.D. Love, P. Carrick, S.N. Hartley, D.L. Bairstow, A. Sidebottom, G.B. Stevenson, C.M. Old.

Yorks v Hants, Bournemouth 1982: G. Boycott, R.G. Lumb, C.W.J. Athey, S.N. Hartley, K. Sharp, D.L. Bairstow, P. Carrick, G.B. Stevenson, C.M. Old, A. Sidebottom, R. Illingworth.

Yorks v Notts, Worksop 1982: G. Boycott, R.G. Lumb, C.W.J. Athey, J.D. Love, S.N. Hartley, D.L. Bairstow, P. Carrick, G.B. Stevenson, C.M. Old, R. Illingworth, A. Sidebottom.

Surrey v Kent & v Gloucs 1984: A.R. Butcher, G.P. Howarth, G.S. Clinton, M.A. Lynch, R.D.V. Knight, A. Needham, C.J. Richards, D.J. Thomas, G. Monkhouse, S.T. Clarke, K. Medlycott.

Kent v Northants, Maidstone 1985: M.R. Benson, S.G. Hinks, N.R. Taylor, D.G. Aslett, C.S. Cowdrey, C. Penn, E.A.E. Baptiste, R.E. Ellison, G.W. Johnson, A.P.E. Knott, D.L. Underwood.

THOMSON RECALLED FOR SCOTLAND

From time to time a cricketer has found there has been a very large gap between two first-class appearances. The most extreme example is that of pace bowler R.H. Moss, an Oxford Blue in 1889. In 1893 he played in a first-class fixture for Liverpool & District against the Australians and made his next, and last, first-class appearance for Worcs v Gloucs in 1925, aged 57 after a 32-year gap. Moss's first-class career details almost defy belief and his feat is likely to remain a record for all time but the recent achievements of Jimmy Thomson, a left-arm spinner from Kilmarnock, certainly deserve comment. The 44-year-old Thomson this season played for Scotland v Ireland at Titwood, 22 years after his only previous first-class appearance in the same game at Greenock. Thomson joins a short list of players with 22 years or more between two first-class appearances, as the table shows. Scottish cricket statistician Richard Miller points out that since Thomson only took wickets in the 1984 game, here was a specialist bowler who took 22 years to obtain his first first-class wicket. W.C. Caesar, second in the table, did even better than Thomson, however. The specialist pace bowler made his début in 1922 and took his first wicket in 1946. As weird as most is the record of Hants stalwart Harry Baldwin. A mightily built slow bowler, Baldwin made his unsuccessful first-class début for Hants as a 16-year-old in 1877 and had to wait until his next game before taking his first wickets. This was in 1895 and he went on to make up for lost time, retiring in 1905 with 580 wickets.

LONGEST GAP BETWEEN FIRST-CLASS APPEARANCES

Player	Matches	Seasons	Gap (yrs)
R.H. Moss	Liverpool & District v Australians	1893	
	Worcs v Gloucs	1925	32
W.C. Caesar	Surrey v Scotland	1922	
	Somerset v Leics	1946	24
H.A. Cursham	Notts v Surrey	1880	
	Notts v South Africans	1904	24
M.B. Elderton	Gents v Cambridge U.	1907	
	Minor Counties v N Zealanders	1931	24
F.H. Hollins	Lancs v Warwicks	1904	
	MCC v Cambridge U.	1927	23
G.S. Tompkinson	Worcs v Cambridge U.	1903	
	Worcs v Derbys	1926	23
S.M. Toyne	Hants v Yorkshire	1905	
	MCC v Ireland	1928	23
E. Whalley-Tooker	Hants v Sussex	1885	
	Hambledon v 'England XII'	1908	23
D.H. Robins	Warwicks v Cambridge U.	1947	
	D.H. Robins XI v W. Indies	1969	22
G.B. Sanderson	Warwicks v London County	1901	
	Worcs v Northants	1923	22
J. Thomson	Scotland v Ireland	1962	
	Scotland v Ireland	1984	22

Harry Baldwin – a long wait for his first wickets.

EARLY CENTURIES FOR LEICESTER PAIR

Chris Balderstone and Peter Willey scored centuries for Leicestershire on April 18, 1984 – the earliest for 78 years. A full list of early centuries is given below.

EARLIEST FIRST-CLASS CENTURIES

Date	Player	Match/Venue	Season
April 14	T.W. Hayward	Surrey v London County, The Oval	1903
April 16	T.W. Hayward	Surrey v London County, The Oval	1900
	E.H.D. Sewell	Gentlemen v Surrey, The Oval	1906
April 18	J.C. Balderstone (earliest outside The Oval)	Leics v Cambridge U., Cambridge	1984
	P. Willey	Leics v Cambridge U., Cambridge	1984 (later same day)
April 19	K.S. McEwan	Essex v Cambridge U., Cambridge	1978
	I.P. Butcher	Leics v Cambridge U., Cambridge	1984
	R.J. Bartlett	Somerset v Oxford U., Oxford	1986
	B.R. Hardie	Essex v Cambridge U., Cambridge	1987
April 20	M.D. Haysman	Leics v Cambridge U., Cambridge	1984
April 21	B.F. Davison	Leics v MCC, Lord's	1976
	D.J.S. Taylor	Somerset v Cambridge U., Cambridge	1976
	A. Jones	Glamorgan v Cambridge U., Cambridge	1982
	C. Gladwin	Essex v Cambridge U., Cambridge	1984
	J.G. Wyatt	Somerset v Oxford U., Oxford	1985
	P.M. Roebuck	Somerset v Oxford U., Oxford	1985
April 22	J.A. Jameson	Warwicks v Cambridge U., Cambridge	1970
	J.A. Jameson	D.H. Robins' XI v Indians, Eastbourne	1974
	D.L. Amiss	D.H. Robins' XI v Indians, Eastbourne	1974
	Sadiq Mohammad	Gloucs v Oxford U., Oxford	1976
	N.H.C. Cooper	Gloucs v Oxford U., Oxford	1976
	A.E. Lea	Cambridge U. v Essex, Cambridge	1984
	J.D. Carr	Oxford U. v Somerset, Oxford	1985
	M.W. Gatting	MCC v Essex, Lord's	1987
	M.R. Benson	Kent v Oxford U., Oxford	1987
	S.G. Hinks	Kent v Oxford U., Oxford	1987

Peter Willey (top) and Chris Balderstone (above) – early birds of the 1984 season.

Tom Hayward – still the earliest century of any season.

HADLEE'S DOUBLE

Inarguably one of the major cricketing feats of recent years was Richard Hadlee's 'double' in England in 1984. The taking of 100 wickets and the scoring of 1,000 runs in one season by one player had been a common occurrence at one time but until Hadlee no-one had achieved the feat since Fred Titmus in 1967. The reduction in the number of first-class fixtures is always given as the main reason for the virtual extinction of this particular feat but really that is only part of the story since a 'double' has been achieved on several occasions in fewer matches than a regular first-class cricketer now plays in an English season. Hadlee achieved his 'double' in his 21st match of the season; the following table shows that in doing this he equalled the post-war record but that his commendable performance has been beaten 22 times, and that the record, shared by W.G. Grace and George Hirst, looks unreachable.

Richard Hadlee, the first 'double' for 17 years.

FEWEST MATCHES FOR DOUBLE

Matches	Players/Seasons
16	W.G. Grace 1875, 1877; G.H. Hirst 1906
17	W.G. Grace 1874; F.R. Foster 1911
18	F.E. Woolley 1920; J.W.H.T. Douglas 1921
19	W.G. Grace 1878; C.T. Studd 1882, 1883; G.A. Davidson 1895; G.H. Hirst 1901; C.B. Llewellyn 1901; F.A. Tarrant 1907, 1908; F.E. Woolley 1922; J.W. Hearne 1923; V.W.C. Jupp 1928
20	C.L. Townsend 1898; J.R. Gunn 1906; F.A. Tarrant 1913, 1914; S.G. Smith 1914; J.W. Hearne 1914, 1920; F.E. Woolley 1919; W.E. Astill 1921
21	W.G. Grace 1876; E.G. Arnold 1903; S.G. Smith 1909; F.A. Tarrant 1910; A.E. Relf 1913; J.W.H.T. Douglas 1914; F.E. Woolley 1921; G.H. Pope 1948; R.J. Hadlee 1984

Hadlee reached his 'double' on August 27, which seems to compare very badly with the record held by the redoubtable Yorkshireman George Hirst. In 1906 George actually added his 100th wicket to his 1,000 runs on June 28, and finally obtained 2,385 runs and 208 wickets for a unique 'double double' feat. Hirst had many more matches of course, so Hadlee's performance is by no means as inferior as the time factor makes it seem. In fact, to judge a 'double' by the number of days it took is now almost meaningless, so disadvantaged is the modern all-rounder.

It is certainly relevant that George Pope and Hadlee both achieved their 21-match 'doubles' in County Championship matches. This is a post-war record but George Hirst reached his Championship 'double' in 1906 in 17 matches, as did F.R. Foster for Warwickshire in 1911, and Frank Woolley (Kent) in 1920. The record for fewest matches needed to reach a County Championship 'double' is held by J.W.H.T. Douglas. His record for Essex in 1921 is so marvellous that I make no excuse for reproducing it match by match.

DOUGLAS'S DOUBLE

Runs	Wkts
44, 27	0–90, 2–17
8, 123★	7–91, 7–65
25, 2	6–99, 5–120
210★	9–47, 2–0
4, 35	4–115
123★, 57	2–72, 1–20
33, 30	0–55
50, 27	4–100, 4–39
50	3–65, 4–55
32	7–17, 7–74
80, 59★	3–34, 5–68
(1,000 runs completed)	
16, 1	3–58, 3–68
33	4–90, 3–35
9, 1	4–63
3	4–57, 0–1
('double' completed)	
7, 24★	0–62
22, 14	1–80
12	4–116, 1–70

1,161 runs and 109 wickets in 18 Championship matches, and the 'double' in only 15. As with with a number of other items in this book, one can set this as a 'milestone' never to be passed, or even reached again.

Johnnie Douglas achieved this record during and after a traumatic spell as one of the least successful and most maligned of all England captains. Such county form at this time adds much to Douglas's already considerable reputation as a man of courage and fortitude. Indeed in the circumstances his previously unsung performances in the 1921 County Championship must rank among the most remarkable in the history of the competition.

INVERARITY PASSES BRADMAN

The Sheffield Shield, which is presented each season to the winner of the Australian domestic first-class competition, was named after the 3rd Lord Sheffield who in 1891–92 organized a tour to Australia and donated £150 for the advancement of cricket in Australia; the money was invested in the Shield which was then competed for by the major colonies (now states).

The initial match commenced on December 16, 1892, played at Adelaide between South Australia and New South Wales. The first ball was bowled to Test player Sammy Jones by South Australia's intrepid skipper, George Giffen – a player who was to have a profound influence in the first years of the competition. The first century was scored in this game by Harry Donnan, born in Bakewell, Derbyshire, but resident in New South Wales for many years. Donnan's five-hour 120 helped his side to a first-innings lead but all-round excellence by George Giffen and a second-innings century by Test veteran Jack Lyons enabled South Australia to register the first Sheffield Shield victory – after following on. Some milestone, that – it didn't happen again in the Sheffield Shield for 73 years, and has still occurred only twice!

Giffen, a far more effective Shield than Test performer, really stamped his personality on the competition in its early days and

WILLS'S CIGARETTES.

GEORGE H. HIRST (YORKSHIRE).

J. W. H. T. DOUGLAS

reached 1,000 runs in only his ninth match. This happened during his 94★ against Victoria at the start of the 1894–95 season and the number of matches needed remained a record until the great Bill Ponsford reached 1,000 runs in his 8th Shield game in 1924–25. Ponsford still holds the record, but Donald Bradman equalled Giffen a few years later. Ponsford and Bradman more than maintained their form in the following years. They still share the record for 2,000 runs – in 14 games, but then Ponsford forged ahead. He reached 3,000 runs in a mere 18 games and 4,000 in 25 games (both still records) but the strain then told and he quietly tailed off. Nonetheless his final total of 5,413 runs (av 83.27) in 43 games compares favourably with all bar Bradman. Bradman reached 5,000 runs in 34 games, 6,000 in 43, 7,000 in 49, 8,000 in 55 and his final total of 8,926 was achieved in 62 matches – a stupendous record which almost defies belief, and should stand for all time. In 1983–84 John Inverarity became the first and so far only batsman to outscore Bradman in the Sheffield Shield – in his 158th game. This takes nothing from Inverarity; the table shows that he is currently without a challenger.

George Giffen, a stalwart of the Sheffield Shield.

LEADING RUN-SCORERS IN SHEFFIELD SHIELD

Player	State(s)	Inns	N.O.	Runs	H.S.	Av'ge	Career
R.J. Inverarity	WA, SA	275	32	9342	187	38.44	1962–85
D.G. Bradman	NSW, SA	96	15	8926	452★	110.19	1927–49
G.S. Chappell	SA, Q'land	173	20	8762	194	57.26	1966–85
S.C. Trimble	Q'land	230	13	8647	252★	39.84	1959–76
L.E. Favell	SA	220	4	8269	164	38.28	1951–70
I.M. Chappell	SA	157	13	7665	205	53.22	1961–80
P.J.P Burge	Q'land	138	12	7084	283	56.22	1952–68
Present-day leaders							
D.W. Hookes	SA	120	5	5728	306★	49.80	1975–
A.R. Border	NSW, Q'land	95	8	4765	200	54.77	1976–

Not only was George Giffen the first to reach 1,000 runs in the competition, he also reached 100 wickets for the first time in his 13th match, in 1895–96. Having already reached his 1,000 he thus completed the 'double'. He remains the record-holder for the quickest 100 wickets and quickest 'double'. Giffen's South Australian colleague, fast bowler Ernest Jones (later well-known as the original 'pommie bastard' hater, still baiting and barracking during the 'Body-line' series of 1932–33), was first to reach 200 wickets in his 37th game in 1902–03, but the remaining records are held by one man – Clarrie Grimmett.

Grimmett didn't start until the age of 32, in 1923–24. He took nine for 98 on his Shield début, for Victoria, but the following season he joined South Australia where he stayed until his 49th year, by which time he had set an aggregate record which will almost certainly never be beaten. Grimmett reached his 100 wickets in 16 matches, 200 in 31, 300 in 46, 400 in 61 and 500 in 78. A remarkably consistent record of 16, 15, 15, 15 and 17 matches for each 100.

Grimmett remains well clear of any possible challengers but in 1985–86 Jeff Thomson of Queensland achieved the remarkably creditable feat of overtaking off-spinner Ashley Mallet to move into second place. Thomson is comfortably the leading wicket-taker of any pace. He played in 84 matches, finishing with a very satisfactory average of 4.2 wickets per match.

Thomson's milestone was excellent for his time. It will be seen that there are no obvious challengers on the current Sheffield Shield scene.

LEADING WICKET-TAKERS IN SHEFFIELD SHIELD

Player	State(s)	Runs	Wkts	Av'ge	Career
C.V. Grimmett	Vict, SA	12976	513	25.29	1923–40
J.R. Thomson	Q'land, NSW	8728	355	24.58	1972–86
A.A. Mallett	SA	8170	344	23.75	1967–81
D.K. Lillee	WA	7544	323	23.35	1969–84
G.A.R. Lock	WA	7216	302	23.89	1962–71
Present-day leaders					
R.J. Bright	Vict	8707	250	34.82	1972–
T.M. Alderman	WA	5569	243	22.91	1974–

Clarrie Grimmett, a late starter but one who certainly made up for lost time.

Another batsman gets his marching orders from Jeff Thomson. This time it's a Test victim, at Headingley in 1985.
Top left Terry Alderman, still a long way to go to catch Jeff Thomson.

COWDREY'S EARLY SUCCESS

C.S. Cowdrey became the 25th bowler to take a wicket in his first over in Test cricket for England when he dismissed India's Kapil Dev in Bombay in 1984–85. The full list is as follows.

BOWLERS TAKING A WICKET IN THEIR FIRST OVER FOR ENGLAND

Bowler/Victim	No. Ball	Match/Venue	Season
A.N. Hornby/F.E. Allan	?	E v A, Melbourne	1878–79
W.M. Bradley/F. Laver	1	E v A, Old Trafford	1899
E.G. Arnold/V.T. Trumper	1	E v A, Sydney	1903–04
G.H.T. Simpson-Hayward/J.W. Zulch	5	E v SA, Johannesburg	1909–10
G.G. Macaulay/G.A.L. Hearne	1	E v SA, Cape Town	1922–23
M.W. Tate/M.J. Susskind	1	E v SA, Edgbaston	1924
M. Leyland/G. Challenor	?	E v WI, The Oval	1928
E.W. Clark/R.H. Catterall	6	E v SA, The Oval	1929
M.S. Nichols/H. Foley	?	E v NZ, Christchurch	1929–30
W. Barber/H.B. Cameron	2	E v SA, Leeds	1935
D.V.P. Wright/J.H.W. Fingleton	4	E v A, Trent Bridge	1938
R. Howorth/D.V. Dyer	1	E v SA, The Oval	1947
J.C. Laker/C.L. Walcott	4	E v WI, Bridgetown	1947–48
R.O. Jenkins/E.A.B. Rowan	3	E v SA, Durban	1948–49
R. Appleyard/Hanif Mohammad	2	E v P, Trent Bridge	1954
H.J. Rhodes/Pankaj Roy	4	E v I, Leeds	1959
L.J. Coldwell/Imtiaz Ahmed	5	E v P, Lord's	1962
M. Hendrick/E.D. Solkar	3	E v I, Old Trafford	1974
D.S. Steele/A.A. Mallett	4	E v A, Lord's	1975
M.W.W. Selvey/R.C. Fredericks	6	E v WI, Old Trafford	1976
J.E. Emburey/B.A. Edgar	4	E v NZ, Lord's	1978
R.D. Jackman/C.G. Greenidge	5	E v WI, Bridgetown	1980–81
D.R. Pringle/Yashpal Sharma	6	E v I, Lord's	1982
E.E. Hemmings/Javed Miandad	4	E v P, Edgbaston	1982
C.S. Cowdrey/Kapil Dev	4	E v I, Bombay	1984–85

W.M. Bradley, an early success in his Test career.

David Steele – a wicket in his first over but only one more in his Test career.

Maurice Tate, the first of many Test wickets at Edgbaston in 1924.

SRI LANKAN GLORY

Sri Lanka passed a notable 'milestone' in the August 1984 Test match which should be given recognition. Both Sidath Wettimuny and L.R.D. Mendis scored more than 200 runs in the match; this is the first time two players from the same side have passed this total in a Lord's Test.

The two Sri Lankans added their names to an even shorter list of batsmen scoring more than 200 runs in their first Lord's Test.

Player/Scores	Match/ Season
K.S. Duleepsinhji	
173+48=221	E v A, 1930
D.G. Bradman 254+1=255	A v E, 1930
K.J. Hughes 117+84=201	A v E, 1980
S. Wettimuny 190+13=203	SL v E, 1984
L.R.D. Mendis 111+94=205	SL v E, 1984

Wettimuny and Mendis share the enjoyment of centuries on their first appearance at Lord's.

GATTING GETS THERE AT LAST

One of the very few bright features of the early part of England's 1984–85 Indian tour was the maiden Test century of Mike Gatting, at Bombay, made in his 54th Test innings and his 31st Test match. Those players who required more Test innings than Gatting to achieve their first hundred were: A.W. Nourse (SA) 64; T.L. Goddard (SA) 62; Intikhab Alam (P) 61; W. Rhodes (E) 59; V. Pollard (NZ) 56. Intikhab Alam passed this 'milestone' in his 37th Test. Rhodes and S.M.H. Kirmani (I) in their 35th, Goddard in his 32nd.

It is interesting to examine the Test record of players who took a long time to achieve a century and I have listed all those who scored more than 1,000 runs before achieving the feat.

Mike Gatting – a long wait for his first Test century.

WILLS'S CIGARETTES.

WILFRED RHODES (YORKSHIRE).

MOST INNINGS BEFORE MAIDEN TEST CENTURY

Player	No. Matches	Inns	N.O.	Runs	H.S.	Av'ge	50s	Other Test Achievements at Time
T.L. Goddard (SA)	32	61	5	1978	99	35.32	15	85 wkts
R.B. Simpson (A)	29	51	5	1653	92	35.93	15	24 wkts
A.W. Nourse (SA)	34	63	8	1639	93★	29.80	12	36 wkts
I.R. Redpath (A)	28	48	4	1491	97	33.89	10	
J.V. Coney (NZ)	25	43	6	1211	84	32.73	10	
W. Rhodes (E)	34	58	15	1202	77	27.95	8	96 wkts
M.W. Gatting (E)	31	53	4	1159	81	23.65	9	
S.M.H. Kirmani (I)	34	50	7	1150	88	26.74	6	59 ct 21 st
Intikhab Alam (P)	37	60	9	1123	68	22.02	7	87 wkts
R.W. Barber (E)	22	35	3	1091	97	34.09	8	31 wkts
G.A. Gooch (E)	21	35	3	1027	99	32.09	8	

FOWLER AND GATTING BOTH PASS 200

The performance of Graeme Fowler and Mike Gatting, who both scored a double century against India at Madras, was unique for England in Tests, and only the sixth example in all Test cricket. I set out to try and find further examples in first-class cricket and although the feat is not as rare as I had expected I feel the list of all those I have traced will be of interest. I have also indicated the result of each match. Without necessarily disputing the long accepted dictum that bowling wins matches, it will be seen that outstanding batting, especially by two in harness, also helps a lot.

K. MILLER

J. de COURCY

TWO DOUBLE CENTURIES IN ONE INNINGS

Players/Scores	Inns Total	Match/Venue	Season	Result
J.T. Brown (300) & J. Tunnicliffe (243)	662	Yorks v Derbys, Chesterfield	1898	Won
R.M. Poore (304) & E.G. Wynyard (225)	672-7 dec	Hants v Somerset, Taunton	1899	Won
C.B. Fry (209) & E.H. Killick (200)	560-5 dec	Sussex v Yorks, Hove	1901	Drawn
J.B. Hobbs (205) & E.G. Hayes (276)	742	Surrey v Hants, The Oval	1909	Won
J.W. Hearne (218*) & E.H. Hendren (201)	608-7 dec	Middlesex v Hants, Lord's	1919	Won
W. Rhodes (210) & C.A.G. Russell (201)	627	MCC v S Australia, Adelaide	1920–21	Won
H.O. Rock (235) & A.F. Kippax (212*)	614	New South Wales v Victoria, Sydney	1924–25	Lost
W.H. Ponsford (352) & J. Ryder (295)	1,107	Victoria v New South Wales, Melbourne	1926–27	Won
D.N. Moore (206) & W.R. Hammond (211*)	627-2 dec	Gloucs v Oxford U., Oxford	1930	Won
G.A. Headley (344*) & C.C. Passailaigue (261*)	702-5 dec	Jamaica v Tennyson's XI, Kingston	1931–32	Won
P. Holmes (224*) & H. Sutcliffe (313)	555-1 dec	Yorks v Essex, Leyton	1932	Won
I.S. Lee (258) & S.O. Quin (210)	560-6 dec	Victoria v Tasmania, Melbourne	1933–34	Drawn
W.H. Ashdown (332) & L.E.G. Ames (202*)	803-4 dec	Kent v Essex, Brentwood	1934	Won
W.H. Ponsford (266) & D.G. Bradman (244)	701	Australia v England, The Oval	1934	Won
A.D. Nourse (240) & I.J. Siedle (207)	664-6 dec	Natal v W. Province, Durban	1936–37	Won
F.M.M. Worrell (308*) & J.D.C. Goddard (218*)	650-3 dec	Barbados v Trinidad, Bridgetown	1943–44	Drawn
V.S. Hazare (200*) & R.S. Modi (201*)	615-4	CC of India v Services, Bombay	1944–45	Won
V.M. Merchant (217) & R.S. Modi (210)	592-6 dec	Bombay v W. India, Bombay	1944–45	Won
F.M.M. Worrell (255*) & C.L. Walcott (314*)	619-3 dec	Barbados v Trinidad, Port of Spain	1945–46	Drawn
Gul Mahomed (319) & V.S. Hazare (288)	784	Baroda v Holkar, Baroda	1946–47	Won
S.G. Barnes (234) & D.G. Bradman (234)	659-8 dec	Australia v England, Sydney	1946–47	Won
D.E. Davies (215) & W.E. Jones (212*)	586-5 dec	Glamorgan v Essex, Brentwood	1948	Won
B.B. Nimbalkar (443*) & K.V. Bhandarkar (205)	826-4	Maharashtra v Kathiawar, Poona	1948–49	Won
J.G. Dewes (204*) & G.H.G. Doggart (219*)	441-1 dec	Cambridge U. v. Essex, Cambridge	1949	Drawn
F.M.M. Worrell (241*) & E.D. Weekes (200*)	628-2 dec	West Indians v. Leics, Leicester	1950	Won
G.S. Ramchand (230*) & D.G. Phadkar (217)	725-3 dec	Bombay v Maharashtra, Bombay	1950–51	Drawn
R.I. Maddocks (271) & J. Hallebone (202)	647	Victoria v Tasmania, Melbourne	1951–52	Drawn
D. Brookes (204*) & D.W. Barrick (211)	532-6 dec	Northants v Essex, Northampton	1952	Drawn
K.R. Miller (262*) & J.H. De Courcy (204)	592-4 dec	Australians v Combined Services, Kingston	1953	Won
W. Watson (257) & T.W. Graveney (231)	607	MCC v British Guiana, Georgetown	1953–54	Won
G.S. Sobers (365*) & C.C. Hunte (260)	790-3 dec	West Indies v Australia, Bridgetown	1964–5	Won
Pervez Akhtar (337*) & Javed Baber (200)	910-6 dec	Railways v Dera Ismael Khan, Lahore	1964–65	Won
W.M. Lawry (210) & R.B. Simpson (201)	650-6 dec	Australia v W Indies, Bridgetown	1964–65	Drawn
Zafar Altaf (268) & Majid Khan (241)	824	Lahore Greens v Bahawalpur, Lahore	1965–66	Drawn
T.L. Goddard (222) & H.M. Ackerman (200*)	524-6 dec	NE Transvaal v W Province, Cape Town,	1967–68	Drawn
C.P.S. Chauhan (207) & M.S. Gupte (200)	560-2 dec	Maharashtra v Vidarbha, Poona	1972–73	Won
J.A. Jameson (240*) & R. Kanhai (213*)	465-1	Warwicks v Gloucs, Edgbaston	1974	Won
Khalid Irtiza (290) & Aslam Ali (236)	656-5 dec	UBL v Multan, Karachi	1975–76	Won
Wahid Mirza (324) & Mansoor Akhtar (224*)	561-1 dec	Karachi Whites v Quetta, Karachi,	1976–77	Won
S. Desai (218*) & R.M.H. Binny (211*)	451-0 dec	Karnataka v Kerala, Chickmagalur,	1977–78	Won
J.M. Weiner (221*) & J.K. Moss (200*)	487-2 dec	Victoria v W Australia, Melbourne	1981–82	Drawn
A.I. Kallicharran (230*) & G.W. Humpage (254*)	523-4 dec	Warwicks v Lancs, Southport	1982	Lost
Mudassar Nazar (231) & Javed Miandad (280*)	581-3 dec	Pakistan v India, Hyderabad	1982–83;	Won
G. Fowler (201) & M.W. Gatting (207)	652-7 dec	England v India, Madras	1984–85	Won
Qasim Omar (206) & Javed Miandad (203*)	555-3	Pakistan v Sr Lanka, Faisalabad	1985–86	Drawn
D.W. Hookes (306*) & W.B. Phillips (213*)	643-3 dec	S Australia v Tasmania, Adelaide	1986–7	Won

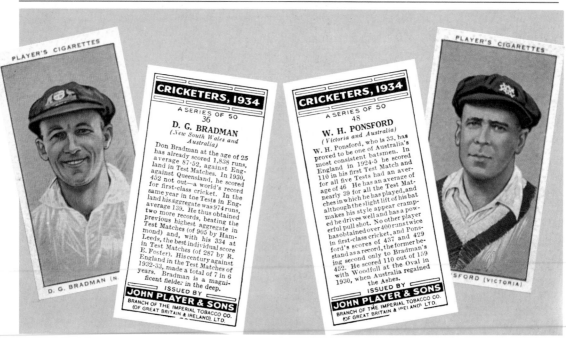

John Jameson and Rohan Kanhai on a memorable day at Edgbaston.

Graeme Fowler hits out on his way to a double century at Madras.

200 RUNS BY TWO BATSMEN FROM THE SAME SIDE IN A TEST MATCH

Players/Scores	Match/Venue	Season
G. Giffen 161+41=202; S.E. Gregory 201+16=217	A v E, Sydney	1894–95
C.A. Roach 209+22=231; G.A. Headley 114+112=226	WI v E, Georgetown	1929–30
W.H. Ponsford 266+22=288; D.G. Bradman 244+77=321	A v E, The Oval	1934
S.G. Barnes 234; D.G. Bradman 234	A v E, Sydney	1946–47
E.D. Weekes 206+1=207; F.M.M. Worrell 167+56=223	WI v E, Port of Spain	1953–54
E.D. Weekes 139+87=226; C.L. Walcott 126+110=236	WI v A, Port of Spain	1955–56
Waqar Hassan 189+17=206; Imtiaz Ahmed 209+0=209	P v NZ, Lahore	1955–56
C.C. Hunte 260; G.S. Sobers 365★	WI v P, Kingston	1957–58
W.M. Lawry 210+58★=268; R.B. Simpson 201+5=206	A v WI, Bridgetown	1964–65
I.M. Chappell 145+121=266; G.S. Chappell 247★+133=380	A v NZ, Wellington	1973–74
Mudassar Nazar 231; Javed Miandad 280★	P v I, Hyderabad	1982–83
S. Wettimuny 190+13=203; L.R.D. Mendis 111+94=205	SL v E, Lord's	1984
G. Fowler 201+2=203; M.W. Gatting 207+10=217	E v I, Madras	1984–85
Qasim Omar 206; Javed Miandad 203★	P v SL, Faisalabad	1985–86

TEST DEBUT FOR 38 YEAR OLD

The Test début for Australia of Bob Holland in the last West Indies series gave a glimmer of hope for lovers and purveyors of spin bowling, and also for those not in the first flush of youth.

Holland, born at Camperdown, South Sydney on October 19, 1946, was 38 years 35 days old on the first day of his Test début at Brisbane, the oldest Test débutant since D.S. de Silva, who first played for Sri Lanka in

Bob Holland, a late entry into Test cricket.

1981–82 aged 40 years 251 days (though officially only 37), and the oldest Australian débutant since D.D. Blackie, 46 years 253 days when playing against England at Sydney in 1928–29. Holland is indeed the third-oldest-ever Australian débutant, and the following list of Australians over 36 on Test début puts his feat into perspective.

The previous oldest post-war Australian débutant was J.B. Iverson, 35 years 156 days on the first day of the Brisbane Test v England in 1950–51.

MATURE AUSTRALIAN TEST DÉBUTANTS

Age (Yrs-days)	Player/Match/Venue	Season
46–253	D.D. Blackie (A v E), Sydney	1928–29
46–237	H. Ironmonger (A v E), Brisbane	1928–29
38–35	R.G. Holland (A v WI), Brisbane	1984–85
37–329	N. Thompson (A v E), Melbourne	1876–77
37–154	R.K. Oxenham (A v E), Melbourne	1928–29

1985

CALCUTTA MARATHON FOR ENGLAND BOWLERS

In the Calcutta Test of the 1984–85 England tour India's score of 437 for seven declared occupied 200 six-ball overs and I was asked how unusual this was. The answer is that in Test cricket as a whole it is not so unusual at all, and in fact according to my records this was the 80th such occurrence in Test cricket. India has however achieved the feat on only five occasions, the full list being as follows:

MOST OVERS IN AN INDIAN TEST INNINGS

Overs	Total	Inns	Match/Venue	Season
241.5	531–7 dec		I v NZ, Delhi	1955–56
227	539–9 dec		I v P, Madras	1960–61
209.2	510		I v E, Leeds	1967
202	520		I v A, Adelaide	1985–86
200.1	362–7 dec		I v WI, Port of Spain	1952–53
200	437–7 dec		I v E, Calcutta	1984–85

The last time the England Test bowlers had to send down 200 or more overs in an innings was when new Zealand scored 551 for nine declared at Lord's in 1973.

As a matter of interest I have drawn up a table giving details of every innings in Test cricket which has occupied 250 or more six-ball overs, or the equivalent in four, five or eight ball overs.

Richard Ellison, the most used bowler in India's long innings at Calcutta with a total of 53 overs but without a wicket to show for all his efforts.

LONGEST INNINGS IN TEST CRICKET

Overs	Balls	Inns Total	Match/Venue	Season
335.2	2012	903–7 dec	E v A, The Oval	1938
319	1914	657–8 dec	P v WI, Bridgetown	1957–58
293.1	1759	611	E v A, Old Trafford	1964
[1]218.2(8)	1746	654–5	E v SA, Durban	1938–39
272.1	1633	636	E v A, Sydney	1928–29
271.3	1629	491	A v E, Melbourne	1928–29
[1]202.6(8)	1622	530	SA v E, Durban	1938–39
268	1608	543–3 dec	NZ v WI, Georgetown	1971–72
258.2	1550	849	E v WI, Kingston	1929–30
258	1548	583–4 dec	E v WI, Edgbaston	1957
256.1	1537	695	A v E, The Oval	1930
255.5	1535	656–8 dec	A v E, Old Trafford	1964

[1] (8) indicates eight-ball overs in use.

In other first-class cricket I have traced only seven further instances of an innings of more than 250 overs; it will be noted that all bar one occurred in India.

LONGEST INNINGS IN OTHER FIRST-CLASS CRICKET

Overs	Balls	Inns Total	Match/Venue	Season
291	1746	784	Baroda v Holkar, Baroda	1946–47
286.1	1717	650	Bombay v Maharashtra, Poona	1940–41
264.5	1589	735	Bombay v Maharashtra, Bombay	1943–44
263.5	1583	798	Maharashtra v N India, Poona	1940–41
256	1536	764	Bombay v Holkar, Bombay	1944–45
[1]190.7(8)	1527	1107	Victoria v New South Wales, Melbourne	1926–27
253.3	1521	620	Bombay v Baroda, Bombay	1948–49

LONGEST INNINGS IN ENGLISH DOMESTIC CRICKET

[2]274.3(5)	1373	887	Yorkshire v Warwicks, Edgbaston	1896

[1] Eight-ball overs.
[2] Five-balls overs.

INDIA'S YOUNG STARS

Although results went against them, two definite credits emerged for India in the 1984–85 series against England. Laxman Sivaramakrishnan's precocity showed the definite spark of cricket genius. In 1982 he had marked his first-class début two months after his 16th birthday with innings figures of seven for 28 against the subsequent Ranji Trophy winners, and in 1983 he achieved his maiden first-class century before his 18th birthday. He celebrated his 19th birthday already having a Test wicket for every year. One hopes his are not talents too fragile to survive and that his subsequent demise is merely temporary; his early performances in first-class cricket are unprecedented.

Mohammed Azharuddin also showed remarkable ability in scoring centuries in each of his first three Tests, a unique feat. Only George Headley had totalled three centuries after his first three Tests before Azharuddin, and he

Mohammed Azharuddin – a third successive century against England at Kanpur.

scored two of these in the third match. Azharuddin also joins the short list of players who have exceeded 400 runs in their first three Tests.

As a matter of interest, L.G. Rowe (WI) holds the record after one Test (314), and R.E. Foster (E) is best after two Tests with 355.

MOST RUNS AFTER THREE TESTS

Player	Inns	N.O.	Runs	Av'ge	100s	Season
Javed Miandad (P)	5	1	504	126.00	2	1976–77
G.A. Headley (WI)	6	0	470	78.33	3	1929–30
C.C. Hunte (WI)	5	1	458	124.50	2	1957–58
M. Azharuddin (I)	5	1	439	109.75	3	1984–85
S.M. Gavaskar (I)	6	3	430	143.33	2	1970–71
H.L. Collins (A)	5	0	424	84.80	2	1920–21
K.S. Ranjitsinhji (E)	6	2	418	104.50	2	1896
Taslim Arif (P)	5	1	412	103.00	1	1979–80

H.L. Collins – the best start for an Australian batsman.

CLIVE LLOYD'S AUSTRALIAN TALLY

It was manifestly appropriate that Clive Lloyd signed off his Test career having just completed 3,000 first-class runs on Test tours to Australia. He is the first non-English tourist to achieve this feat, and it is sufficiently rare to justify a list being drawn up.

3000 RUNS ON TEST TOURS TO AUSTRALIA

Player	Match	Inns	N.O.	Runs	H.S.	Av'ge	100s	Tours	Span
J.B. Hobbs	57	94	5	4570	187	51.35	14	5	1907–29
M.C. Cowdrey	68	122	14	4405	307	40.79	10	6	1954–75
W.R. Hammond	47	70	4	4340	251	65.76	17	4	1928–47
E.H. Hendren	38	59	5	3444	271	63.78	10	3	1920–29
L. Hutton	38	63	9	3425	156★	63.43	10	3	1946–55
H. Sutcliffe	36	53	1	3420	194	65.77	12	3	1924–33
G. Boycott	41	75	14	3322	173	54.46	9	4	1965–80
D.C.S. Compton	37	62	10	3173	182	59.87	12	3	1946–55
C.H. Lloyd	45	74	5	3016	149	43.71	6	5	1968–85

Jack Hobbs, one of the most prolific visitors to Australia.
Top Clive Lloyd enjoying Australian hospitality at Adelaide in 1980.

GOOCH'S FLIER: EARLIEST EVER 500 RUNS

Graham Gooch's flying start to the 1985 season – something in which he specializes – was in fact better than was generally realized. Gooch reached 500 first-class runs on May 2, annihilating the old record, which he himself shared, by no fewer than seven days.

W.G. Grace was the first batsman to score 500 runs by the end of May, in 1871. The table shows the earliest dates to 500 first-class runs in an English season and the subsequent progress of the record, plus other outstanding efforts.

EARLIEST TO 500 RUNS

Date	Player	Scores
†May 29, 1871	W.G. Grace (Gloucs)	181, 23, 98, 118, 178
†May 25, 1888	W.G. Grace (Gloucs)	10, 4, 73, 16, 14, 39, 41, 13, 215, 5, 64, 33
†May 24, 1895	W.G. Grace (Gloucs)	13, 103, 18, 25, 288, 52, 257
†May 12, 1896	R. Abel (Surrey)	138, 152, 231
May 14, 1900	T.W. Hayward (Surrey)	120★, 55, 108, 131★, 55, 193
May 13, 1905	C.B. Fry (Sussex)	23, 45★, 156, 106, 97, 201★
†May 10, 1906	T.W. Hayward (Surrey)	39, 82, 25, 5, 219, 135
May 12, 1938	W.J. Edrich (Middlesex)	104, 37, 115, 63, 20★, 182
May 12, 1960	E.R. Dexter (Sussex)	23, 93, 18, 133, 96, 76, 4, 151★
May 11, 1971	D.L. Amiss (Warwicks)	20, 82, 5★, 44, 88, 41, 96, 112, 46
May 12, 1973	G.M. Turner (NZ)	41, 151★, 143, 85, 7, 8, 17★, 81
†May 9, 1980	G.A. Gooch (Essex)	44, 4, 205, 47, 108★, 29★, 16★, 37, 122
May 9, 1984	G.A. Gooch (Essex)	89, 78, 8, 220, 10★, 10, 84, 1
May 9, 1984	A.I. Kallicharran (Warwicks)	200★, 117★, 17, 8, 180
†May 2, 1985	G.A. Gooch (Essex)	99, 88, 15, 41, 8, 61, 67, 202

† Record at the time.
The record for an Australian Touring team is May 14, held jointly by D.G. Bradman (1930) and W.H. Ponsford (1934).

Graham Gooch, a prolific run-scorer in the first weeks of the season.

Bobby Abel (above) and Ted Dexter (right), who both reached 500 runs on May 12th. Abel required only three innings to achieve this in 1896 whereas Dexter needed seven innings in 1960.

Below Alvin Kallicharran, whose early success continued into the 1984 season including this innings of 70 at Lords in the Benson & Hedges final.

BOTHAM'S SIXES AND FOURS

A reader pointed out to me that against Glamorgan at Taunton in May 1985, Ian Botham, in his innings of 112, obtained more sixes (8) than fours (7) and suggested this was unusual. A bit of research certainly confirms this and below I have listed all those instances of an innings of more than 100 runs containing more sixes than fours.

CENTURIES CONTAINING MORE 6s THAN 4s

Score	Sixes/Fours	Player	Match/Venue	Season
109★	9-6; 7-4	P.J. Heather	Transvaal v Border, Durban	1910–11
¹113	10-6; ?-4	H. Sutcliffe	Yorks v Northants, Kettering	1933
135	11-6; 9-4	R. Benaud	Australians v T.N. Pearce's XI, Scarborough	1953
102	8-6; 5-4	I.L. Bula	Fiji v Canterbury, Christchurch	1953–54
101	8-6; 5-4	F.M.M. Worrell	A.E.R. Gilligan's XI v N Zealanders, Hastings	1958
104	8-6; 7-4	W.J. Stewart	Warwicks v Somerset, Street	1961
122	10-6; 7-4	H.R. Lance	Transvaal v E Province, J'burg	1966–67
147★	13-6; 10-4	Majid Khan	Pakistanis v Glamorgan, Swansea	1967
113	8-6; 7-4	K.D. Boyce	Essex v Leics, Chelmsford	1975
112	8-6; 7-4	I.T. Botham	Somerset v Glamorgan, Taunton	1985

¹ I was unable to verify the number of fours in Sutcliffe's innings but it was certainly fewer than 10. C.I. Thornton hit nine sixes in his 124 for Kent v Sussex at Tunbridge Wells in 1869; he too may qualify but the number of fours is unobtainable.

Herbert Sutcliffe, who found the Northants bowling very much to his liking at Kettering in 1933.
Top Richie Benaud, often remembered more for his bowling, obviously enjoyed his Festival innings at Scarborough in 1953.

Another big hit from Ian Botham.

HICK'S DOUBLE DELIGHT

Something of a sensation was caused at The Parks at Oxford in June 1985 when Graeme Hick, the Zimbabwean batsman, achieved his maiden first-class century and went on to score 230. The first table below confirms that although it is far from being the highest-ever maiden century, it is high on the list in English cricket. The table includes all players I have found who reached a score of 230 or more.

From the second table it will be seen that Hick comes much higher on the list where high scores at The Parks are concerned. Indeed his 230 appears to be the fourth best score ever obtained on the ground.

Finally, Hick achieved his first double century at the age of 19 years 19 days. This is not the youngest ever, of course, but it is interesting to compare his achievement with that of Graeme Pollock who scored a double century for an Eastern Province XI v Cavaliers at Port Elizabeth in 1962–63. His age? 19 years 19 days!

Graeme Hick, who made such a memorable start to the Zimbabwe tour.

HIGHEST MAIDEN HUNDREDS

Score	Player	Match/Venue	Season
337*	Pervez Akhtar	Railways v Dera Ismael Khan, Lahore	1964–65
324	Waheed Mirza	Karachi Whites v Quetta, Karachi	1976–77
292*	V.T. Trumper	New South Wales v Tasmania, Sydney	1898–99
290	W.N. Carson	Auckland v Otago, Dunedin	1936–37
290	Khalid Irtiza	United Bank v Multan, Karachi	1975–76
282	H.L. Collins	New South Wales v Tasmania, Hobart	1912–13
276	Altaf Shah	House Building & Finance Corp v Multan, Multan	1976–77
275	W.A. Farmer	Barbados v Jamaica, Bridgetown	1951–52
274	G.A. Davidson	Derbyshire v Lancs, Old Trafford	1896
271	R.I. Maddocks	Victoria v Tasmania, Melbourne	1951–52
268	C.R.N. Maxwell	Sir Julien Cahn's XI v Leics, W Bridgford	1935
268	H.P. Bayley	British Guiana v Barbados, Georgetown	1937–38
264	P. Vaulkhard	Derbys v Notts, Trent Bridge	1946
264*	R.G. Flockton	New South Wales v S Australia, Sydney	1959–60
262*	G.L. Wight	British Guiana v Barbados, Georgetown	1951–52
261*	S.S.L. Steyn	Western Province v Border, Cape Town	1929–30
261	I.R. Redpath	Victoria v Queensland, Melbourne	1962–63
253	L.S. Birkett	Trinidad v British Guiana, Georgetown	1929–30
247	R.H. Spooner	Lancashire v Notts, Trent Bridge	1903
246*	R.F. Surti	Rajasthan v Uttar Pradesh, Udaipur	1959–60
¹240	W.F.E. Marx	Transvaal v Griqualand West, Johannesburg	1920–21
237	B.S. Groves	Natal B v Orange Free State, Bloemfontein	1967–68
237	P.L. Corbett	NE Transvaal v Transvaal B, Johannesburg	1962–63
236*	H. Ashton	Cambridge U. v Free Foresters, Cambridge	1920
234	S. Strydom	Orange Free State v Transvaal B, Vereeniging	1965–66
233	H.D. Kanga	Parsees v Europeans, Poona	1905–06
¹232*	S.J.E. Loxton	Victoria v Queensland, Melbourne	1946–47
230*	W.H. Denton	Northants v Essex, Leyton	1913
230*	K.C. Ibrahim	Bombay v West India States, Bombay	1941–42
230*	G.S. Ramchand	Bombay v Maharashtra, Bombay	1950–51
¹230	G.R. Viswanath	Mysore v Andhra, Vijayawada	1967–68
230	G.A. Hick	Zimbabweans v Oxford U, The Parks	1985

¹ Denotes first-class début.

HIGHEST AT THE PARKS

266*	W. Place	Lancashire v Oxford University	1947
239	W.J. Edrich	Middlesex v Oxford University	1952
236	E.R.T. Holmes	Oxford University v Free Foresters	1927
230	G.A. Hick	Zimbabweans v Oxford University	1985

Graeme Pollock, a good man for Graeme Hick to emulate.

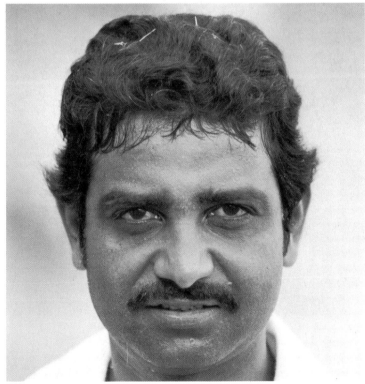

G.R. Viswanath, 230 on his début.

FOUR IN A ROW FOR BORDER

The feat of Australian skipper Allan Border in scoring centuries in his first four innings of the 1985 season deservedly attracted a great deal of attention, and certainly nothing like it has ever been achieved before at the start of an English season, whether by a tourist or a domestic player. However, for tourists in general, Border only equalled W.R. Hammond and P.B.H. May in scoring four centuries at the start of a tour, and finished one short of E.D. Weekes's record.

123

FIVE CENTURIES BY A TOURIST FROM START OF TOUR

Player	Scores	Tour	Season
E.D. Weekes	156, 148, 123, 119★, 103	W Indians in New Zealand	1955–56

FOUR CENTURIES FROM START

Player	Scores	Tour	Season
W.R. Hammond	141, 107, 104, 136	MCC in Australia	1936–37
P.B.H. May	162, 118, 124★, 205	MCC in South Africa	1956–57
A.R. Border	106, 135, 125, 100	Australians in England	1985

The record for most consecutive centuries from the start of a season is held by D.G. Bradman of South Australia who started the 1938–39 Australian season with the following consecutive scores: 118, 143, 225, 107, 186, 135★.

For an English season Border is the first-ever batsman to score four consecutive centuries from the start. The previous record was three, held jointly by the following players.

BEST STARTS TO AN ENGLISH DOMESTIC SEASON

Player	Scores	Season
R. Abel (Surrey)	138; 152; 231	1896
R.M. Poore (Hants)	104; 119★; 111	1899
R.E. Foster (Oxford U.)	128; 100★; 169	1900
J.A. Jameson (Warwicks)	110; 111; 115	1974

Allan Border, an immovable object as far as the bowlers were concerned in 1985.
Top R.M. Poore, who had an impressive start to the 1899 season.

AMISS REACHES 40,000

When Dennis Amiss became the 14th cricketer to score 40,000 first-class runs, during the Warwickshire game with the Zimbabweans in 1985, much was made in some reports of the fact that he was the only batsman to have passed this milestone and yet not scored one hundred centuries. Well, although it is correct that all the others had reached the 'ton' by the time they retired, Amiss was not alone in passing 40,000 when still short of 100 centuries. The accompanying table shows the number of hundreds each batsman had obtained when he passed 40,000, as well as the number of innings required and career record at the time of reaching the total.

Although this record is far from being the best, Amiss most certainly does not pale into insignificance and one wonders why this most unselfish of batsmen, always able and willing to adapt his approach and methods according to the needs of his side, has won so little recognition; certainly he is the most accomplished of modern English cricketers not to have been awarded a British Empire Membership or Order.

An interesting facet of the list, as shown in the last column, is that nine of the 14 reached 40,000 runs during an innings of more than a century.

Dennis Amiss, still accumulating runs for Warwickshire long after the end of his Test career.
Top Peter May – four centuries in a row in South Africa.

CAREER RECORD AT TIME OF REACHING 40,000 FIRST-CLASS RUNS

HENDREN

Player	Match	Inns	N.O.	Av'ge	100s	Season	Age	Score
W.G. Grace	622	1062	82	42.55	94	1894	45	196
T.W. Hayward	636	1014	89	43.24	96	1912	41	182
J.B. Hobbs	573	939	72	46.14	114	1925	42	109
C.P. Mead	573	939	119	48.78	112	1928	41	180
F.E. Woolley	680	1029	65	41.49	100	1929	42	176
E.H. Hendren	582	893	122	51.88	118	1930–31	41	86
H. Sutcliffe	579	832	98	54.50	121	1934	39	203
A. Sandham	616	954	78	45.66	105	1937	45	21
W.R. Hammond	516	826	89	54.27	127	1937	34	121
L. Hutton	511	811	91	55.56	129	1957	40	76
T.W. Graveney	592	1002	120	45.35	107	1965	38	104
M.C. Cowdrey	635	1038	123	43.72	100	1973	40	28
G. Boycott	506	838	128	56.34	125	1981–82	41	105
D.L. Amiss	591	1022	116	44.15	94	1985	42	18★

Tom Graveney who passed forty thousand runs at the age of 38. Only Walter Hammond reached this milestone at a younger age.

ONTONG'S ALL-ROUND EXCELLENCE

Rodney Ontong produced a real captain's performance for Glamorgan against Nottinghamshire at Trent Bridge in late August 1985, when he scored 130 in his only innings and had match figures of 13 wickets for 106. His really was an exceptional performance, as the list of such feats shows. Not surprisingly, most, like Ontong's, were match-winning efforts.

For Glamorgan alone Ontong's are the best-ever all-round match figures. On only one previous occasion has any one player scored 100 runs and taken even 10 wickets in a match for them. He is the late B.L. Muncer, who scored 107★ and took 10 for 57 when Glamorgan defeated Derbyshire at Chesterfield in 1951.

Trevor Bailey, a regular contributor with both bat and ball throughout the 1950s for both Essex and England.

Below Johnny Briggs – an impressive all-round performance in an early Roses match.

100 RUNS AND 13 WICKETS IN A FIRST-CLASS MATCH

Player	Runs/Wkts	Match/Venue	Season	Result
T.E. Bailey	59, 71★; 6–32, 8–49	Essex v Hants, Romford	1957	Won
I.T. Botham	114; 6-58, 7-48	England v India, Bombay	1979–80	Won
J. Briggs	115; 8-113, 5-96	Lancs v Yorks, Old Trafford	1892	Won
C.R. Browne	102; 5-77, 8-58	B Guiana v Barbados, Port of Spain	1925–26	Won
L.N. Constantine	107; 7-45, 6-67	W Indians v Northants, Northampton	1928	Won
J.W.H.T. Douglas	8, 123★; 7-91, 7-65	Essex v Worcs, Leyton	1921	Won
G. Giffen	20, 82; 9-91, 8-110	S Australia v Victoria, Adelaide	1885–86	Won
G. Giffen	166; 8-65, 6-60	S Australia v Victoria, Adelaide	1887–88	Won
G. Giffen	135, 19; 6-82, 7-77	S Australia v Victoria, Melbourne	1888–89	Lost
G. Giffen	271; 9-96, 7-70	S Australia v Victoria, Adelaide	1891–92	Won
G. Giffen	81, 97★; 7-75, 8-110	S Australia v Victoria, Adelaide	1902–03	Lost
W.G. Grace	150; 8-33, 7-46	Gloucs v Yorks, Sheffield	1872	Won
A.E.V. Hartkopf	86, 14★; 5-23, 8-105	Victoria v MCC, Melbourne	1922–23	Won
J.W. Hearne	106★; 7-54, 7-92	Middlesex v Essex, Leyton	1914	Won
W.R. Hillyer	26, 83; 7 wkts, 6 wkts	MCC v Oxford U., Oxford	1847	Won
R. Illingworth	135; 7-49, 7-52	Yorks v Kent, Dover	1964	Won
Imran Khan	111★; 7-;53, 6-46	Worcs v Lancs, Worcester	1976	Won
J.A. Newman	66, 42★; 8-61, 6-87	Hants v Gloucs, Bournemouth	1926	Won
M.S. Nicholls	159; 9-37, 6-126	Essex v Gloucs, Gloucester	1938	Won
R.C. Ontong	130; 5-39, 8-67	Glamorgan v Notts, Trent Bridge	1985	Won
A.D. Pougher	5, 109★; 6-29, 8-60	Leics v Essex, Leyton	1894	Won
M.J. Procter	108; 7-35, 6-38	Gloucs v Worcs, Cheltenham	1977	Won
M.J. Procter	73, 35; 7-16, 7-60	Gloucs v Worcs, Cheltenham	1980	Won
A.E. Relf	103★; 8-41, 7-36	Sussex v Leics, Hove	1912	Won
F.A. Tarrant	14, 101★; 9-105, 7-71	Middlesex v Lancs, Old Trafford	1914	Won
V.E. Walker	20★, 108; 10-74, 4-17	England v Surrey, The Oval	1859	Won
Wasim Raja	85, 50; 6-118, 8-65	Pakistan U-25 v Sri Lanka U-25, Colombo	1973–74	Won

Rodney Ontong, some impressive all-round performances but as yet unrecognized at Test level.

Mike Gatting in action against Australia during his consistent run which ended at The Oval in 1985.

GATTING'S DOUBLE-FIGURE SEQUENCE

A reader of *The Cricketer* pointed out that M.W. Gatting had achieved a run of 18 consecutive double-figure Test innings during the period 1984–85. Gatting's run, which started against West Indies at Lord's and finished at The Oval against Australia, went as follows: 29, 15, 136, 26, 30★, 48, 207, 10★, 62, 41★, 53, 12, 14, 75★, 74, 35★, 160, 100★. Although a creditable run, against some pretty ordinary Test bowling, it is by no means a record, and I have drawn up a detailed list of all those players I have traced who have equalled or beaten Gatting. If the figures are to be taken seriously the most consistent of all among Test batsmen was Rohan Kanhai; a number of names more associated with soundness and reliability do not appear in the list at all.

BATSMEN WITH MOST CONSECUTIVE DOUBLE FIGURE INNINGS IN TEST CRICKET

Inns	Player	Span	Scores
25	L. Hutton (E)	1950–53	156★, 45, 79, 60★, 28, 57, 29, 63, 11, 12, 12★, 27, 98★, 100, 28, 27, 10, 10, 150, 39★, 104, 86, 43, 60★, 145
	R.B. Kanhai (WI)	1960–65	117, 115, 38, 31, 24, 138, 89, 139, 20, 44, 41, 90, 73, 21, 32, 38, 92, 44, 30, 77, 17, 16, 27, 53, 89
23	J.B. Hobbs (E)	1912–24	66, 32, 82, 23, 92, 41, 64, 97, 33, 11★, 49, 59, 122, 20, 18, 123, 27, 13, 40, 34, 76, 211, 31
	Majid Khan (P)	1974–77	17, 100, 18, 23, 21, 98, 112, 50, 15, 47, 76, 35, 48, 26★, 88, 28, 47, 54, 23, 167, 92, 16, 11
21	R.B. Kanhai (WI)	1968–73	17, 69, 11, 80, 44, 18, 56, 158★, 37, 27, 25, 85, 11, 13, 21, 84, 105, 56, 14, 57, 23
20	A.D. Nourse (SA)	1938–49	27, 38, 103, 25, 149, 61, 58, 23, 115, 51, 57, 10, 97, 37, 32, 32, 56★, 112, 34, 129★
	S.M. Gavaskar (I)	1978–80	120, 40, 61, 68, 42, 59, 78, 13, 221, 50, 10, 76, 12, 115, 14, 25, 123, 88, 31, 21
19	V.L. Manjrekar (I)	1959–62	
	C.H. Lloyd (WI)	1976–80	
	G.S. Chappell (A)	1979–81	
	I.V.A. Richards (WI)	1977–81	
18	F.E. Woolley (E)	1924–30	
	J.B. Stollmeyer (WI)	1939–50	
	R.W. Barber (E)	1961–65	
	R.B. Kanhai (WI)	1966–68	
	M.W. Gatting (E)	1984–85	

EVERY ONE A VICTIM

In Bill Frindall's *Wisden Book of Cricket Records* a very small but fascinating item appears in the Test record section on page 616 – a list of the three bowlers who have taken the wicket of all eleven members of the opposition in the same Test match. The rarity of this achievement in Test cricket comes as a considerable surprise to some people, and the fact that the great match performances of Syd Barnes, Bob Massie and, recently, Richard Hadlee did not see them dismissing all of the opposition. I set myself the task of producing an up to date and (one hopes) accurate list of those bowlers who have performed the feat in any first-class match. On the face of it the list is long yet an average of less than one per year throughout first-class cricket history is in fact very small. It will be seen that the feat has become very rare in recent years; the most recent I can trace was by Mohammed Riaz for Zone D v Habib Bank at Rawalpindi in the 1985–86 Qaid-I-Azam competition. The last time in England was by Phil Edmonds in 1977.

Phil Edmonds, too good for all 11 Gloucestershire opponents in 1977.

Dudley Nourse, a successful sequence that stretched either side of the Second World War.

BOWLER TAKING THE WICKET OF ALL ELEVEN OPPONENTS IN A MATCH

Player	Match/Venue	Season	Analysis
F.W. Lillywhite	Slow Bowlers v Fast Bowlers, Lord's	1841	14 wkts
F.W. Lillywhite	MCC v Cambridge U., Cambridge	1844	14 wkts
F.P. Fenner	Cambridge Town v Cambridge U., Cambridge	1844	17 wkts
W. Clarke	Notts v Kent, Trent Bridge	1845	16–67
W. Clarke	North v MCC, Trent Bridge	1845	13 wkts
W. Hillyer	Kent v Surrey, Aylesford	1847	13 wkts
E. Hinkley	Kent v England, Lord's	1848	16 wkts
J. Chester	MCC v Cambridge U., Cambridge	1850	15 wkts
J. Wisden	North v South, Lord's	1850	13 wkts
D. Day	Surrey v England XI, The Oval	1850	13 wkts
W. Clarke	North v South, The Oval	1851	15–98
J. Wisden	Utd England XI v England XI, Lord's	1857	12–96
J. Jackson	Notts v Surrey, The Oval	1860	15–73
H.A. Arkwright	MCC v Gents of Kent, Canterbury (12-a-side match)	1861	18–96
E.M. Grace	Gents of MCC v Gents of Kent, Canterbury (12-a-side match)	1862	15–146
T. Emmett	Yorks v Cambridgeshire, Hunslet	1869	16–38
S.E. Butler	Oxford U. v Cambridge U., Lord's	1871	15–95
I.J. Salmon	Wellington v Nelson, Wellington	1873–74	13–58
E. Willsher	Kent v Derbys, Wirksworth	1874	13–58
J. Southerton	South v North, Lord's	1875	16–52
J. Southerton	Surrey v Middlesex, The Oval	1877	14–92
W.G. Grace	Gloucs v Notts, Cheltenham	1877	17–89
E. Barratt	C.I. Thornton's XI v Australians, Twickenham	1878	12–141
A.G. Steel	Cambridge U. v Yorks, Cambridge	1878	13–85
G.G. Hearne	Kent v MCC, Lord's	1879	14–45
E. Barratt	Surrey v Lancs, The Oval	1880	13–161
A. Shaw	Notts v Australians, Trent Bridge (Australians only had 10 men)	1880	12–95
G. Giffen	Australian XI v Combined XI, Sydney	1883–84	13–128
H. Rotheram	Gents v Oxford U., Oxford	1884	14–150
F.R. Spofforth	Australians v England XI, Aston	1884	14–37
F.R. Spofforth	Australians v I Zingari, Scarborough	1884	14–185
W. Attewell	Notts v Australians, Trent Bridge	1888	12–96
C.T.B. Turner	Australians v England XI, Hastings	1888	17–50
W.C. Hedley	Kent v Middlesex, Lord's	1888	14–109
R. Peel	Yorks v Gloucs, Halifax	1888	13–84
G.A. Lohmann	Surrey v Sussex, Hove	1889	15–98
A.E. Moss	Canterbury v Wellington, Wellington	1889–90	13–72
S.M.J. Woods	Cambridge U. v C.I. Thornton's XI, Cambridge	1890	15–88
W.A. Woof	Gloucs v Surrey, Cheltenham	1890	11–70
W. Wright	Kent v Middlesex, Lord's	1890	13–106
A.W. Mold	Lancs v Somerset, Taunton	1891	15–131
G. Giffen	S Australia v Victoria, Adelaide	1891–92	16–166
J. Briggs	Lancs v Yorks, Old Trafford	1892	13–209
T. Richardson	Surrey v Notts, Trent Bridge	1894	13–99
W. Mead	Essex v Hants, Southampton	1895	17–119
T. Richardson	Surrey v Warwicks, Edgbaston	1895	14–161
C.L. Townsend	Gloucs v Notts, Trent Bridge	1895	16–122
C.L. Townsend	Gloucs v Yorks, Cheltenham	1895	15–184
S.T. Callaway	New South Wales v New Zealand XI, Christchurch	1895–96	15–175
J.T. Hearne	MCC v Oxford U., Oxford	1897	15–110
T. Richardson	Surrey v Yorks, Headingley	1897	15–154
F.G. Roberts	Gloucs v Kent, Maidstone	1897	15–123
C.L. Townsend	Gloucs v Middlesex, Lord's	1898	15–134
H. Trumble	Victoria v S Australia, Melbourne	1898–99	11–96
W. Rhodes	Yorks v Hants, Hull	1900	14–66
W. Rhodes	Yorks v Leics, Leicester	1901	13–96
A.E. Trott	Middlesex v Sussex, Lord's	1901	15–187
F.W. Tate	Sussex v Middlesex, Lord's	1902	15–68
H. Trumble	Australians v England XI, Eastbourne	1902	14–84
H. Trumble	Australians v South, Bournemouth	1902	15–68
E.G. Arnold	South v Australians, Bournemouth	1902	12–87
W.P. Howell	Australians v Western Province, Cape Town	1902–03	17–54
B. Cranfield	Somerset v Gloucs, Gloucester	1903	13–102
J.R. Gunn	Notts v Surrey, The Oval	1903	14–132
C. Blythe	Kent v Hants, Southampton	1904	13–91
W. Brearley	Lancs v Yorks, Sheffield	1905	13–157
E.G. Dennett	Gloucs v Worcs, Cheltenham	1906	15–140
A. Fielder	Players v Gents, Lord's	1906	14–221
G.J. Thompson	Northants v Worcs, Worcester	1906	16–69
T.G. Wass	Notts v Lancs, Liverpool	1906	16–69
A.E.E. Vogler	E Province v Orange Free State, Johannesburg	1906–07	14–58
L.C. Braund	Somerset v Warwicks, Bath	1907	14–141
E.G. Dennett	Gloucs v Northants, Northampton	1907	15–97
S. Haigh	Yorks v Warwicks, Sheffield	1907	13–40
E.G. Dennett	Gloucs v Middlesex, Bristol	1908	13–120

H.V. Hordern	Philadelphians v Jamaica, Kingston	1908–09	13–113
C. Blythe	Kent v Leics, Leicester	1909	16–102
C. Blythe	Kent v Northants, Northampton	1909	14–75
W. Brearley	Lancs v Middlesex, Old Trafford	1909	13–126
H. Dean	Lancs v Somerset, Old Trafford	1909	14–77
C.H. Kilminster	Colombo v South of India, Colombo	1909–10	12–35
H. Dean	Lancs v Somerset, Bath	1910	16–103
J.A. Newman	Hants v Yorks, Bradford	1910	12–153
A.R. Litteljohn	Middlesex v Lancs, Lord's	1911	15–189
F.A. Tarrant	Middlesex v Yorks, Headingley	1912	11–91
E.G. Dennett	Gloucs v Surrey, Bristol	1913	15–195
J.W. Hitch	Surrey v Kent, The Oval	1913	13–163
D. McBeath	Canterbury v Auckland, Auckland	1918–19	15–168
A.G. Dipper	Gloucs v Leics, Cheltenham	1919	14–104
J.W.H.T. Douglas	Essex v Worcs, Leyton	1921	14–156
A.A. Mailey	Australians v Gloucs, Cheltenham	1921	13–87
C.H. Parkin	Lancs v Glamorgan, Blackpool	1923	15–95
C.W.L. Parker	Gloucs v Somerset, Taunton	1924	11–113
C.W.L. Parker	Gloucs v Derbys, Derby	1924	15–109
V.W.C. Jupp	Northants v Glamorgan, Swansea	1925	15–52
C.W.L. Parker	Gloucs v Essex, Gloucester	1925	17–56
G.R. Cox	Sussex v Warwicks, Horsham	1926	17–106
A.A. Mailey	Australians v Notts, Trent Bridge	1926	15–193
J.A. Newman	Hants v Somerset, Weston-super-Mare	1927	16–88
C.W.L. Parker	Gloucs v Northants, Northampton	1927	14–96
R.J.O. Meyer	Europeans v Mohammedans, Bombay	1927–28	16–188
W.R. Hammond	Gloucs v Worcs, Cheltenham	1928	15–128
R.K. Tyldesley	Lancs v Northants, Old Trafford	1928	11–91
A.P. Freeman	Kent v Essex, Southend	1930	16–94
C.W.L. Parker	Gloucs v Warwicks, Cheltenham	1930	14–97
E.P. Nupen	Transvaal v Griqualand West, Johannesburg	1931–32	16–136
C.V. Grimmett	S Australia v Queensland, Adelaide	1934–35	16–289
W.E. Bowes	Yorks v Northants, Kettering	1935	16–35
H. Verity	Yorks v Leics, Headingley	1935	13–97
H. Verity	Yorks v Middlesex, Headingley	1935	11–73
C.V. Grimmett	Australia v S Africa, Durban	1935–36	13–173
H.L. Hazell	Somerset v Northants, Kettering	1936	14–139
J.C. Clay	Glamorgan v Worcs, Swansea	1937	17–212
T.W.J. Goddard	Gloucs v Hants, Bristol	1937	14–146
T.W.J. Goddard	Gloucs v Worcs, Cheltenham	1937	16–181
J.C. Clay	Glamorgan v Hants, Cardiff	1938	12–147
A.R. Gover	Surrey v Worcs, Kidderminster	1938	14–85
Azim Khan	Rajputna v Delhi, Delhi	1938–39	12–85
C.S. Nayudu	Baroda v Nawanagar, Baroda	1938–39	13–176
T.W.J. Goddard	Gloucs v Worcs, Bristol	1939	16–99
T.W.J. Goddard	Gloucs v Kent, Bristol	1939	17–106
T.F. Smailes	Yorks v Derbys, Sheffield	1939	14–58
Amir Elahi	Mohammedans v The Rest, Bombay	1940–41	14–192
G.E. Tribe	Victoria v Queensland, Brisbane	1945–46	11–156
D.C.S. Compton	Middlesex v Surrey, The Oval	1947	12–174
D.V.P. Wright	Kent v Sussex, Hastings	1947	15–173
J.E. Walsh	Leics v Sussex, Hove	1948	15–100
J.E. Walsh	Leics v Notts, Loughborough	1949	15–164
A.M.B. Rowan	Transvaal v Australians, Johannesburg	1949–50	15–68
T.B. Burtt	Canterbury v Central District, Palmerston N	1950–51	12–130
J.E. McConnon	Glamorgan v Derbys, Cardiff	1951	14–153
E.P. Robinson	Somerset v Sussex, Weston-Super-Mare	1951	15–78
C. Gladwin	North v South, Kingston	1951	14–182
R.G. Marlar	Sussex v Glamorgan, Swansea	1952	15–133
C.W. Grove	Warwicks v Sussex, Edgbaston	1952	12–87
P.J. Loader	Surrey v Warwicks, Edgbaston	1953	12–117
J.E. Walsh	Leics v Oxford U., Oxford	1953	16–225
R. Tattersall	Lancs v Somerset, Bath	1953	13–69
S.K. Girdhari	Assam v Bihar, Jarhat	1953–54	12–66
J.H. Wardle	Yorks v Sussex, Hull	1954	16–112
F. Fee	Ireland v MCC, Dublin	1956	14–100
G.A.R. Lock	Surrey v Kent, Blackheath	1956	16–85
G.A.R. Lock	Surrey v Notts, Trent Bridge	1956	13–144
J.C. Laker	England v Australia, Old Trafford	1956	19–90
R. Tattersall	Lancs v Yorks, Headingley	1956	14–90
S. Ramadhin	West Indians v Oxford U., Oxford	1957	13–47
G.E. Tribe	Northants v Worcs, Northampton	1958	13–99
D.J. Halfyard	Kent v Worcs, Maidstone	1959	15–117
A. Hagemann	Border v Griqualand, Kimberley	1960–61	14–59
S. Venkataraghavan	India v New Zealand, Delhi	1964–65	12–152
S. Venkataraghavan	Madras v Andra, Coinbataire	1964–65	12–82
G.A.R. Lock	Leics v Glamorgan, Leicester	1967	13–116
M.L. Jaisimha	Hyderabad v Madras, Hyderabad	1968–69	11–112
Shahid Mahmood	Karachi Whites v Khairpair, Karachi	1969–70	12–77
J.W. Holder	Hants v Gloucs, Gloucester	1972	13–128
P.G. Lee	Lancs v Warwicks, Edgbaston	1975	12–62

Doug Wright (above) and Johnny Wardle (right), both of whom on separate occasions disposed of all eleven Sussex opponents.

P.H. Edmonds	Middlesex v Gloucs, Lord's	1977	14–150
D.L. Hobson	W Province v E Province, Cape Town	1978–79	12–126
S. Madan Lal	Delhi v Haryana, Delhi	1979–80	13–64
D.R. Parry	Combined Islands v Jamaica, Kingston	1979–80	15–101
G. Dymock	Australia v India, Kanpur	1979–80	12–166
Mohammed Riaz	Zone D v Habib Bank, Rawalpindi	1985–86	15–144

RANJI GOEL RETIRES WITH HIS RECORD

The Ranji Trophy was presented to the Indian Cricket Board of Control in 1934 by the then Maharaja of Patiala for annual competition between the Provincial Cricket Associations of India. It was named after K.S. Ranjitsinhji, the first great Indian batsman who had died a year before. The inaugural match started on November 4, and took place at Madras between Madras and Mysore. Unhappily Madras won by an innings in a single day, with Ram Singh, a left-arm spinner, achieving match figures of 11–35 in 27.5 overs. The competition has subsequently developed apace and is now the largest first-class domestic cricket competition in the world.

First bowler to take 100 wickets in the competition was Nawanagar pace bowler Amar Singh, a magnificent cricketer who had played for India in their initial Test, in 1932, opening the bowling and scoring their first Test half-century. The following season he became the first to complete a career 'double' in the Ranji Trophy (1,000 runs and 100 wickets) and shortly afterwards died from typhoid.

The increase in matches over the years made it inevitable that eventually a career total of 500 wickets would be passed, and with India's history of fine spin bowlers – Mankad, Gupte, Chandrasekhar, Bedi et al – it seemed likely that the 'milestone' would be passed by a spinner. It finally happened in 1981–82 and the bowler was Rajinder Goel. Who? Ranji Goel, a left-arm spinner who made his Ranji Trophy début for Patiala in 1958–59, transferred to Delhi in 1963–64 and finally moved on to Haryana in 1973–74 where he stayed for 12 seasons before finishing his career aged 42 in 1984–85, heavy with Ranji Trophy wickets (a record of 636 which will stand for probably the rest of the century) but short on honours. The nearest he came to a Test cap was at Bangalore in November 1974; Bedi was disciplined and Goel brought in for the first West Indies Test. He invested in new boots, bat and kit, but was left out on the first morning. Poor Goel; his Test career was aborted on the day, and he was never given a Test tour, so robbing him of his Indian colours. Even his Lancashire League career failed to get off the ground: he came, saw, and went back home, frightened away by the Northern English attitude to life.

But . . . he was the first to take 500 Ranji Trophy wickets. Future Test batsman Raman Lamba of Delhi was the 500th victim while another accomplished player, Kirti Azad, had been No. 499. Goel's 636th and final victim was L.S. Rajput of Bombay; it was in the 1984–85 Ranji Trophy quarter-final and no fault of Goel's that Haryana lost. Goel's retirement was not announced – simply, and typically, he has just never played again.

One last point: in 1984 Indian batsman Sunil Gavaskar produced *Idols* – a book of essays on his 31 favourite cricketers. Goel, the least famous of all, stole the show.

LEADING WICKET-TAKERS IN RANJI TROPHY

Player	Runs	Wkts	Av'ge
R. Goel	10950	636	17.21
S. Venkataraghavan	9655	530	18.21
B.S. Chandrasekhar	8352	436	19.15
V.V. Kumar	7756	417	18.59
B.S. Bedi	5926	402	14.74

During the 1984–85 season Bombay annexed the Ranji Trophy for the 30th time in its 51-season existence, when for the second time running they defeated Delhi in the final. A large part in Bombay's win was played by their talented Test all-rounder Ravi Shastri. His second-innings analysis of eight for 91, and match figures of 12 for 182 represented some of the best figures in the history of Ranji Trophy finals, as these lists of outstanding performances show.

B.S. Chandrasekhar, a leading wicket taker in the Ranji Trophy.

11 OR MORE WICKETS IN RANJI TROPHY FINAL

Analysis	Player	Match/Venue	Season	Result
13–34	P.K. Shivalkar	Bombay v Tamil Nadu, Madras	1972–73	Won
12–81	B.S. Chandrasekhar	Karnataka v Uttar Pradesh, Mohannaggar	1977–78	Won
12–182	Ravi Shastri	Bombay v Delhi, Bombay	1984–85	Won
11–59	J.B. Khot	Bombay v Mysore, Bombay	1941–42	Won
11–81	C.S. Nayudu	Baroda v Hyderabad, Secunderabad	1942–43	Won
11–120	R.B. Desai	Bombay v Rajasthan, Udaipur	1960–61	Won
11–120	Maninder Singh	Delhi v Haryana, Delhi	1985–86	Won
11–428	C.S. Nayudu	Holkar v Bombay, Bombay	1944–45	Lost

(most runs conceded by one bowler in any first-class match)

EIGHT OR MORE WICKETS IN ONE INNINGS IN RANJI TROPHY FINAL

Analysis	Player	Match/Venue	Season	Result
9–152	R.S. Hans	Uttar Pradesh v Karnataka, Mohannagar	1977–78	Lost
8–16	P.K. Shivalkar	Bombay v Tamil Nadu, Madras	1972–73	Won
8–39	M.S. Hardikar	Bombay v Bengal, Calcutta	1955–56	Won
8–40	H.J. Vajifdar	Bombay v Northern India, Bombay	1934–35	Won
8–54	Maninder Singh	Delhi v Haryana, Delhi	1985–86	Won
8–91	R.J. Shastri	Bombay v Delhi, Bombay	1984–85	Won
8–99	A. Durani	Rajasthan v Bombay, Udaipur	1950–61	Lost
8–118	S. Madan Lal	Delhi v Bombay, Bombay	1980–81	Lost

Madan Lal, whose solo effort for Delhi in 1981 ended vainly, seen here in action against England at Calcutta the following year.

Maninder Singh (above left) and Ravi Shastri (above right) – impressive performances in successive finals of the Ranji Trophy.

IMPRESSIVE CONSISTENCY BY RICHARDS

Vivian Richards's nine hundreds in 24 innings during the 1985 English season was a very high average indeed and set me wondering about his position as a century-scorer among leading batsmen of all time. Using a qualification of 50 centuries in a career, I drew up a list of batsmen who averaged a century every eight innings or less.

Among those short of 50 centuries, West Indian George Headley achieved the outstanding average 4.97 innings for each of his 33 centuries (the 'Black Bradman' indeed!). W.M. Woodfull scored 49 centuries at a rate of one per 5 innings, and W.H. Ponsford obtained 47 at exactly the same average. Indian master Vijay Merchant averaged 5.21 innings for his 44 centuries and Arthur Morris of Australia achieved 5.44 for each of his 46 centuries. Among current players, the Pakistanis Mudassar Nazar and Shafiq Ahmed both average less than 7.50.

On the main list Bradman of course goes 'off the graph'. Whatever 'excuses' are put forward for his phenomenal run scoring the fact remains that on all known statistical measures of a batsman's ability Bradman comes out top, and always by a considerable margin over the runner-up. Vivian Richards's position is very impressive and on the whole some modern batsmen are higher in the list than had been expected, while some from the past are lower.

MOST PROLIFIC CENTURY-SCORERS IN FIRST-CLASS CRICKET

(Qualification: over 50 centuries and a century every eight innings or less)

Player	Centuries	Inns	Av'ge Inns per 100
D.G. Bradman	117	338	2.89
A.L. Hassett	59	322	5.46
W.R. Hammond	167	1005	6.02
V.S. Hazare	60	367	6.12
L. Hutton	129	814	6.31
K.S. Duleepsinhji	50	333	6.66
J.B. Hobbs	197	1315	6.68
G. Boycott	151	1014	6.71
I.V.A. Richards	93	626	6.73
Hanif Mohammad	55	370	6.73
D.C.S. Compton	123	839	6.82
R.N. Harvey	67	461	6.88
R.G. Pollock	64	437	6.82
K.S. Ranjitsinhji	72	500	6.94
Zaheer Abbas	107	747	6.98
C.B. Fry	94	658	7.00
S.M. Gavaskar	80	562	7.02
G.S. Sobers	86	609	7.08
W. Bardsley	53	376	7.09
B.A. Richards	80	576	7.20
P.B.H. May	85	618	7.27
R.B. Simpson	60	436	7.27
H. Sutcliffe	149	1088	7.30
G.S. Chappell	74	542	7.32
I.M. Chappell	59	448	7.59
E.H. Hendren	170	1300	7.65
G.M. Turner	103	792	7.69

Lindsay Hassett, left, and Len Hutton, two of the most prolific century scorers, toss before the Lord's Test of 1953.

Viv Richards, the most regular century-scorer in cricket today.

15 WICKETS FOR HADLEE IN BRISBANE TEST

The phenomenal bowling success of Richard Hadlee in Australia in 1985–86 tended to obscure the fact that he has been (and still is) a fine batsman. It was pointed out to me that Hadlee's 15 wickets in the Brisbane Test meant that he had joined a fairly short list of cricketers who have scored a double century in an innings as well as taking 15 wickets in a match in their first-class career.

Hadlee's achievement is obviously extremely unusual, he being only the sixth player to join the list since World War II. Even Hadlee seems unlikely ever to challenge W.G. Grace, however. The 'Doctor' remains alone in having achieved a triple century (three times) and taken 17 wickets in a match (once) in first-class cricket.

Richard Hadlee in full flight.

DOUBLE CENTURY IN AN INNINGS AND 15 WICKETS IN A MATCH

Player	Inns	Match	Season	Analysis	Match	Season
B.J.T. Bosanquet	214	The Rest v Yorks	1908	15–65	Oxford U. v Sussex	1900
L.C. Braund	257*	Somerset v Worcs	1913	15–71	Somerset v Yorks	1902
T.W. Cartwright	210	Warwicks v Middlesex	1962	15–89	Warwicks v Glamorgan	1967
G.A. Davidson	274	Derbys v Lancs	1896	15–116	Derbys v Essex	1898
G. Giffen	203	S Australia v G.F. Vernon's XI	1887–88 (4)	17–201	S Australia v Victoria	1885–86 (6)
W.G. Grace	224*	England v Surrey	1866 (13)	15–79	Gloucs v Yorks	1872 (5)
R.J. Hadlee	210*	Notts v Middlesex	1984	15–123	NZ v Australia	1985–86
W.R. Hammond	250*	Gloucs v Lancs	1925 (36)	15–128	Gloucs v Worcs	1928
G.H. Hirst	214	Yorks v Worcs	1901 (4)	15–63	Yorks v Leics	1907
J.L. Hopwood	220	Lancs v Gloucs	1934	15–112	Lancs v Worcs	1934
V.W.C. Jupp	217*	Sussex v Worcs	1914	15–52	Northants v Glamorgan	1925
R.J.O. Meyer	202*	Somerset v Lancs	1936	16–188	Europeans v Mohammedans	1927–28
M.S. Nichols	205	Essex v Hants	1936	15–165	Essex v Gloucs	1938
R. Peel	210*	Yorks v Warwicks	1896	15–50	Yorks v Somerset	1895
W. Rhodes	201	Yorks v Somerset	1905 (3)	15–56	Yorks v Essex	1899 (2)
S.G. Smith	204	Northants v Gloucs	1910 (2)	16–85	W Indies XI v R.A. Bennett's XI	1901–02
F.A. Tarrant	206	Victoria v NSW	1907–08 (4)	15–47	Middlesex v Hants	1913 (2)
C.L. Townsend	224*	Gloucs v Essex	1899 (2)	16–122	Gloucs v Notts	1895 (5)
J. Vine	202	Sussex v Northants	1920	15–161	Sussex v Notts	1901
S.M.J. Woods	215	Somerset v Sussex	1895	15–88	Camb U. v Gents XI	1890 (2)

Notes. The figure in parentheses after some entries indicates the total number of such feats in a player's career. Only the first instance is quoted.

W.G. Grace, always heavily involved in any match in which he played.

Tom Cartwright, a great all-rounder for two decades.

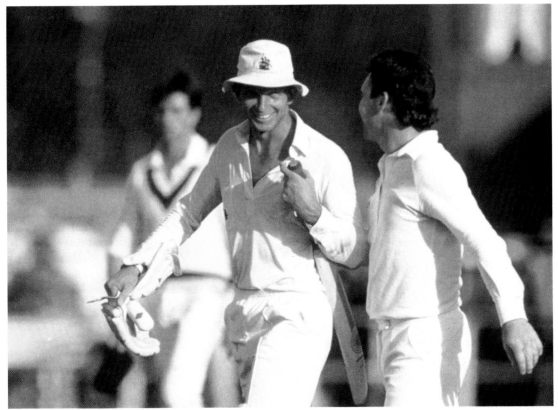

David Gower chats to rival captain Allan Border at the end of another fine innings during the most enjoyable period of his England captaincy.

GOWER'S TEST TALLY – A CAPTAIN'S CONTRIBUTION

In 1985 David Gower became the first England captain to score more than 700 runs in a series, beating Len Hutton's total of 677 runs against the West Indies in 1953–54. He also became the first captain of any country to score more than 600 runs in a series against Australia. His total is also the highest made by any captain – home or visiting – in England.

Only nine captains have been able to score more than 600 runs in a Test series. Only one captain has done so on three occasions: inevitably, Don Bradman. No other captain has exceeded 600 runs in a series more than once. Below is a list of all the occasions when this feat was achieved.

D. G. BRADMAN
NEW SOUTH WALES

HIGH SCORING TEST CAPTAINS

Captain	Series	Season	Tests	Inns	N.O.	H.S.	Runs	Av'ge	100s	50s
D.G. Bradman	A v E	1936–37	5	9	–	270	810	90.00	3	1
S.M. Gavaskar	I v WI	1978–79	5	9	–	205	732	91.50	4	1
D.I. Gower	E v A	1985	6	9	1	215	732	81.33	3	1
G.S. Sobers	WI v E	1966	5	8	1	174	722	103.14	3	2
D.G. Bradman	A v I	1947–48	5	6	2	201	715	178.75	4	1
G.S. Chappell	A v WI	1975–76	6	11	5	182*	702	117.00	3	3
D.G. Bradman	A v E	1946–47	5	8	1	234	680	97.14	2	3
L. Hutton	E v WI	1953–54	5	8	1	205	677	96.71	2	3
W.M. Lawry	A v WI	1968–69	5	8	1	205	677	83.37	3	2
C.H. Lloyd	WI v I	1974–75	5	9	1	242*	636	79.20	2	1
W.R. Hammond	E v SA	1938–39	5	8	1	181	609	87.00	3	2

LETHAL COMBINATION FOR GLOUCESTERSHIRE

Gloucestershire showed a dramatic improvement in the 1985 Britannic Assurance County Championship; they rose from last to third place, their best position since 1977, and it was suggested that one of the reasons for the county's advance was the fact that five of its bowlers featured in the top 18 positions in the first-class averages. This had never happened before to Gloucestershire and only ever on seven previous occasions overall. The table below reveals that the team with such a lethal attack usually won the title, yet when Yorkshire had six in the top 18, in 1921, they only finished third.

COUNTIES WITH FIVE OR MORE BOWLERS IN TOP 18 OF FIRST-CLASS AVERAGES

1898 Yorks 1st

Posn	Player	Wkts	Av'ge
1	E. Smith	13	9.46
4	W. Rhodes	154	14.60
5	E. Wainwright	69	14.90
8	F.S. Jackson	104	15.67
18	S. Haigh	102	18.43

1905 Yorks 1st

2	S. Haigh	129	15.37
4	W. Rhodes	182	16.95
9	W. Ringrose	73	19.20
11	H. Myers	72	19.43
15	G.H. Hirst	110	19.94

1919 Yorks 1st

2	W. Rhodes	164	14.42
8	E.R. Wilson	40	17.47
11	R. Kilner	45	18.31
16	A. Waddington	100	18.74
17	A.C. Williams	25	18.88

1921 Yorks 3rd

1	E.R. Wilson	51	11.19
2	W. Rhodes	141	13.27
7	G.G. Macaulay	101	17.33
14	R. Kilner	61	18.80
15	A. Waddington	105	18.92
17	H.D. Badger	15	19.40

(This is the only instance of six bowlers in the top 18)

1922 Yorks 1st

1	W. Rhodes	119	12.19
8	G.G. Macaulay	133	14.67
9	R. Kilner	122	14.73
12	E.R. Wilson	26	15.84
13	A. Waddington	133	16.08

1956 Lancs 2nd

3	M.J. Hilton	158	13.96
7	R. Tattersall	117	14.71
8	J.B. Statham	91	14.84
14	T. Greenhough	62	16.83
15	F. Moore	17	17.11

1957 Surrey 1st

1	G.A.R. Lock	212	12.02
4	J.C. Laker	126	15.24
5	E.A. Bedser	77	15.42
6	P.J. Loader	133	15.47
12	A.V. Bedser	131	16.56

1985 Gloucs 3rd

4	G.E. Sainsbury	27	17.81
5	C.A. Walsh	85	20.07
14	K.M. Curran	61	23.26
16	D.V. Lawrence	85	24.62
18	D.A. Graveney	41	24.70

AMISS PASSES ANOTHER MILESTONE

In 1986 Dennis Amiss passed 30,000 Championship runs, finishing the season with an aggregate of 30,341. This is a very considerable feat, especially for a present-day cricketer. The best current player after Amiss is Keith Fletcher with a total of 25,955, a long way short of 30,000 and still some way short of the Essex best – the 27,703 runs scored by P.A. Perrin.

At the start of 1987 Amiss needed 1,125 runs to overtake Wm Quaife for the Warwickshire record. All things being equal, he should certainly do this and will then reach seventh place in the table below, which lists all such achievements since the beginning of the County Championship. Eventually Amiss could well finish in sixth position.

Although Tom Graveney narrowly failed to reach 30,000 runs in the County Championship, he does nevertheless hold a record so far

C.P. Mead, the Hampshire run-machine and Don Kenyon (top), leading batsman in the County Championship in the post-war period.

BATSMEN WITH 30,000 RUNS FOR A COUNTY IN THE COUNTY CHAMPIONSHIP

Player/County	Runs	Av'ge	Career
C.P. Mead (Hants)	46268	48.31	1906–36
F.E. Woolley (Kent)	43703	41.26	1906–38
J.B. Hobbs (Surrey)	38737	48.97	1905–34
E.H. Hendren (Middlesex)	37418	50.49	1907–37
H. Sutcliffe (Yorks)	32814	50.71	1919–39
G.E. Tyldesley (Lancs)	31903	45.90	1909–35
Wm Quaife (Warwicks)	31465	36.72	1895–1928
D. Kenyon (Worcs)	31375	34.06	1946–67
W.R. Hammond (Gloucs)	31344	56.67	1920–51
T.W. Hayward (Surrey)	30972	41.85	1893–1914
J.T. Tyldesley (Lancs)	30865	42.63	1896–1923
H.T.W. Hardinge (Kent)	30774	36.89	1902–33
A. Jones (Glamorgan)	30704	32.77	1957–83
J.G. Langridge (Sussex)	30343	37.50	1928–55
D.L. Amiss (Warwicks)	30341	41.84	1960–86

unmatched by any other first-class cricketer. He is the only batsman to have scored over 10,000 runs in the Championship for two different counties. His record is as follows:

County	Seasons	Inns	N.O.	Runs	Av'ge
Gloucs	1948–60	452	44	17525	42.95
Worcs	1962–70	323	59	11842	44.85

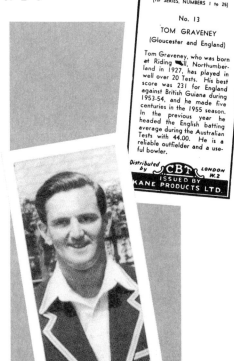

John Dyson, who stood firm while all others fell around him.

DYSON CARRIES HIS BAT FOR 18

In the third international four-day match between the South African and Australian XIs at Johannesburg in 1985–86, John Dyson carried his bat through the Australian second innings for 18 not out in a total of 61. I was asked how this compared with other such feats, and whether Dyson's percentage of the total score – 29.5 – was unusually low.

In the first table below I list all those instances I have traced in which a batsman carried his bat with a lower score than Dyson's. It will be seen that carrying one's bat for a really low score is now extremely rare in first-class cricket, and that Dyson is high on the all-time list. Dyson's is a record low for all first-class cricket in South Africa, beating the previous record of 26* out of 47 which had been held by A.B. Tancred since 1888–89. Tancred was playing for South Africa v England at Cape Town. His was the first instance of a batsman carrying his bat in first-class cricket in South Africa and also the first in Test cricket, and it remains the lowest score for a batsman carrying his bat in a Test.

LOWEST SCORES FOR CARRYING BAT IN FIRST-CLASS CRICKET

Score	Inns Total	Batsman	Match/Venue	Season
5*	69	R.G. Barlow	Lancs v Notts, Trent Bridge	1882
7*	60	A.C. Bannerman	Australians v Kent, Canterbury	1893
8*	19	W. Hooker	Sussex v Surrey, Godalming	1830
8*	33	N. Bezbarua	Assam v Bengal, Jorhat	1974–75
9*	28	W.H. Scotton	England XI v Australians, Stoke	1888
10*	47	R.G. Barlow	Lancs v Yorks, Old Trafford	1880
12*	48	Richard Daft	Notts v Lancs, Trent Bridge	1877
12*	51	G.W. Beldam	Middlesex v Sussex, Lord's	1902
12*	32	P. Hearn	Kent v Hants, Southampton	1952
13*	42	T.R. Morgan	Glamorgan v Lancs, Swansea	1922
14*	60	F.A. Midlane	Wellington v Canterbury, Christchurch	1910–11
14*	40	W. Adams	Northants v Yorks, Northampton	1920
14*	47	T.R. Morgan	Glamorgan v Notts, Cardiff	1922
15*	73	M. Howell	Surrey v Kent, Blackheath	1920
16*	76	W.E. Midwinter	Australians v Notts, Trent Bridge	1878
17*	58	W.H. Scotton	Notts v Yorks, Sheffield	1888
18*	38	F.W. Lillywhite	MCC v Cambridge U., Cambridge	1845
18*	70	S.A.P. Kitcat	Gloucs v Yorks, Hull	1901
18*	67	G.C. Collins	Kent v Northants, Gravesend	1924
18*	61	J. Dyson	Australian XI v S. African XI, J'burg	1985–86

R.G. Barlow (above) and A.C. Bannerman (right), both dour defenders in disastrous circumstances.

The second table reveals that Dyson's percentage of the innings was low but did not approach the record of Lancashire's R.G. Barlow, which is quite mind-boggling.

The same match was also notable for the fact that South African bowlers Clive Rice and Garth le Roux *both* performed the hat-trick. This appears to be unique, though there have been a number of instances of two hat-tricks in the same first-class match.

LOWEST PERCENTAGE OF TOTAL SCORE AFTER CARRYING BAT

Per cent	Score	Inns Total	Batsman	Match/Venue	Season
7.2	5*	69	R.G. Barlow	Lancs v Notts, Trent Bridge	1882
11.6	7*	60	A.C. Bannerman	Australians v Kent, Canterbury	1893
15.6	23*	147	A. Berry	Cambridge v Notts, Trent Bridge	1862
17.5	46*	262	C.J.B. Wood	Leics v Sussex, Leicester	1903
18.2	34*	187	R.G. Barlow	Lancs v Kent, Maidstone	1876
19	19*	100	J. Vine	Sussex v Lancs, Liverpool	1910
19.5	24*	123	E.L. Griffiths	Gloucs v Notts, Trent Bridge	1885
19.7	36*	182	I. Grimshaw	Yorks v Kent, Maidstone	1881

ANSARI'S REMARKABLE DOUBLE CENTURY

S. Ansari's innings of 200 for Madhya Pradesh, after his side had been asked to follow on, was a splendidly defiant gesture but not by any means unique. Listed below are all the other instances that I have managed to trace. Overall the scoring of a double century in a second innings is comparatively common but I thought it might be of interest to list those scoring over 300. The leader in the list, Don Bradman (of whom the writer is an unashamed admirer), is likely to retain his position for a very long time indeed.

W. M. WOODFULL

No. 9

COLIN McDONALD
(Victoria and Australia)

Victorian opening batsman, 27-year-old Colin McDonald from Melbourne toured England in 1953, making 757 runs, but did not play in a Test match. In two Tests against England in 1954-5 he made 186 runs at an average of 46.5, and then hit 449 runs in five Tests during the 1955 West Indies tour.

Distributed by CBT LONDON W.2
ISSUED BY
KANE PRODUCTS LTD.

BATSMEN SCORING DOUBLE CENTURY FOR TEAM FOLLOWING-ON

Player	Score	Match/Venue	Season
S. Ansari	200	Madhya Pradesh v Uttar Pradesh, Kanpur	1984–85
D.G. Aslett	221★	Kent v Sri Lankans, Canterbury	1984
J.T. Bell	209★	Wales v MCC, Lord's	1927
D.G. Bradman	225	W.M. Woodfull's XI v J. Ryder's XI, Sydney	1929–30
M.C. Cowdrey	204★	Kent v Cambridge U., Cambridge	1956
G. Cox	234★	Sussex v Indians, Hove	1946
C.B. Fry	219★	Sussex v Oxford U., Eastbourne	1901
C.B. Fry	232★	Gents v Players, Lord's	1903
G. Giffen	203	S Australia v G.F. Vernon's XI, Adelaide	1887–88
W.G. Grace	344	MCC v Kent, Canterbury	1876
W. Gunn	236★	Notts v Surrey, The Oval	1898
Hanif Mohammad	337	Pakistan v West Indies, Bridgetown	1957–58
E.H. Hendren	200	Middlesex v Hampshire, Lord's	1928
Imtiaz Ahmed	300★	Prime Minister's XI v Commonwealth XI, Bombay	1950–51
J.G. Langridge	200★	Sussex v Derbys, Derby	1951
A.E. Lewis	201★	Somerset v Kent, Taunton	1909
A.R. Lewis	223	Glamorgan v Kent, Gravesend	1966
C.C McDonald	207	Victoria v NSW, Sydney	1951–52
D.J. McGlew	213★	Natal v Border, Durban	1957–58
A.C. MacLaren	226★	Lancs v Kent, Canterbury	1896
C.P. Mead	200★	Hants v Essex, Southampton	1927
R.J.O. Meyer	202★	Somerset v Lancs, Taunton	1936
Nadeem Yousuf	202★	Muslim Commercial Bank v National Bank, Lahore	1981–82
W. Newham	201★	Sussex v Somerset, Hove	1896
Nawab of Pataudi	231★	Worcs v Essex, Worcester	1933
C.E. Pellew	271	S Australia v Victoria, Adelaide	1919–20
J. Potter	221	Victoria v NSW, Melbourne	1965–66
D.N. Sardesai	200★	India v New Zealand, Bombay	1964–65
S. Strydom	234	Orange Free State v Transvaal B, Vereeniging	1965–66
S.C. Trimble	252★	Queensland v NSW, Sydney	1963–64
E. Tyldesley	236	Lancs v Surrey, The Oval	1923
K.C. Wessels	254	Sussex v Middlesex, Hove	1980
W.M. Woodfull	212★	Victoria v Canterbury, Christchurch	1924–25
K.P. Ziebell	212★	Queensland v Victoria, Melbourne	1966–67

HIGHEST INDIVIDUAL SCORES IN SECOND INNINGS

Score	Player	Match/Venue	Season
452★	D.G. Bradman	New South Wales v Queensland, Sydney	1929–30
344	W.G. Grace	MCC v Kent, Canterbury	1876
338★	R.C. Blunt	Otago v Canterbury, Christchurch	1931–32
337	Hanif Mohammad	Pakistan v West Indies, Bridgetown	1957–58
314★	C.L. Walcott	Barbados v Trinidad, Port of Spain	1945–46
300★	Imtiaz Ahmed	Prime Minister's XI v Commonwealth XI, Bombay	1950–51

Hanif Mohammad, scorer of the largest innings for any team asked to follow-on.

1986

LARRY GOMES BECOMES TOP TRINIDADIAN

Comparatively little is heard about the West Indian inter-territory competition, the Shell Shield. Yet in its 20-year existence it has undoubtedly proved itself as a breeding ground for future stars of West Indies Test (and English county) teams. The 1985–86 season was particularly noteworthy since according to my records that fine cricketer Larry Gomes became the first batsman to reach 3,000 runs for Trinidad in the competition, and I felt it would be of interest to list the most prolific scorers in the competition since its inception in 1966. All batsmen with more than 2,000 runs are included.

MOST RUNS IN THE SHELL SHIELD

Player/Team	M	I	N.O.	Runs	H.S.	Av'ge	Seasons
M.L.C. Foster (J)	48	75	7	3887	234	57.15	1966–78
R.C. Fredericks (G)	38	62	6	3565	250	63.66	1966–83
H.A. Gomes (T)	42	76	8	3151	171★	46.34	1974–
L.T. Shillingford (W/I)	56	96	6	3068	120	34.09	1966–82
L.C. Sebastien (W/I)	57	99	9	3044	122	33.82	1966–
R.S. Gabriel (T)	52	92	5	2862	129	32.90	1969–
P.D. Lashley (B)	35	55	6	2736	204	55.84	1966–75
C.H. Lloyd (G)	33	47	8	2676	194	68.62	1966–83
H.S. Chang (J)	42	68	5	2491	155	39.54	1973–83
I.V.A. Richards (L/I)	37	66	2	2429	168★	37.92	1972–
L.G. Rowe (J)	40	70	4	2348	204	35.58	1969–82
A.I. Kallicharran (G)	32	49	4	2205	197	49.00	1967–81
P.J. Dujon (J)	42	66	9	2172	135★	38.10	1975–
D.L. Haynes (B)	32	53	3	2069	160	41.38	1977–

Note: J = Jamaica, G = Guyana, T = Trinidad & Tobago, W = Windwards, I = Combined Islands, B = Barbados, L = Leewards.

Maurice Foster (above left), and Irving Shillingford (above right), two of the leading batsmen in the Shell Shield although neither had great success in Test cricket.

SENSATIONAL START FOR JEAN-JACQUES

The first-class début of Derbyshire's Dominican-born Martin Jean-Jacques in 1986 proved to be pretty sensational. He obtained a wicket in his first over but even more noteworthy was his batting. Going in at number 11, Jean-Jacques scored 73, and added 132 for the 10th wicket with Alan Hill.

The stand was the best for the last wicket for Derbyshire in all first-class cricket, beating the previous record of 93 set by J. Humphries and J. Horsley against Lancashire at Derby as long ago as 1914. This was the only record stand for any wicket for any county which was less than 100, so Derbyshire seem to have lost a perhaps unwanted record.

That the stand was made on Jean-Jacques's first-class début makes it far more interesting. Of all last-wicket century stands I

have found only nine involving a number 11 making his first-class début, and the latest instance is a record for a County Championship match. The second table indicates that so far as I can trace Jean-Jacques's is the third best score on début by a number 11, and a record for the County Championship. Finally, the third table shows that Jean-Jacques is pretty high on the list among *all* number 11 batsmen in County Championship cricket.

LAST-WICKET CENTURY STANDS WITH NUMBER 11 MAKING FIRST-CLASS DÉBUT

Runs	No 11 & Partner	Match/Venue	Season
169	C. McKew (29) & R.B. Minnett (216★)	NSW v Victoria, Sydney	1911–12
154★	K.C. Martin (54★) & N.A. McDonald (100★)	Natal B v Griqualand W, Kimberley	1965–66
154	J.P. Lanigan (64★) & F. Buttesworth (100)	W Australia v Victoria, Perth	1921–22
149	B.A. Collins (83★)& F.H. Hollins (84)	Oxford U. v MCC, Oxford	1901
132	M. Jean-Jacques (73) & A. Hill (172★)	Derbys v Yorks, Sheffield	1986
131★	W.D. Hughes (70★) & C.C. Smart (114★)	Glamorgan v S Africans, Cardiff	1935
122	N. Dodds (36) & W.G. Ward (97★)	Tasmania v Victoria, Hobart	1898–99
102	W.E. Phillipson (27) & P.T. Eckersley (85★)	Lancs v Sussex, Old Trafford	1933

HIGHEST SCORE BY NUMBER 11 ON FIRST-CLASS DÉBUT

Score	Player	Match/Venue	Season
83★	B.A. Collins	Oxford U. v MCC, Oxford	1901
73	M. Jean-Jacques	Derbys v Yorks, Sheffield	1986
70★	W.D. Hughes	Glamorgan v S Africans, Cardiff	1935
64★	J.P. Lanigan	W Australia v Victoria, Perth	1921–22

BEST SCORES BY NUMBER 11 IN COUNTY CHAMPIONSHIP

Score	Player	Match/Venue	Season
163	T.P.B. Smith	Essex v Derbys, Chesterfield	1947
(this is the best score by a number 11 in all first-class cricket)			
115★	G.B. Stevenson	Yorks v Warwicks, Edgbaston	1982
112★	A. Fielder	Kent v Worcs, Stourbridge	1909
99★	J. Bridges	Somerset v Essex, Weston-super-Mare	1919
98	K. Higgs	Leics v Northants, Leicester	1977
90★	J.V. Murdin	Northants v Glamorgan, Northampton	1925
85	A.B. Hipkin	Essex v Somerset, Taunton	1926
82	J.W. Hitch	Surrey v Warwicks, Edgbaston	1911
77	G.E. Stannard	Sussex v Essex, Hove	1919
74★	W. Roche	Middlesex v Kent, Lord's	1899
74★	J.M. Mayer	Warwicks v Surrey, The Oval	1927
73★	W.J. Abel	Surrey v Middlesex, The Oval	1919
73	S.A.B. Daniels	Glamorgan v Gloucs, Swansea	1982
73	M. Jean-Jacques	Derbys v Yorks, Sheffield	1986

Keith Fletcher swoops in an attempt to catch Viswanath at Delhi in 1981.

Top Another catch for Colin Cowdrey. This time the victim is Graeme Pollock in the Second Test at Trent Bridge in 1965.

FLETCHER AMONG THE SAFEST HANDS

During the match between Essex and Kent at Chelmsford, Keith Fletcher became the 23rd cricketer to take 600 first-class catches, wicket-keepers excepted. Although variations in scorecards make if difficult to produce an agreed list of best career records with regard to catches in the field, I feel that the table which follows is about right. In any event the effect of any possible discrepancies with other versions is negligible. The figures for average catches per match may also be of interest. Are Graham Roope and Peter Walker the most effective catchers of all time?

600 CATCHES IN FIRST-CLASS CAREER

Player/Career	Catches	Av'ge per match
F.E. Woolley (1906–38)	1018	1.04
W.G. Grace (1865–1908)	874	1.00
G.A.R. Lock (1946–71)	831	1.27
W.R. Hammond (1920–51)	819	1.29
D.B. Close (1949–86)	813	1.03
J.G. Langridge (1928–55)	786	1.37
W. Rhodes (1898–1930)	764	0.69
C.A. Milton (1948–74)	758	1.22
E.H. Hendren (1907–38)	754	0.91
P.M. Walker (1956–72)	697	1.49
J. Tunnicliffe (1891–1907)	695	1.40
J. Seymour (1900–26)	675	1.22
C.P. Mead (1905–36)	671	0.82
M.C. Cowdrey (1950–76)	638	0.92
M.J. Stewart (1954–72)	634	1.19
K.W.R. Fletcher (1962–86)	623	0.89
P.J. Sainsbury (1954–76)	617	1.00
P.J. Sharpe (1956–76)	616	1.25
K.J. Grieves (1945–64)	610	1.25
E.G. Hayes (1896–1926)	609	1.09
G.H. Hirst (1891–1929)	607	0.74
G.R.J. Roope (1964–86)	602	1.49
P.G.H. Fender (1910–36)	600	1.08

WARWICKSHIRE'S RECORD-BREAKING OPENERS

Warwickshire's tyro opening pair, Paul Smith and Andy Moles, achieved an outstanding feat in adding more than 150 for the first wicket in both innings of their match with Somerset at Weston-super-Mare. Not only is the feat unique for a Warwickshire pair but it is only the fifth time such a feat has been achieved in the whole history of the County Championship. The list shows that Paul and Andy are in exalted company.

OPENING PAIR ADDING MORE THAN 150 IN BOTH INNINGS OF
CHAMPIONSHIP MATCH

Inns	Players	Match/Venue	Season
170 179	C.B. Fry & J. Vine	Sussex v Leics, Hove	1903
184 210*	P. Holmes & H. Sutcliffe	Yorks v Notts, Trent Bridge	1928
172 154	M.J. Harris & J.B. Bolus	Notts v Lancs, Trent Bridge	1970
195 152*	P.M. Roebuck & J.W. Lloyds	Somerset v Northants, Northampton	1982
161 155	P.A. Smith & A.J. Moles	Warwicks v Somerset, Weston-s-Mare	1986

In first-class cricket as a whole the feat has been achieved on only 12 occasions.

Paul Smith, one half of Warwickshire's opening pair at Weston-super-Mare.

Holmes and Sutcliffe, a challenge to any opening attack.

HICK ET UBIQUE

A feature of the 1986 season was the great form of Worcestershire's Zimbabwean, Graeme Hick. Hick's completion of 2,000 runs in the last match of his first full season set one wondering whether he may be the youngest-ever batsman to perform this feat, and a bit of research confirmed that not only was this surmise correct, but that he beat the previous record by a quite considerable margin.

Below I have listed the 20 youngest batsmen to score 2,000 runs. It will be seen that with two exceptions – Bradman and W.G. Grace, surely the most famous cricketers ever – Hick's record compares very favourably with all the others, while he is part of a list containing some of the greatest names in English batsmanship.

Only one never played Test cricket (not counting Hick, who has had no opportunity as yet). This single exception is Graham Atkinson, last heard of by the writer in Rugby League administration. Why, one wonders, was he unable to capitalize on his Glad Season?

YOUNGEST BATSMEN TO SCORE 2,000 RUNS IN AN ENGLISH SEASON

Age (Yrs–days)	Player	Inns	N.O.	Runs	Av'ge	Season
20–111	G.A. Hick (Worcs)	37	6	2004	64.64	1986
21–33	L. Hutton (Yorks)	58	7	2888	56.62	1937
21–65	D.C.S. Compton (Middlesex)	50	6	2468	56.09	1939
21–163	W.J. Edrich (Middlesex)	53	5	2154	44.87	1937
21–233	P.B.H. May (Camb U./Surrey)	43	9	2339	68.79	1951
21–319	D.G. Bradman (Australians)	36	6	2960	98.66	1930
22–54	P.E. Richardson (Worcs)	61	3	2294	39.55	1953
22–68	R.G.A. Headley (Worcs)	69	5	2040	31.87	1961
22–120	J.M. Brearley (Camb U./Middlesex)	54	5	2178	44.44	1964
22–163	D.S. Sheppard (Camb U./Sussex)	43	3	2014	52.60	1951
22–211	J.W. Hearne (Middlesex)	49	3	2036	44.26	1913
22–285	C.L. Townsend (Gloucs)	54	7	2440	51.91	1899
23–20	W.G. Grace (Gloucs)	39	4	2379	78.25	1871
23–38	B.A. Richards (Hants)	55	5	2395	47.90	1968
23–46	A.E. Fagg (Kent)	53	6	2456	52.25	1938
23–47	C.J. Barnett (Gloucs)	59	3	2280	40.71	1933
23–91	G.M. Turner (Worcs)	46	7	2379	61.00	1970
23–136	R.E. Foster (Worcs)	44	2	2128	50.66	1901
23–150	G. Atkinson (Somerset)	57	1	2078	37.10	1961
23–298	J.G. Dewes (Camb U./Middlesex)	45	4	2432	59.31	1950

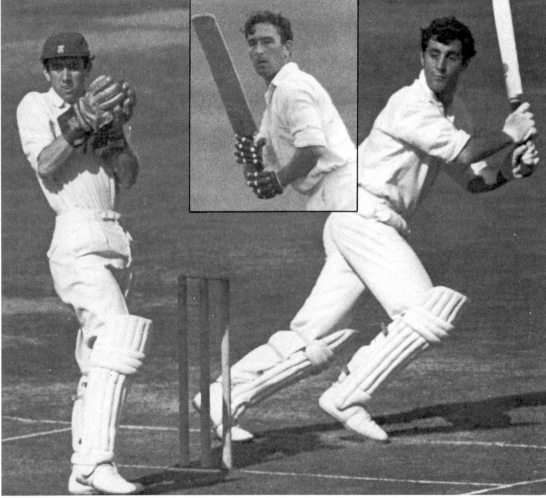

Denis Compton (inset), and Mike Brearley, two Middlesex players who achieved success at an early age.

DEADLY PAIRINGS

An old friend who assists with the records section of the Gloucestershire Yearbook suggested that something unusual had occurred during Gloucestershire's innings defeat of Somerset at Bristol in the late season. In the Somerset first innings most damage was done by West Indian paceman Courtney Walsh, who finished with the outstanding figures of nine for 72, but scarcely less impressive were Phil Bainbridge's figures of eight for 53 which heralded another Somerset collapse in their second effort. How rare is it for a bowler to take at least nine wickets in one innings of a match and a different bowler to take at least eight wickets for the same side in the same match? The table confirms that it is a very rare happening indeed. I have traced only eight instances in the whole history of first-class cricket.

Phil Bainbridge (above) and Courtney Walsh (below), alternately successful against Somerset.

TWO BOWLERS TAKING AT LEAST NINE AND EIGHT WICKETS IN AN INNINGS FOR ONE TEAM IN SAME MATCH

First Innings	Second Innings	Match/Venue	Season
T. Richardson 9–47	W.H. Lockwood 8–39	Surrey v Yorks, Sheffield	1893
G.A. Davidson 8–33	J.J. Hulme 9–27	Derbys v Yorks, Sheffield	1894
H. Pickett 10–32	C.J. Kortright 8–63	Essex v Leics, Leyton	1895
W. Brearley 9–80	W. Huddleston 8–24	Lancs v Yorks, Old Trafford	1909
J.M. Sims 8–47	J.W. Hearne 9–61	Mid'sex v Derbys, Chesterf'd	1933
R.A. Sinfield 8–40	T.W.J. Goddard 9–37	Gloucs v Leics, Bristol	1934
J.S. Pressdee 9–43	D.J. Shepherd 9–48	Glamorgan v Yorks, Swansea	1965
C.A. Walsh 9–72	P. Bainbridge 8–53	Gloucs v Somerset, Bristol	1986

Pickett (left) and Kortright (right), a devastating combination against Leics in 1895.

MARSHALL AMONG THE FASTEST

Malcolm Marshall's achievement in 1986 when he took his 1,000th first-class wicket in his 228th match caused much discussion as to whether this may have been a record low number of matches. This was, of course, out of the question; my mind immediately went to another fast bowler, Tom Richardson, and investigation revealed that he took his 1,000 first-class wickets in an amazing 134 matches. This is a record which is most unlikely to be approached, let alone beaten. It is hardly surprising that Richardson was past his best before his 30th birthday, but he continued to try

to dig some life out of the Oval pitch, and reached 2,000 wickets in only 327 matches – itself also a record. Small wonder that Richardson's heart gave out when he was only 41 – '. . . an age when other bowlers were still gently trundling to a packed outfield' as Denzil Batchelor so eloquently put it in his essay on Richardson in *The Book of Cricket* (1952).

The first table shows that Malcolm Marshall is well down the list for the number of matches needed for 1,000 wickets. This does not detract from his performance. The game is now different and he is well ahead of

any of his fast-bowling contemporaries.

The 1986 season saw another bowling achievement granted to few when Norman Gifford of Warwickshire took his 2,000th first-class wicket. The second table shows that in number of matches and years required 'Babe' Gifford is well down the list, but again one should not denigrate a performance which requires considerable skill and staying power, plus an unflagging will to continue to succeed in the game.

Malcolm Marshall, the most successful fast bowler in recent years, is surrounded by his West Indian teammates after claiming yet another victim.

BOWLERS REACHING 1,000 FIRST-CLASS WICKETS IN FEWEST MATCHES

Player	No. matches	Years	Final Total	Age at 1000th wkt
T. Richardson (Surrey)	134	1892–96	2105	26
E.G. Dennett (Gloucs)	147	1903–09	2218	29
A.W. Mold (Lancs)	149	1889–1905	1673	32
J.T. Hearne (Middlesex)	156	1888–96	3061	29
G.A. Lohmann (Surrey)	159	1884–88	1805	23
A.E. Trott (Middlesex)	164	1892–1902	1674	29
J. Southerton (Surrey)	166	1854–72	1681	44
W. Rhodes (Yorks)	168	1898–1902	4187	24
J.C. White (Somerset)	171	1909–24	2356	33
C.V. Grimmett (S Australia)	176	1911–41	1424	42
F. Morley (Notts)	181	1871–80	1274	29
C.H. Parkin (Lancs)	183	1906–25	1048	39
E. Peate (Yorkshire)	185	1879–85	1076	29
C. Blythe (Kent)	187	1899–1907	2503	27
A.P. Freeman (Kent)	187	1914–25	3776	36
T.G. Wass (Notts)	190	1896–1908	1666	34
H. Dean (Lancs)	193	1906–13	1301	28
E.A. McDonald (Lancs)	194	1909–28	1395	37
E. Willsher (Kent)	195	1850–69	1329	40
W. Mead (Essex)	197	1892–1901	1916	33
H. Verity (Yorks)	199	1930–35	1956	30
T.L. Richmond (Notts)	201	1912–26	1176	36
James Lillywhite (Sussex)	202	1862–77	1210	35
A. Fielder (Kent)	203	1900–11	1277	33
A. Watson (Lancs)	205	1872–87	1383	42
W.E. Bowes (Yorks)	206	1928–35	1639	27
W.G. Grace (Gloucs)	207	1865–77	2876	28
A. Shaw (Notts)	207	1864–76	2027	34
B. Dooland (Notts)	207	1945–57	1016	33
G.J. Thompson (Northants)	209	1897–1910	1591	32
T.B. Mitchell (Derbys)	214	1928–35	1483	32
W. Attewell (Notts)	217	1881–91	1950	30
G.E. Tribe (Northants)	218	1945–57	1378	36
F. Martin (Kent)	221	1885–95	1317	33
G.G. Macaulay (Yorks)	222	1920–27	1837	29
J.W. Hitch (Surrey)	223	1907–19	1387	33
C. Gladwin (Derbys)	224	1939–53	1653	37
J.H. Wardle (Yorks)	225	1946–54	1846	31
J.E. Walsh (Leics)	225	1936–54	1190	41
B.S. Bedi (Delhi)	225	1961–76	1560	29
B.S. Chandrasekhar (Mysore)	226	1963–79	1063	33
M.D. Marshall (Hants)	228	1977–86	1000	28

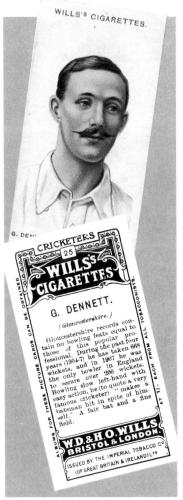

BOWLERS WHO HAVE TAKEN 2,000 FIRST-CLASS WICKETS

Player	No. matches	Years	Final Total	Age at 2000th wkt
T. Richardson (Surrey)	327	1892–1903	2105	32
J.T. Hearne (Middlesex)	347	1888–1902	3061	35
E.G. Dennett (Gloucs)	349	1903–24	2218	43
C. Blythe (Kent)	350	1899–1912	2503	33
A.P. Freeman (Kent)	350	1914–29	3776	41
W. Rhodes (Yorks)	365	1898–1908	4187	30
J.C. White (Somerset)	381	1909–31	2356	40
A. Shaw (Notts)	399	1864–94	2027	51
C.W.L. Parker (Gloucs)	400	1903–27	3278	44
T.W.J. Goddard (Gloucs)	414	1922–39	2979	38
W.G. Grace (Gloucs)	420	1865–87	2876	38
W.E. Hollies (Warwicks)	435	1932–55	2323	42
G.A.R. Lock (Surrey)	438	1946–62	2844	32
A.S. Kennedy (Hants)	450	1907–28	2874	37
D. Shackleton (Hants)	460	1948–62	2857	37
M.W. Tate (Sussex)	469	1912–31	2784	35
D.V.P. Wright (Kent)	473	1932–56	2056	41
G. Geary (Leics)	474	1912–37	2063	44
J.B. Statham (Lancs)	474	1950–66	2260	35
J. Briggs (Lancs)	481	1879–98	2221	36
F.S. Trueman (Yorks)	498	1949–65	2304	34
D.L. Underwood (Kent)	518	1963–81	2420	36
R.T.D. Perks (Worcs)	537	1930–53	2233	41
J.A. Newman (Hants)	547	1906–30	2032	45
F.J. Titmus (Middlesex)	548	1949–68	2830	35
S. Haigh (Yorks)	554	1895–1913	2012	42
G.H. Hirst (Yorks)	561	1891–1908	2733	36
W.E. Astill (Leics)	566	1906–31	2431	43
D.J. Shepherd (Glamorgan)	596	1950–69	2218	42
T.E. Bailey (Essex)	639	1945–65	2082	41
N. Gifford (Warwicks)	664	1960–86	2001	46
R. Illingworth (Leics)	735	1951–77	2072	35
F.E. Woolley (Kent)	824	1906–33	2068	46

Bishen Bedi, the most successful Indian bowler.

Frank Woolley who, although usually best remembered for his batting, is also numbered among those who achieved over 2000 first-class wickets.

HICK FIRST TO 1,000 RUNS

Although the run-scoring in 1986 was generally up to current 'average' and there was some top-class batting from various players from time to time, there was a somewhat anti-heroic feature to the season – the fact that in June and July the weeks went by with no-one being able to reach 1,000 runs. The 'milestone' was eventually passed by Graeme Hick – most appropriately since he was unarguably the batsman of the season – but he waited until July 17 to do it. This was the latest date since 1894, a season when the fixture list was extended and so theoretically an early date was likely. As with 1986, there appears to have been no obvious reason for the late date.

In *The Cricketer* for September 1986 I produced a list of the first batsman to reach 1,000 runs for every season since 1894; I have now extended the list back to 1866. In various seasons before that year *Lillywhite's Guide* produced averages for matches described variously as 'first-class' or 'important', but these averages are so full of ambiguities and illogicalities that I feel no important purpose is served in seeking to ascertain such records as are in this section. Anyone wishing to study cricket before 1866 is advised to equip himself with a set of *Lillywhite's Guides*, a set of *Scores & Biographies*, a complete run of *Bells' Life*, unlimited time and patience, ice packs and black coffee!

FIRST BATSMAN TO REACH 1,000
RUNS IN A SEASON

Season/Player	Date
1866 H. Jupp (Surrey)	Aug 17
1867 –	
1868 –	
1869 W.G. Grace (various teams)	Jul 26
1870 W.G. Grace (Gloucs)	Jul 18
1871 W.G. Grace (Gloucs)	Jul 3
1872 W.G. Grace (Gloucs)	Jul 8
1873 W.G. Grace (Gloucs)	Jul 21
1874 W.G. Grace (Gloucs)	Jul 27
1875 W.G. Grace (Gloucs)	Jul 26
1876 W.G. Grace (Gloucs)	Jul 21
1877 W.G. Grace (Gloucs)	Jul 24
1878 W.G. Grace (Gloucs)	Aug 16
1879 –	
1880 W. Barnes (Notts)	Aug 20

1881 A.N. Hornby (Lancs)   Jul 21
1882 W.L. Murdoch (Australians)   Jul 20
1883 G. Ulyett (Yorks)   Jul 19
1884 W.G. Grace (Gloucs)   Aug 7
1885 W. Gunn (Notts)   Jul 10
1886 W.G. Grace (Gloucs)   Jul 30
1887 W.G. Grace (Gloucs)   Jul 12
1888 W.G. Grace (Gloucs)   Jul 16
1889 W. Barnes (Notts)   Jul 18
1890 A. Shrewsbury (Notts)   Jun 26
1891 R. Abel (Surrey)   Aug 18
1892 A. Shrewsbury (Notts)   Aug 4
1893 A.E. Stoddart (Middlesex)   Jun 23
1894 W. Brockwell (Surrey)   Jul 30
1895 W.G. Grace (Gloucs)   May 30
1896 R. Abel (Surrey)   Jun 19
1897 R. Abel (Surrey)   Jun 24
1898 J.T. Tyldesley (Lancs)   Jul 15
1899 K.S. Ranjitsinhji (Sussex)   Jun 26
1900 T.W. Hayward (Surrey)   May 31
1901 T.W. Hayward (Surrey)   Jun 11
1902 R. Abel (Surrey)   Jun 23
1903 C.B. Fry (Sussex)   Jun 13
1904 C.B. Fry (Sussex)   Jun 14
1905 C.B. Fry (Sussex)   Jun 6
1906 T.W. Hayward (Surrey)   Jun 6
1907 J.T. Tyldesley (Lancs)   Jun 26
1908 T.W. Hayward (Surrey)   Jun 29
1909 J.B. Hobbs (Surrey)   Jun 5
1910 J.T. Tyldesley (Lancs)   Jun 18
1911 J. Vine (Sussex)   Jun 23
1912 C.G. Macartney (Australians)   Jun 19
1913 C.P. Mead (Hants)   Jun 14
1914 F.A. Tarrant (Middlesex)   Jun 15
1919 E.H. Hendren (Middlesex)   Jun 30
1920 J.B. Hobbs (Surrey)   Jun 23
1921 A.M. Ducat (Surrey)   Jun 17
1922 A.C. Russell (Essex)   Jun 7
1923 E.H. Hendren (Middlesex)   Jun 15
1924 W.W. Whysall (Notts)   Jun 25
1925 J.B. Hobbs (Surrey)   Jun 15
1926 E.H. Hendren (Middlesex)   Jun 22
1927 W.R. Hammond (Gloucs)   May 28
1928 C. Hallows (Lancs)   May 31
1929 E.H. Bowley (Sussex)   Jun 15
1930 D.G. Bradman (Australians)   May 31
1931 J.B. Hobbs (Surrey)   Jun 15
1932 H. Sutcliffe (Yorks)   Jun 16
1933 C.F. Walters (Worcs)   Jun 7
1934 J. O'Connor (Essex)   Jun 9
     E. Tyldesley (Lancs)   Jun 9
1935 I.J. Siedle (S Africans)   Jun 24
1936 E.H. Hendren (Middlesex)   Jun 20
1937 J.H. Parks (Sussex)   Jun 3
1938 D.G. Bradman (Australians)   May 27
1939 W.R. Hammond (Gloucs)   Jun 8
1945   —
1946 L.B. Fishlock (Surrey)   Jun 27
1947 D.C.S. Compton (Middlesex)   Jun 11
1948 D.G. Bradman (Australians)   Jun 10
1949 J.G. Langridge (Sussex)   Jun 1
1950 R.T. Simpson (Notts)   Jun 6
1951 D.C.S. Compton (Middlesex)   Jun 11
1952 J.D. Robertson (Middlesex)   Jun 17
1953 D. Kenyon (Worcs)   Jun 18
1954 D. Kenyon (Worcs)   Jun 5
1955 D.J. Insole (Essex)   Jun 28
1956 D.J. Insole (Essex)   Jun 19
1957 T.W. Graveney (Gloucs)   Jun 12
1958 P.B.H. May (Surrey)   Jun 19
1959 M.R. Hallam (Leics)   Jun 4
1960 E.R. Dexter (Sussex)   Jun 6
1961 W.E. Russell (Middlesex)   Jun 9
1962 W.J. Stewart (Warwicks)   Jun 12
1963 P.E. Richardson (Kent)   Jun 24
1964 M.J. Horton (Worcs)   Jun 19
1965 J.H. Edrich (Surrey)   Jun 17
1966 C. Milburn (Northants)   Jun 21
1967 W.E. Russell (Middlesex)   Jun 26
1968 R. Kanhai (Warwicks)   Jun 30
1969 Younis Ahmed (Surrey)   Jun 30

W.L. Murdoch, the first tourist to reach 1,000 runs ahead of his English hosts.
Top W.G. Grace, consistently first to 1000 runs throughout the 1870s.

1970 R. Kanhai (Warwicks)   Jun 13
1971 Zaheer Abbas (Pakistanis) Jun 4
1972 Mushtaq Mohammad
     (Northants)   Jul 10
1973 G.M. Turner (N Zealanders) May 31
1974 J.A. Jameson (Warwicks)   Jun 29
1975 G. Boycott (Yorks)   Jun 28
1976 D.L. Amiss (Warwicks)   Jun 17
1977 I.V.A. Richards (Somerset) Jun 30
1978 Zaheer Abbas (Gloucs)   Jun 30
1979 R.G. Lumb (Yorks)   Jun 13
1980 G.A. Gooch (Essex)   Jun 19
1981 Zaheer Abbas (Gloucs)   Jun 30
1982 M.W. Gatting (Middlesex)   Jun 26
1983 K.S. McEwan (Essex)   Jun 22
1984 A.I. Kallicharran (Warwicks) Jun 14
1985 C.L. Smith (Hants)   Jun 13
1986 G.A. Hick (Worcs)   Jul 17
In the blank years no batsman reached
1,000 runs.

In 1938 Bill Edrich reached 1,000 runs before the end of May but still came second – to the remarkable Bradman. Furthermore, Edrich's runs were all scored at Lord's, the only time a player has achieved this feat on one ground.

Whereas, in 1986, the target of 1,000 runs was reached at a later date than in any season since 1894, Gloucestershire's Courtney Walsh was first to 100 wickets on August 11, the earliest date since 1971. As with the batsmen, I have computed the complete list of bowlers who were first to 100 wickets since 1866. Not too much should be read into the generally later dates of recent years. After all, there is less cricket nowadays; even so the difference since the 1930s is quite startling and, one feels, out of all proportion to the admitted reduction in first-class cricket. Whatever the future for bowlers in England, one can be pretty sure that the record, June 12, held jointly by J.T. Hearne (1896) and Charlie Parker (1931) will remain for all time.

Richard Lumb, whose early success in 1979 put him in contention for a Test place.
Top K.S. Ranjitsinhji, who was first past the post in 1899.

J.T. Hearne, still fastest to 100 wickets, a record which he shares with Charlie Parker.

FIRST BOWLER TO REACH 100 WICKETS IN A SEASON

Season/Player	Date
1866 G. Wootton (Notts)	Aug 2
1867 G. Wootton (Notts)	Jun 27
1868 J. Southerton (Surrey, Sussex)	Jul 30
1869 G. Wootton (Notts)	Jul 26
1870 A. Shaw (Notts)	Sep 12
1871 J. Southerton (Surrey, Sussex)	Jul 27
1872 J. Southerton (Surrey, Sussex)	Jul 12
1873 J. Southerton (Surrey)	Jul 29
1874 J. Southerton (Surrey)	Aug 7
1875 W.G. Grace (Gloucs)	Jul 22
1876 A. Shaw (Notts)	Jul 12
1877 W. Mycroft (Derbys)	Jul 9
1878 A. Shaw (Notts)	Jul 2
1879 F. Morley (Notts)	Aug 2
1880 F. Morley (Notts)	Jul 15
1881 E. Peate (Yorks)	Jul 22
1882 E. Peate (Yorks)	Jul 25
1883 E. Barratt (Surrey)	Aug 3
1884 F.R. Spofforth (Australians)	Jul 11
1885 G.A. Lohmann (Surrey)	Jul 23
1886 G. Giffen (Australians)	Jul 28
1887 G.A. Lohmann (Surrey)	Aug 18
1888 C.T.B. Turner (Australians)	Jun 28
1889 G.A. Lohmann (Surrey)	Jul 9
1890 G.A. Lohmann (Surrey)	Jul 4
1891 W. Attewell (Notts)	Jul 24
1892 J.T. Hearne (Middlesex)	Jun 28
1893 J.T. Hearne (Middlesex)	Jun 20
1894 T. Richardson (Surrey)	Jun 18
1895 T. Richardson (Surrey)	Jun 21
1896 J.T. Hearne (Middlesex)	Jun 12
1897 J.T. Hearne (Middlesex)	Jun 26
1898 J.T. Hearne (Middlesex)	Jun 27
1899 A.E. Trott (Middlesex)	Jun 19
1900 W. Rhodes (Yorks)	Jun 21
1901 W. Rhodes (Yorks)	Jun 21
1902 F.W. Tate (Sussex)	Jun 24
1903 S.F. Barnes (Lancs)	Jul 24
1904 J.T. Hearne (Middlesex)	Jul 15
1905 W.S. Lees (Surrey)	Jul 4
1906 G.H. Hirst (Yorks)	Jun 28
1907 F.A. Tarrant (Middlesex)	Jun 26
1908 W. Brearley (Lancs)	Jun 26
1909 C. Blythe (Kent)	Jun 28
1910 W.C. Smith (Surrey)	Jun 28
1911 H. Dean (Lancs)	Jul 14
1912 S.J. Pegler (S Africans)	Jul 9
1913 M.W. Booth (Yorks)	Jul 8
1914 A.S. Kennedy (Hants)	Jul 10
1919 W. Rhodes (Yorks)	Jul 25
1920 H. Howell (Warwicks)	Jul 17
1921 A.P. Freeman (Kent)	Jul 6
1922 C.H. Parkin (Lancs)	Jun 29
1923 M.W. Tate (Sussex)	Jun 30
1924 M.W. Tate (Sussex)	Jun 21
1925 M.W. Tate (Sussex)	Jun 17
1926 C.W.L. Parker (Gloucs)	Jun 26
1927 A.P. Freeman (Kent)	Jul 13
1928 A.P. Freeman (Kent)	Jun 21
1929 T.W.J. Goddard (Gloucs)	Jun 25
1930 A.P. Freeman (Kent)	Jun 14
1931 C.W.L. Parker (Gloucs)	Jun 12
1932 A.P. Freeman (Kent)	Jun 17
1933 A.P. Freeman (Kent)	Jun 28
1934 A.P. Freeman (Kent)	Jul 5
1935 H. Verity (Yorks)	Jun 27
1936 H. Verity (Yorks)	Jun 19
1937 T.W.J. Goddard (Gloucs)	Jun 30
1938 R. Pollard (Lancs)	Jul 6
1939 T.W.J. Goddard (Gloucs)	Jul 3
1945	—
1946 T.W.J. Goddard (Gloucs)	Jul 19
1947 T.W.J. Goddard (Gloucs)	Jul 1
1948 T.L. Pritchard (Warwicks)	Jul 10
1949 R.O. Jenkins (Worcs)	Jul 14
1950 J.H. Wardle (Yorks)	Jul 11

Alfred Shaw, who in 1870 had to wait until September 12th to become the first bowler to 100 wickets.

Neal Radford, whose 100 wickets in 1985 earned him a Test place the following year.

Season/Player	Date
1951 J.C. Laker (Surrey)	Jul 11
1952 J.A. Young (Middlesex)	Jul 19
1953 A.V. Bedser (Surrey)	Jul 14
1954 B. Dooland (Notts)	Jul 7
1955 G.A.R. Lock (Surrey)	Jul 2
1956 D.J. Shepherd (Glamorgan)	Jul 2
1957 G.A.R. Lock (Surrey)	Jul 6
1958 G.A.R. Lock (Surrey)	Jul 18
1959 H.L. Jackson (Derbys)	Jul 27
1960 F.S. Trueman (Yorks)	Jul 5
1961 J.A. Flavell (Worcs)	Jul 7
1962 D. Shackleton (Hants)	Jul 11
1963 B.R. Knight (Essex)	Jul 24
1964 D. Shackleton (Hants)	Aug 1
1965 J.B. Statham (Lancs)	Jul 26
1966 D.L. Underwood (Kent)	Jul 28
1967 D.L. Underwood (Kent)	Jul 30
1968 R.M.H. Cottam (Hants)	Jul 27
1969 M.J. Procter (Gloucs)	Aug 14
1970 D.J. Shepherd (Glam)	Aug 31
1971 L.R. Gibbs (Warwicks)	Aug 5
1972	—
1973 B.S. Bedi (Northants)	Aug 27
1974 A.M.E. Roberts (Hants)	Aug 17
1975 P.G. Lee (Lancs)	Sept 2
1976	—
1977 M.J. Procter (Gloucs)	Sep 2
1978 D.L. Underwood (Kent)	Aug 25
1979 J.K. Lever (Essex)	Aug 28
1980 R.D. Jackman (Surrey)	Aug 18
1981 R.J. Hadlee (Notts)	Sep 12
1982 M.D. Marshall (Hants)	Aug 25
1983 J.E. Emburey (Middlesex)	Sep 1
1984 J.K. Lever (Essex)	Aug 18
1985 N.V. Radford (Worcs)	Sep 18
1986 C.A. Walsh (Gloucs)	Aug 11

In the blank years no bowler reached 100 wickets.

BOTHAM PASSES UNDERWOOD AT THE OVAL

A little-noticed 'milestone' passed by Ian Botham during his partially 'lost' 1986 season was when he took his 46th wicket in Oval Tests, thus passing Derek Underwood's previous best wicket total there. In the season before Botham had set the record for Lord's Tests, passing Fred Trueman, and I decided to see which bowlers had done best with regard to wicket-taking at other Test grounds.

It soon became apparent that to keep this section within acceptable bounds only the 'main' grounds could be listed. None of those Test venues which have been omitted has had a bowler with a substantial number of wickets. The outstanding single feat is manifestly that of Dennis Lillee at Melbourne; it is even further beyond any challenge than is Alec Bedser's excellent record at Old Trafford.

Ian Botham, record wicket-taker at both Lord's and The Oval.

MOST WICKETS AT MAJOR TEST GROUNDS

Ground	Player	Runs	Wkts	Av'ge
Lord's	I.T. Botham (E)	1643	68	24.16
	F.S. Trueman (E)	1394	63	22.12
The Oval	I.T. Botham (E)	1095	46	23.80
	D.L. Underwood (E)	1251	45	27.80
Old Trafford	A.V. Bedser (E)	686	51	13.45
	J.C. Laker (E)	325	27	12.03
Headingley	F.S. Trueman (E)	795	44	18.06
	R.G.D. Willis (E)	771	40	19.27
Trent Bridge	A.V. Bedser (E)	829	41	20.21
Edgbaston	F.S. Trueman (E)	798	39	20.46
Melbourne	D.K. Lillee (A)	1798	82	21.92
	G.D. McKenzie (A)	1019	45	22.64
Sydney	C.T.B. Turner (A)	602	45	13.37
	D.K. Lillee (A)	1036	43	24.09
	R.R. Lindwall (A)	726	42	17.28
Adelaide	D.K. Lillee (A)	1206	45	26.80
Brisbane (Gabba)	D.K. Lillee (A)	625	31	20.16
Perth	D.K. Lillee (A)	817	30	27.23
Port of Spain	L.R. Gibbs (WI)	1646	52	31.65
	G.S. Sobers (WI)	1434	41	34.97
Kingston	G.S. Sobers (WI)	879	27	32.55
Bridgetown	J. Garner (WI)	762	31	24.58
	A.M.E. Roberts (WI)	692	28	24.71
	M.D. Marshall (WI)	470	26	18.07
Georgetown	L.R. Gibbs (WI)	578	28	20.64
Wellington	R.J. Hadlee (NZ)	865	42	20.59
Auckland	R.J. Hadlee (NZ)	1263	42	30.07
Christchurch	R.J. Hadlee (NZ)	1471	69	21.31
Madras (Cheepauk)	Kapil Dev (I)	1074	37	29.02
	E.A.S. Prasanna (I)	672	36	18.66
Calcutta	B.S. Bedi (I)	639	29	22.03
Delhi	Kapil Dev (I)	750	27	27.77
Karachi	Imran Khan (P)	916	57	16.07
Lahore	Imran Khan (P)	698	48	14.54

Fred Trueman (top left), in action at Lord's, and Derek Underwood (above), collecting another wicket at The Oval: both their records were passed by Ian Botham.
Top right Lance Gibbs, who still holds the record at Port of Spain and Georgetown, ahead of any West Indian fast bowler.

Kapil Dev, who has taken most Test wickets at Madras and Delhi.

To complete the record, I then studied the batsmen at each ground. Gavaskar is still setting records in India while Cowdrey's Edgbaston record is under siege from David Gower; otherwise the standing records are likely to remain for many years.

MOST RUNS AT MAJOR TEST GROUNDS

Ground	Player	Inns	N.O.	Runs	Av'ge
Lord's	G. Boycott (E)	29	2	1183	43.81
	D.I. Gower (E)	23	1	951	43.22
The Oval	L. Hutton (E)	19	2	1521	89.47
	H. Sutcliffe (E)	13	1	938	78.16
Old Trafford	D.C.S. Compton (E)	13	3	818	81.80
Headingley	D.G. Bradman (A)	6	1	963	192.60
	G. Boycott (E)	16	2	903	64.50
Trent Bridge	D.C.S. Compton (E)	10	0	955	95.50
Edgbaston	M.C. Cowdrey (E)	13	0	737	56.69
	D.I. Gower (E)	11	1	690	69.00
Melbourne	D.G. Bradman (A)	17	4	1671	128.53
	G.S. Chappell (A)	31	4	1257	46.55
	J.B. Hobbs (E)	18	1	1178	69.29
Sydney	G.S. Chappell (A)	22	3	1150	60.52
	K.D. Walters (A)	19	2	900	52.94
Adelaide	D.G. Bradman (A)	11	2	970	107.77
Bridgetown	G.S. Sobers (WI)	14	2	914	76.16
	C.H. Lloyd (WI)	13	1	807	67.25
Kingston	G.S. Sobers (WI)	18	5	1354	104.15
	C.L. Walcott (WI)	12	2	924	92.40
Port of Spain	R. Kanhai (WI)	31	3	1212	43.28
	E.D. Weekes (WI)	13	2	1074	97.63
	C.H. Lloyd (WI)	28	2	1035	39.80
Bombay	S.M. Gavaskar (I)	21	0	1225	58.33
Madras	S.M. Gavaskar (I)	23	4	1124	59.15
	G.R. Viswanath (I)	17	1	785	49.06
Lahore	Zaheer Abbas (P)	15	4	1093	99.36

Gary Sobers, leading run-scorer at Bridgetown and Kingston.
Top Greg Chappell, leading run-scorer on the Sydney Cricket Ground, here adds to his tally at Perth in 1982.

1,000 RUNS AT NEW ROAD FOR GRAEME HICK

During his wonderful season for Worcestershire in 1986 Graeme Hick scored more than 1,000 runs at the Worcestershire County Ground at New Road. Out of interest I decided to find who else had scored 1,000 runs in a season on this ground and it seems that Hick is only the sixth player to do this. Glenn Turner holds the record for most runs there, but Hick, at 21, is the youngest to reach four figures.

With regard to other grounds I found that Allan Lamb beat the record for Northampton in 1981 – overtaking the legendary big-hitting Bob Haywood after 60 years – but further investigations revealed that most of the other ground records have stood for a long time. As for the bowlers, no-one seems to take wickets any more. Just for the record, however, I have produced the best for the major grounds. The symbol † denotes the progress of a record where it has passed from one player to at least one other.

ESSEX

1,000 RUNS IN ONE SEASON AT LEYTON

Player	Inns	N.O.	Runs	Av'ge	Season
†C.P. McGahey	18	5	1019	78.38	1901
†C.P. McGahey	20	2	1086	60.33	1905
†A.C. Russell	17	2	1250	83.33	1921

MOST WICKETS IN A SEASON AT LEYTON

Player	Runs	Wkts	Av'ge	Season
W. Mead	985	70	14.07	1899

GLOUCS

MOST RUNS IN ONE SEASON AT BRISTOL

Player	Inns	N.O.	Runs	Av'ge	Season
W.R. Hammond	12	2	951	95.10	1933

MOST WICKETS IN ONE SEASON AT BRISTOL

Player	Runs	Wkts	Av'ge	Season
T.W.J. Goddard	673	84	8.01	1939

HANTS

MOST RUNS IN ONE SEASON AT SOUTHAMPTON

Player	Inns	N.O.	Runs	Av'ge	Season
†C.B. Fry	12	1	889	80.81	1911
†C.P. Mead	18	1	987	58.05	1913
†C.P. Mead	13	2	990	90.00	1914

LEICS

1,000 RUNS IN ONE SEASON AT GRACE ROAD, LEICESTER

Player	Inns	N.O.	Runs	Av'ge	Season
†M. Tompkin	26	2	1041	43.37	1950
C.H. Palmer	17	2	1002	66.80	1951
†M.R. Hallam	20	1	1100	57.89	1959
W. Watson	18	5	1037	79.76	1959
B.F. Davison	19	6	1026	78.92	1976

MOST WICKETS IN A SEASON AT GRACE ROAD

Player	Runs	Wkts	Av'ge	Season
G.A.R. Lock	1231	88	13.98	1967

MOST RUNS IN ONE SEASON AT AYLESTONE ROAD, LEICESTER

Player	Inns	N.O.	Runs	Av'ge	Season
†C.J.B. Wood	21	3	948	54.66	1905
†L.G. Berry	20	1	1229	64.68	1937

MOST WICKETS IN ONE SEASON AT AYLESTONE ROAD

Player	Runs	Wkts	Av'ge	Season
T. Jayes	1334	66	20.21	1906

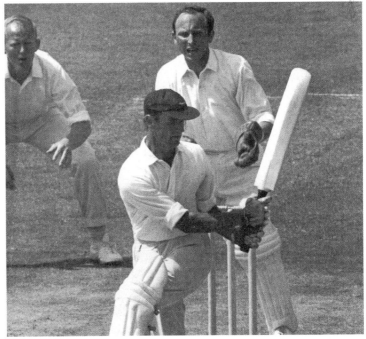

Tony Lock (above left), most wickets at Grace Road, Leicester and Maurice Hallam (above right), who holds the record for most runs.

LANCS

1,000 RUNS IN ONE SEASON AT OLD TRAFFORD

Player	Inns	N.O.	Runs	Av'ge	Season
†J.T. Tyldesley	18	1	1048	61.64	1904
†J.W.H. Makepeace	23	2	1128	53.71	1919
E. Tyldesley	18	1	1016	59.76	1926
C. Hallows	17	7	1004	100.40	1927
†F.B. Watson	13	2	1183	107.54	1928
E. Paynter	19	0	1128	59.36	1937
†C. Washbrook	19	4	1300	86.66	1947
G. Pullar	25	3	1098	49.90	1961

MOST WICKETS IN ONE SEASON AT OLD TRAFFORD

Player	Runs	Wkts	Av'ge	Season
†J. Briggs	701	79	8.87	1888
†A.W. Mold	898	89	10.08	1894
W. Brearley	1322	87	15.19	1908

MIDDLESEX

MOST RUNS IN ONE SEASON AT LORD'S

Player	Inns	N.O.	Runs	Av'ge	Season
†W.G. Grace	16	2	1070	76.42	1871
†A.E. Stoddart	23	1	1083	49.22	1893
†J.W. Hearne	23	3	1099	54.95	1914
†E.H. Hendren	18	3	1500	100.00	1920
†E.H. Hendren	31	1	1760	62.85	1928
E.H. Hendren	32	1	1514	48.83	1936
W.J. Edrich	30	5	1592	63.68	1938
D.C.S. Compton	29	2	1614	59.77	1939
J.D.B. Robertson	30	3	1563	57.88	1947
†D.C.S. Compton	28	3	2048	81.92	1947
J.D.B. Robertson	33	2	1650	53.22	1951

The above table charts the progress of the record, and also lists all instances of 1,500 runs or more in a Lord's season. Hendren scored 1,000 runs at Lord's in 14 seasons, Edrich in 10, Robertson and Compton in nine.

MOST WICKETS IN ONE SEASON AT LORD'S

Player	Runs	Wkts	Av'ge	Season
†G. Wootton	590	79	7.46	1867
†J.T. Hearne	1544	104	14.84	1892
†J.T. Hearne	2123	122	17.40	1893
†J.T. Hearne	1845	141	13.08	1896
J.T. Hearne	1603	124	12.92	1898
†A.E. Trott	2637	173	15.24	1899*
A.E. Trott	3011	148	20.34	1901

* In 1899 A.E. Trott also scored 913 runs (av 26.08) at Lord's; this is the nearest approach ever to a 'double' on one ground during a season. J.T. Hearne took more than 100 wickets at Lord's in six seasons, A.E. Trott in three seasons, and F.A. Tarrant, C.I.J. Smith and F.J. Titmus once each. A.E. Trott's 173 wickets at Lord's in 1899 is the most ever by one bowler at one ground during one season.

NORTHANTS

1,000 RUNS IN ONE SEASON AT NORTHAMPTON COUNTY GROUND

Player	Inns	N.O.	Runs	H.S.	Av'ge	Season
†R.A. Haywood	25	0	1127	198	45.08	1921
D. Brookes	18	3	1022	204*	68.13	1952
†A.J. Lamb	21	5	1310	162	81.87	1981

MOST WICKETS IN ONE SEASON AT NORTHAMPTON COUNTY GROUND

Player	Runs	Wkts	Av'ge	Season
G.J. Thompson	994	77	12.90	1912

NOTTS

MOST RUNS IN ONE SEASON AT TRENT BRIDGE

Player	Inns	N.O.	Runs	Av'ge	Season
†J. Iremonger	13	0	1019	78.38	1904
†J. Iremonger	18	0	1152	64.00	1905
†J. Iremonger	21	4	1222	71.76	1906
†W.W. Whysall	29	1	1358	48.50	1928
†R.T. Simpson	26	4	1507	68.50	1953

The above table shows the progress of the record. W.W. Whysall scored 1,000 runs at Trent Bridge in six seasons, W.W. Keeton and R.T. Simpson in four, J. Iremonger and J. Hardstaff Jr in three each.

MOST WICKETS IN ONE SEASON AT TRENT BRIDGE

Player	Runs	Wkts	Av'ge	Season
†T.G. Wass	1280	85	15.05	1907
†H. Larwood	934	89	10.49	1932
†B. Dooland	1500	97	15.46	1953
†B. Dooland	1591	125	12.72	1954

The table shows the progress of the record. T.L. Richmond took 85 wickets in the 1920 and 1926 seasons. Dooland also took 86 wickets in 1956 and 90 in 1957.

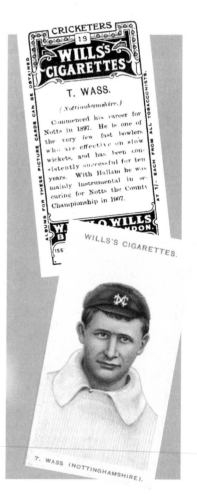

CRICKETERS 19

WILLS's CIGARETTES

T. WASS.
(Nottinghamshire.)

Commenced his career for Notts in 1897. He is one of the very few fast bowlers who are effective on slow wickets, and has been consistently successful for ten years. With Hallam he was mainly instrumental in securing for Notts the County Championship in 1907.

ALBUMS FOR THESE PICTURE CARDS CAN BE OBTAINED

AT 1/- EACH FROM ALL TOBACCONISTS.

WILLS'S CIGARETTES.

T. WASS (NOTTINGHAMSHIRE).

Denis Compton (above) and Albert Trott (above left), both still holders of the records for most runs and wickets at Lord's.

SOMERSET

MOST RUNS IN ONE SEASON AT TAUNTON

Player	Inns	N.O.	Runs	Av'ge	Season
†L.C.H. Palairet	17	1	875	54.68	1895
†W.E. Alley	11	3	908	113.50	1961

MOST WICKETS IN ONE SEASON AT TAUNTON

Player	Runs	Wkts	Av'ge	Season
E.J. Tyler	1416	71	19.94	1895

SURREY

MOST RUNS IN ONE SEASON AT THE OVAL

Player	Inns	N.O.	Runs	Av'ge	Season
†R. Abel	24	1	1009	43.86	1895
†R. Abel	25	2	1428	62.08	1896
†R. Abel	25	4	1895	90.23	1899
T.W. Hayward	21	2	1542	81.15	1899
R. Abel	22	3	1525	80.26	1900
R. Abel	29	4	1521	60.84	1901
T.W. Hayward	32	2	1783	59.43	1904
T.W. Hayward	33	4	1752	60.41	1906
J.B. Hobbs	29	5	1605	66.87	1919
A. Sandham	28	4	1556	64.83	1921
R.J. Gregory	32	3	1544	53.24	1934

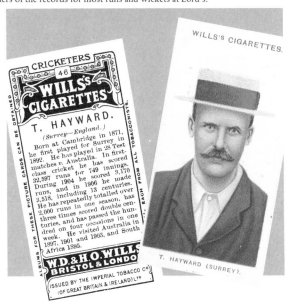

The table charts the progress of the record, and also lists every instance of 1,500 runs in an Oval season.

MOST WICKETS IN ONE SEASON AT THE OVAL

Player	Runs	Wkts	Av'ge	Season
†J. Southerton	1605	95	16.89	1870
†G.A. Lohmann	1177	100	11.77	1888
†T. Richardson	2087	132	15.81	1895
T. Richardson	2004	132	15.18	1896
T. Richardson	2015	110	18.31	1897
W.K. Lees	1699	104	16.33	1905
W.C. Smith	1497	107	13.99	1910
A.R. Gover	2008	113	17.76	1937
G.A.R. Lock	953	101	9.43	1957

The table charts the progress of the record and lists every instance of 100 wickets in an Oval season.

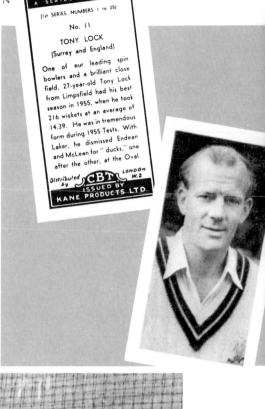

SUSSEX

MOST RUNS IN A SEASON AT HOVE

Player	Inns	N.O.	Runs	Av'ge	Season
†K.S. Ranjitsinhji	20	4	1198	74.87	1895
†K.S. Ranjitsinhji	15	2	1348	103.69	1900
†C.B. Fry	18	3	1382	92.13	1903
†C.B. Fry	20	0	1679	83.95	1904

The table charts the progress of the record. Ranjitsinhji scored 1,000 runs in four seasons, C.B. Fry in three seasons, and E.H. Bowley (1928), John Langridge (1935) and A.S.M. Oakman (1961) one each.

MOST WICKETS IN A SEASON AT HOVE

Player	Runs	Wkts	Av'ge	Season
†W.A. Humphreys	1529	84	18.20	1893
†G.R. Cox	1424	86	16.55	1905

C.B. Fry, still unsurpassed at Hove.

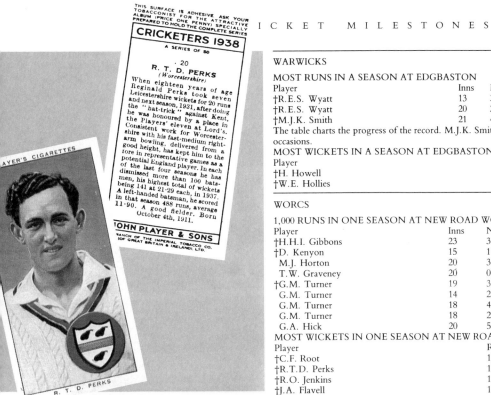

WARWICKS

MOST RUNS IN A SEASON AT EDGBASTON

Player	Inns	N.O.	Run	Av'ge	Season
†R.E.S. Wyatt	13	3	1098	109.80	1929
†R.E.S. Wyatt	20	2	1175	65.27	1937
†M.J.K. Smith	21	4	1271	74.76	1959

The table charts the progress of the record. M.J.K. Smith scored 1,000 runs on three occasions.

MOST WICKETS IN A SEASON AT EDGBASTON

Player	Runs	Wkts	Av'ge	Season
†H. Howell	1573	84	18.72	1923
†W.E. Hollies	1315	92	14.29	1946

WORCS

1,000 RUNS IN ONE SEASON AT NEW ROAD WORCESTER

Player	Inns	N.O.	Runs	Av'ge	Season
†H.H.I. Gibbons	23	3	1034	50.17	1934
†D. Kenyon	15	1	1115	79.64	1953
M.J. Horton	20	3	1017	59.82	1959
T.W. Graveney	20	0	1034	51.70	1964
†G.M. Turner	19	3	1236	77.25	1970
G.M. Turner	14	2	1000	83.33	1979
G.M. Turner	18	4	1095	78.21	1980
G.M. Turner	18	2	1044	65.25	1981
G.A. Hick	20	5	1028	68.53	1986

MOST WICKETS IN ONE SEASON AT NEW ROAD, WORCESTER

Player	Runs	Wkts	Av'ge	Season
†C.F. Root	1332	68	19.58	1923
†R.T.D. Perks	1237	81	15.27	1937
†R.O. Jenkins	1567	78	20.08	1949
†J.A. Flavell	1042	83	12.55	1965

R.E.S. Wyatt (above left) and M.J.K. Smith (above right), successive record-holders at Edgbaston.

RADLEY COMPLETES A FULL SET

By scoring 113★ for Middlesex v Somerset at Lord's during 1986, Clive Radley completed the estimable feat of recording at least one century for his county against every other first-class county. A period of 21 years between his first and 16th century compares rather unfavourably with the record of M.J.K. Smith, who took only six years, but it is still a feat not to be undervalued, calling for run-scoring ability on all sorts of pitches and grounds. Radley is number 31 on the list which includes many great names and, undoubtedly, a few surprises.

Only first-class matches have been taken into account.

For present-day cricket-watchers the following comments on current batsmen close to achieving the feat may be of interest. Keith Fletcher of Essex has required a hundred against Hants to complete his set for several years, while team-mate and skipper Graham Gcoch needs only Sussex. Hampshire's Gordon Greenidge has in fact scored centuries against the sixteen counties other than his own but the Leics century was for West Indies. Alvin Kallicharran needs Derbyshire, while his Warwicks team-mate Geoff Humpage requires hundreds against Middlesex and Notts to complete a rare set of every other county

and both universities. Leics skipper Peter Willey requires Gloucs while his Notts counterpart Clive Rice needs only Surrey, and ex-Lancs skipper Clive Lloyd has long been seeking an Essex hundred to complete his set. Sussex's Paul Parker has completed centuries against all counties bar Sussex, but the one against Yorkshire was for Cambridge University.

Finally, think with sympathy of Mike Harris, of Middlesex and Notts, who needed only a century against Leicestershire for a unique feat of county championship hundreds against *every* county, but found the ultimate task beyond him.

John Edrich, who enjoyed success against every other county.

BATSMEN SCORING A CENTURY AGAINST EVERY OTHER COUNTY

Player	County	First 100	16th 100
L.E.G. Ames	Kent	1927	1939
D.L. Amiss	Warwicks	1967	1977
G. Boycott	Yorks	1963	1975
D. Brookes	Northants	1938	1957
J.H. Edrich	Surrey	1959	1968
W.J. Edrich	Middlesex	1937	1952
W.R. Hammond	Glous	1923	1933
J. Hardstaff Jr	Notts	1931	1949
E.H. Hendren	Middlesex	1911	1933
J.B. Hobbs	Surrey	1905	1925
L. Hutton	Yorkshire	1934	1951
J. Iddon	Lancashire	1927	1939
D.J. Insole	Essex	1947	1957
W.W. Keeton	Notts	1931	1947
W. Larkins	Northants	1975	1985
K.S. McEwan	Essex	1974	1981
C.P. Mead	Hampshire	1906	1932
J. O'Connor	Essex	1922	1932
W.G.A. Parkhouse	Glamorgan	1948	1960
C.T. Radley	Middlesex	1965	1986
I.V.A. Richards	Somerset	1974	1985
J.D.B. Robertson	Middlesex	1939	1953
A.C. Russell	Essex	1913	1929
R.T. Simpson	Notts	1946	1957
M.J.K. Smith	Warwicks	1957	1963
H.S. Squires	Surrey	1929	1949
H. Sutcliffe	Yorkshire	1919	1928
K.G. Suttle	Sussex	1952	1968
G.M. Turner	Worcestershire	1968	1979
E. Tyldesley	Lancashire	1912	1927
F.E. Woolley	Kent	1906	1932

Joe Hardstaff Jr, one of three Notts batsmen to share the same distinction.

G.M. Turner and I.V.A. Richards actually scored a century against every county, the ones against their own county being scored for touring teams.

Clive Radley in action against Surrey in 1982.

1,000 RUNS AGAINST EVERY COUNTY BAR THEIR OWN

Player	County	Runs	Av'ge	Seasons
D.L. Amiss	Warwicks	33846	42.25	1960–86
L.G. Berry	Leics	30143	30.32	1924–51
G. Boycott	Yorks	32458	57.85	1962–86
D. Brookes	Northants	28980	36.13	1934–59
K.W.R. Fletcher	Essex	28152	37.33	1962–86
A. Jones	Glamorgan	34056	33.03	1957–83
D. Kenyon	Worcs	33490	33.19	1946–67
James Langridge	Sussex	28884	35.79	1924–53
J.G. Langridge	Sussex	34152	37.70	1928–55
R.E. Marshall	Hampshire	30303	36.03	1953–72
C.A. Milton	Gloucs	30218	33.65	1948–74
J.M. Parks	Sussex	29138	35.97	1949–72
M.J.K. Smith	Warwicks	27672	43.10	1956–75
K.G. Suttle	Sussex	29375	30.92	1949–71

HARPER'S 234 AT No. 7

During the 1986 season Roger Harper, the West Indian Test all-rounder, played an innings of 234 – his maiden double century – for Northants against Gloucs from No. 7 in the order. Not only was this the best first-class score for the county from No. 7, it was the best for all English first-class cricket. The list for English cricket for each position follows.

To some extent this performance goes with the previous one, though it is in fact a good deal more difficult to achieve, requiring as it does great consistency over a long period. The next batsman to join the select band will probably be Clive Radley of Middlesex, who required only 24 runs against Warwickshire.

Radley would then join another even more accomplished group of batsmen who have scored over 1,000 runs and at least one century for their county against every other one. This list currently consists of Dennis Amiss, Geoffrey Boycott, Dennis Brookes, Mike Smith and Ken Suttle; perhaps they can claim to be the most accomplished all-round county batsmen of all time.

Roger Harper, who savaged the Gloucester attack.

Roy Marshall – regular runs against every opposition.

BEST SCORES FROM EACH POSITION IN THE ORDER IN ENGLISH CRICKET

Posn	Score	Player	Match/Venue	Season
1	424	A.C. MacLaren	Lancs v Somerset, Taunton	1895
2	322	E. Paynter	Lancs v Sussex, Hove	1937
3	345	C.G. Macartney	Australians v Notts, Trent Bridge	1921
4	322	I.V.A. Richards	Somerset v Warwicks, Taunton	1985
5	341	G.H. Hirst	Yorks v Leics, Leicester	1905
6	260	A.P.F. Chapman	Kent v Lancs, Maidstone	1927
7	234	R.A. Harper	Northants v Gloucs, Northampton	1986
8	268	C.R.N. Maxwell	Sir Julien Cahn's XI v Leics, W. Bridgford	1935
9	189	E.B. Alletson	Notts v Sussex, Hove	1911
10	165	J. Chapman	Derbys v Warwicks, Blackwell Colliery	1910
11	163	T.P.B. Smith	Essex v Derbys, Chesterfield	1947

Eddie Paynter, the best score in England at number two.

The list for all first-class cricket may also be of interest despite the slightly freakish appearance of its lower reaches. Trumper was not of course a regular at either No. 7 or No. 9, while Chapman and Peter Smith usually went in somewhat higher than listed here.

BEST SCORES FROM EACH POSITION IN THE ORDER IN ALL FIRST-CLASS CRICKET

Posn	Score	Player	Match/Venue	Season
1	499	Hanif Mohammad	Karachi v Behawalpur, Karachi	1958–59
2	437	W.H. Ponsford	Victoria v Queensland, Melbourne	1926–27
3	452★	D.G. Bradman	New South Wales v Queensland, Sydney	1929–30
4	428	Aftab Baloch	Sind v Bahawalpur, Karachi	1973–74
5	429	W.H. Ponsford	Victoria v Tasmania, Melbourne	1922–23
6	260	A.P.F. Chapman	Kent v Lancs, Maidstone	1927
7	292★	V.T. Trumper	New South Wales v Tasmania, Sydney	1898–99
8	268	C.R.N. Maxwell	Sir Julian Cahn's XI v Leics, W Bridgford	1935
9	293	V.T. Trumper	Arthur Sims's XI v Canterbury, Christchurch	1913–14
10	165	J. Chapman	Derbys v Warwicks, Blackwell Colliery	1910
11	163	T.P.B. Smith	Essex v Derbys, Chesterfield	1947

BEST SCORES FROM EACH POSITION IN THE ORDER IN TEST CRICKET

Posn	Score	Player	Match/Venue	Season
1	354	L. Hutton,	England v Australia, The Oval	1938
2	325	A. Sandham	England v West Indies, Kingston	1929–30
3	365★	G.S. Sobers	West Indies v Pakistan, Kingston	1957–58
4	307	R.M. Cowper	Australia v England, Melbourne	1965–66
5	304	D.G. Bradman	Australia v England, Headingley	1934
6	250	K.D. Walters	Australia v New Zealand, Christchurch	1976–77
7	270	D.G. Bradman	Australia v England, Melbourne	1936–37
8	209	Imtiaz Ahmed	Pakistan v New Zealand, Bagh-i-Jinnah, Lahore	1955–56
9	160	C. Hill	Australia v England, Adelaide	1907–98
10	117	W.W. Read	England v Australia, The Oval	1884
11	68★	R.O. Collinge	New Zealand v Pakistan, Auckland	1972–73

A.P.F. Chapman, world best at number six.

R.O. Collinge's 68 not out is still the best in Test cricket for a number eleven.

FRIENDLY NEIGHBOURS FOR DENNIS AMISS

This somewhat cryptic heading was the least cumbersome I could invent for a series of records which really aroused my interest during the 1986 county season.

For many people 1986 was memorable for Dennis Amiss reaching 100 first-class centuries, but during Warwickshire's home match with Worcestershire Amiss established a Warwicks record which I regarded as of at least equal interest. At the end of the Worcs match Amiss had scored 3,330 runs for Warwicks against the local rivals, thus passing W.G.

Quaife's total of 3,269 runs against Hampshire, the previous Warwickshire record against any one other team. It will be seen that Amiss has a good chance of becoming the heaviest scorer for any one county *against* Worcs. Unfortunately, so far as I can tell, no other record in this particular set is likely to be beaten in the near future.

MOST RUNS FOR ONE COUNTY AGAINST ANY ONE TEAM

County	Player	Inns	N.O.	Runs	H.S.	Av'ge	Seasons	Opponents
Derbys	D. Smith	43	4	1835	202*	47.05	1930–50	Notts
Essex	P.A. Perrin	77	11	3178	343*	48.15	1896–1925	Derbys
Glamorgan	A. Jones	82	1	2900	167	35.80	1957–83	Gloucs
Gloucs	W.R. Hammond	47	4	2823	271	65.65	1920–46	Lancs
Hants	C.P. Mead	92	9	4369	198	52.63	1906–36	Kent
Kent	F.E. Woolley	85	5	3710	172	46.37	1907–38	Sussex
Lancs	J.T. Tyldesley	59	10	3036	209	61.95	1895–1919	Warwicks
Leics	L.G. Berry	69	6	2661	184*	42.23	1925–51	Northants
Middlesex	E.H. Hendren	88	11	4030	199	52.33	1909–37	Surrey
Northants	D. Brookes	62	6	2450	210	43.75	1935–59	Leics
Notts	G. Gunn	84	5	2981	191	37.73	1902–32	Surrey
Somerset	H. Gimblett	37	3	1832	167*	53.88	1936–53	Northants
Surrey	J.B. Hobbs	63	5	3742	215	64.51	1905–34	Warwicks
Sussex	J.G. Langridge	60	4	2408	234*	43.00	1931–55	Derbys
Warwicks	D.L. Amiss	74	13	3330	167	54.59	1965–86	Worcs
Worcs	F.L. Bowley	68	3	2799	276	43.06	1900–23	Hants
Yorks	H. Sutcliffe	61	4	3006	195	52.73	1919–39	Lancs

MOST RUNS AGAINST ONE COUNTY FOR ANY ONE TEAM

Opponents	Player	Inns	N.O.	Runs	H.S.	Av'ge	Seasons	For County
Derbys	P.A. Perrin	77	11	3178	343*	48.15	1896–1925	Essex
Essex	H.T.W. Hardinge	74	7	3379	176	50.43	1904–33	Kent
Glamorgan	W.R. Hammond	42	7	2774	302*	79.25	1923–46	Gloucs
Gloucs	C.P. Mead	82	10	3409	187	47.34	1907–36	Hants
Hants	F.E. Woolley	84	3	3625	188	44.75	1906–38	Kent
Kent	C.P. Mead	92	9	4369	198	52.63	1906–36	Hants
Lancs	H. Sutcliffe	61	4	3006	195	52.73	1919–39	Yorks
Leics	C.P. Mead	76	10	3419	159*	51.80	1907–36	Hants
Middlesex	J.B. Hobbs	70	7	3510	316*	55.73	1905–33	Surrey
Northants	F.E. Woolley	63	5	2719	217	46.87	1907–37	Kent
Notts	E.H. Hendren	73	9	3531	232	55.17	1908–37	Middlesex
Somerset	C.P. Mead	86	15	3450	176*	48.59	1907–35	Hants
Surrey	E.H. Hendren	88	11	4030	199	52.33	1909–37	Middlesex
Sussex	F.E. Woolley	85	5	3710	172	46.37	1907–38	Kent
Warwicks	J.B. Hobbs	63	5	3742	215	64.51	1905–34	Surrey
Worcs	C.P. Mead	75	13	3391	235	54.69	1906–36	Hants
Yorks	C.P. Mead	88	17	3197	213	45.02	1906–36	Hants

MOST WICKETS FOR ONE COUNTY AGAINST ANY ONE TEAM

County	Player	Runs	Wkts	Av'ge	Seasons	Opponents
Derbys	H.L. Jackson	1865	150	12.43	1948–63	Leics
Essex	W. Mead	2622	154	17.02	1894–1912	Yorks
Glamorgan	J. Mercer	2906	169	17.19	1923–39	Worcs
Gloucs	C.W.L. Parker	4943	309	15.99	1907–35	Worcs
Hants	D. Shackleton	3383	229	14.77	1948–69	Sussex
Kent	A.P. Freeman	4427	269	16.45	1919–36	Essex
Lancs	A.W. Mold	2194	171	12.83	1889–1901	Sussex
Leics	W.E. Astill	3634	181	20.07	1907–38	Northants
Middlesex	J.T. Hearne	4476	256	17.48	1890–1914	Yorks
Northants	G.J. Thompson	2143	146	14.67	1905–22	Derbys
Notts	T.G. Wass	3436	220	15.61	1898–1914	Derbys
Somerset	J.C. White	2489	218	11.41	1910–35	Worcs
Surrey	T. Richardson	2568	147	17.46	1892–1904	Somerset
Sussex	M.W. Tate	3334	170	19.61	1919–37	Kent
Warwicks	W.E. Hollies	3730	193	19.32	1933–57	Worcs
Worcs	R.T.D. Perks	3301	162	20.37	1931–55	Somerset
Yorks	W. Rhodes	3595	264	13.61	1898–1930	Essex

W. ASTILL.

MOST WICKETS AGAINST ONE COUNTY FOR ANY ONE TEAM

Opponents	Player	Runs	Wkts	Av'ge	Seasons	For County
Derbys	T.G. Wass	3436	220	15.61	1898–1914	Notts
Essex	A.P. Freeman	4427	269	16.45	1919–36	Kent
Glamorgan	C.W.L. Parker	2786	187	14.89	1921–35	Gloucs
Gloucs	A.P. Freeman	3497	241	14.51	1920–36	Kent
Hants	T.W.J. Goddard	4482	264	16.97	1923–52	Gloucs
Kent	J.T. Hearne	3798	244	15.56	1890–1914	Middlesex
Lancs	W. Rhodes	4053	237	17.10	1898–1930	Yorks
Leics	A.P. Freeman	2679	231	11.59	1919–35	Kent
Middlesex	W. Rhodes	4447	223	19.94	1898–1929	Yorks
Northants	A.P. Freeman	2965	253	11.71	1920–34	Kent
Notts	W. Rhodes	3857	231	16.69	1898–1930	Yorks
Somerset	C.W.L. Parker	4588	302	15.19	1907–35	Gloucs
Surrey	W. Rhodes	4425	231	19.15	1898–1930	Yorks
Sussex	A.P. Freeman	4498	244	18.43	1919–36	Kent
Warwicks	W. Rhodes	3874	256	15.13	1898–1930	Yorks
Worcs	C.W.L. Parker	4943	309	15.99	1907–35	Gloucs
Yorks	J.T. Hearne	4476	254	17.62	1890–1914	Middlesex

BOYCOTT'S RUNS AFTER 40

When he finally retired in 1986, Geoff Boycott had scored 10,802 runs after his 40th birthday. In some circles it was queried whether this was some sort of record. The table below shows that it was nowhere near a record and it puts Boycott's highly creditable figures into their true historical perspective.

MOST RUNS AFTER 40 – TOP FIVE

Player	Runs	Inns	N.O.	Av'ge	100s
J.B. Hobbs	26441	498	47	58.63	98
F.E. Woolley	25963	640	31	42.63	68
E.H. Hendren	24039	551	65	49.46	68
W.G. Grace	22199	696	39	33.79	39
C.P. Mead	19561	475	81	49.65	59

In post-war cricket the following scored more than 10,000 runs after their 40th birthday.

Player	Runs	Inns	N.O.	Av'ge	100s
L.B. Fishlock	12323	342	21	38.39	28
J.G. Langridge	10431	327	19	33.87	20
G.M. Emmett	10353	373	15	28.92	16
G. Boycott	10802	232	43	57.15	31

AUSTRALIAN AND ENGLISH TEST CRICKETERS
A Series of Forty Actual Photographs

No. 12.

J. B. HOBBS.
(Surrey.)
Born December 16th. 1882.

For fifteen years the greatest batsman in the world, with an amazing record in Test matches. A beautiful player on any type of wicket against any type of bowling, and a splendid fieldsman at cover point. Has made more hundreds than any other batsman in first class cricket.

Issued by
MAJOR DRAPKIN & CO.
Branch of The United Kingdom
Tobacco Co. Ltd. LONDON.

Laurie Fishlock, more runs after his fortieth birthday than any other post-war batsman.

CLOSE JOINS THE VENERABLE VETERANS

I was asked shortly after the end of the 1986 season whether Brian Close passed any 'milestones' when he played for his own XI v New Zealanders at Scarborough in September. The answer is no, but he certainly consolidated his reputation as a cricketer who does remarkable things. He is in fact the oldest first class cricketer to play in the British Isles since 1971 and it will be seen from the first table that he is fairly high on the all-time list for first-class cricket in his country. The ages I give are for the last day of the match and must be taken with the reservations mentioned under the table.

One can be sure that even the redoubtable Close will have to go some to beat Benjamin Aislabie's record. Aislabie was immortalized in *Tom Brown's Schooldays* when the boys bowled him 'slow cobs'; such was his bulk by this time that he usually had someone to field for him and always had a runner. According to Haygarth, 'Mr Aislabie's wonderful good nature, pleasantry and untiring zeal caused the eyes of all to be turned on him in the field.' Haygarth adds that despite his long first-class career 'he could not bat in the least, and his average . . . ridiculously small. He was also no field . . .' – an epitaph which Close will certainly not be saddled with.

Aislabie is not the oldest first-class cricketer ever. Indian veteran C.K. Nayudu made his last first-class appearance in 1963–64 for the Maharashtra Governor's XI v Maharashtra Chief Minister's XI in a Defence Fund match at Nagpur and was 68 years and four days old on the final day, but the ultimate accolade surely goes to another Indian, Rajah Maharaj Singh, who made his first and only first-class appearance for the Bombay Governor's XI – (himself – he was the first native Indian to hold that position) against the 1950–51 Commonwealth Tourists at Bombay. Born at Kapurthala, India on May 17, 1878, he was 72 years 192 days old when he batted, scoring four runs, on the opening day. For the remainder of the match he was 'absent ill'!

As Kunwar Singh he attended Harrow and Balliol College. Oxford, where he represented the University as a featherweight boxer; back in India he was national tennis champion. In 1946 he was Indian delegate to the United Nations and in 1948 he became Governor of Bombay. He died aged 81 on June 6, 1959, and although the holder of a unique and surely everlasting cricket record he was not obituarized in any cricket publication. I have to thank my old friend Brain Croudy for this information and much of the research into personal details.

What else did Close achieve in 1986 season? Well, he played first-class cricket more than 37 years after his début and again, though by no means a record for English cricket, he is pretty high on this list (the second table, below). It is likely that W. Beldham, George Brown and John Small from the first table should appear in this list but I am unable to trace their early careers which, tragically for such great players, are shrouded in the mists of antiquity.

The statue of C.K. Nayudu at Indore.

OLDEST PLAYERS IN FIRST-CLASS CRICKET IN BRITISH ISLES

Age (Yrs–days)	Player	Date of birth	Match/Season
67–169	B. Aislabie	14.1.1774	MCC v Cambridge U., 1841
61–106	J. Small Sr	19.4.1737	Hants v MCC, 1798
61–44	F.W. Lillywhite	13.6.1792	Sussex v England, 1853
	(his benefit match; commenced bowling on day 1 but after 11 overs retired ill)		
60–151	Lord Harris	3.2.1851	Kent v Indians, 1911
59–278	W.G. Grace	18.7.1848	Gents v Surrey, 1908
59–186	A.E. Green-Price	11.2.1860	H.K. Foster's XI v Worcs, 1919
	(his only first class match)		
59–167	A.N. Hornby	10.2.1847	England XI v West Indians, 1906
	(withdrew injured on day 2, without batting or bowling)		
58–261	E. Smith	19.10.1869	Leveson Gower's XI v Oxford U., 1928
58–56	H.D.G. Leveson Gower	8.5.1873	Leveson Gower's XI v Cambridge U., 1931
58–6	G.H. Hirst	7.9.1871	Yorks v MCC, 1929
57–125	S.F. Barnes	19.4.1873	Wales v MCC, 1930
57–91	R.H. Moss	24.2.1868	Worcs v Gloucs, 1925
	(oldest player in County Championship: penultimate appearance had been in 1893)		
57–5	D.H. Robins	27.6.1914	D.H. Robins' XI v Indians, 1971
56–237	W. Clarke	24.12.1798	Notts v England XI, 1855
56–143	W.G. Quaife	17.3.1872	Warwicks v Derbys, 1928
	(and scored a century!)		
56–138	I.M. Balfour Melville	9.3.1854	Scotland v Ireland, 1910
56–90	J.T. Hearne	3.5.1867	Middlesex v Scotland, 1923
56–47	R.E.S. Wyatt	2.5.1901	Free Foresters v Oxford, 1957
56–39	J. Bayley	17.5.1794	MCC v Sussex, 1850
56–24	C.E. De Trafford	21.5.1864	Leics v Sussex, 1920
55–345	J.R. Gunn	19.7.1876	Sir Julien Cahn's XI v S Americans, 1932
55–300	R. Daft	2.11.1835	Notts v Middlesex, 1891
55–294	P.F. Warner	2.10.1873	MCC v Navy, 1929
55–276	H. Elliott	2.11.1891	Derbys v Warwicks, 1947
55–190	D.B. Close	24.2.1931	D.B. Close's XI v New Zealanders, 1986
55–111	W. Beldham	21.3.1766	Godalming, etc v MCC, 1821
55–53	G. Brown	27.4.1783	Sussex v England, 1838

Notes. It should be emphasized that prior to 1837 births cannot be verified at the Birth Registration Office since registration was not compulsory until this time. It may be thought that those born before 1837 should not be included in the list, which is probably incomplete anyway for cricket before 1864, since by no means all cricketers have been positively identified.

Three of the oldest players to have appeared in English first-class cricket, Lord Harris (above), George Hirst (top left) and C.E. De Trafford (top right).

PLAYERS WITH LONG CAREERS IN BRITISH FIRST-CLASS CRICKET

Player	First and Last Appearance	No. Years
W.G. Grace	1865–1908	43
Lord Harris	1870–1911	41
E. Smith	1888–1928	40
A.N. Hornby	1867–1906	39
R.H. Moss	1887–1925	38
G.H. Hirst	1891–1929	38
H.D.G. Leveson Gower	1893–1931	38
D.B. Close	1949–1986	37
C.E. De Trafford	1894–1930	36
S.F. Barnes	1894–1930	36
J.R. Gunn	1896–1932	36
J. Shuter	1874–1909	35
J.T. Hearne	1888–1923	35
P.F. Warner	1894–1929	35

Notes Close does hold one record. It will be seen that he is the only one in the list whose cricket has all been played in the same century.

W.G. Grace does not hold the world record. This belongs to the remarkable C.K. Nayudu, whose first-class début was for the Hindus team in 1916–17; he finally signed off 47 years later in 1963–64

Finally, Close's 1986 appearance was his 786th in first-class cricket, again not a record but high in the list as the next table shows. There is some quite intense disagreement among statisticians and historians as to the status of some pre-1947 matches; the totals which follow are based on my own personal opinions

MOST APPEARANCES IN FIRST-CLASS CRICKET

W. Rhodes	1106
F.E. Woolley	978
W.G. Grace	872
E.H. Hendren	831
J.B. Hobbs	825
G.H. Hirst	824
C.P. Mead	814
F.J. Titmus	792
R. Illingworth	787
D.B. Close	786

Fred Titmus – more appearances than any other player in modern times.

John Shuter (top left), who had already been playing first-class cricket for 21 years in 1895 and 'Plum' Warner (above), whose career had just begun.

1 9 8 7

GRAEME POLLOCK HANGS UP HIS BAT

The Currie Cup was presented when the first English team toured South Africa in 1888–89 and was awarded to Kimberley for their efforts in defeating and then drawing with the Tourists. Their feats lose some of their gloss when one realizes that they had 18 players against the more usual 11 in the English side, but in the context of cricket in Southern Africa at the time they were estimable performances, well worthy of the lovely new trophy donated by Scottish shipowner and philanthropist Sir Donald Currie. Two years later Transvaal successfully challenged the holders and the Currie Cup quickly replaced the soon-defunct Champion Bat Tournament as the accepted championship of South Africa.

The first major batting 'milestone' was passed in 1910–11, when Transvaal's Louis Tancred, one of a family of first-class cricketers, completed 1,000 runs in the competition during an innings of 85 against Griqualand West at Durban. Tancred remained the only four-figure batsman in the competition until December 16, 1920, when H.W. Taylor emulated the feat during an innings of 150 for Natal v Orange Free State at Durban; amazingly, a matter of minutes later his partner in a stand of 164, Dave Nourse, also reached four figures. 'Dave', who was seemingly ignorant of the fact that when he was born in Surrey in 1878 his parents wished him to be known as 'Arthur William', showed great staying power. He was the first to 2,000, in 1923–24, and then further distinguished himself by being the first to 3,000 runs a few weeks short of his 52nd birthday in December, 1929. During the next competition in 1931–32, Dave Nourse actually opposed his son Dudley and in January 1951 the youngster became the first to pass 4,000 runs in the Currie Cup.

An increase in the fixture list has seen subsequent 'milestones' being more frequently passed. Ali Bacher, South Africa's last internationally recognized skipper, became the first to 5,000 runs in 1973–74, the season after passing Nourse's old record total. Barry Richards became the first to 6,000 runs in 1975–76; the next season he was passed by Graeme Pollock and this marvellous left-hander has since remained dominant. In 1977–78 he was the first to 7,000 runs and he remains the only batsman to pass 8,000 (1978–79), 9,000 (1979–80), 10,000 (1981–82), 11,000 (1983–84) and 12,000 (1985–86) runs in the competition. The table shows that his lead is virtually unassailable, at least for the foreseeable future. The first bowler to take 100 wickets in the Currie Cup was Jimmie Sinclair, a fine pace bowler and mighty hitter. Sinclair passed this 'milestone' playing for Transvaal v Eastern Province at Port Elizabeth in April, 1903; Sinclair's 13 wickets in the game won the match and the Currie Cup for his side.

Sinclair, who died tragically young, was sadly soon forgotten. The 200-wicket mark was not passed until 1952–53, and then it was done by another fine player never given his just desserts. Jack Waddington made his first-class début for Griqualand West in 1934 aged 15 and remains the youngest player in South African first-class cricket. In 1952–53 he took his 200th wicket against Transvaal, and was the first to 300 playing for Griquas against NE Transvaal at Pretoria in 1958–59. Waddington's total of 317 remained a record until overtaken by M.J. Procter in 1976–77, yet this fine slow bowler never played a Test and his death in 1985 went unnoticed for nearly a year afterwards.

The record has lately been dominated by Vintcent van der Bijl. The big Natal paceman, who tragically missed Test cricket, was first to 400 wickets, in 1979–80, and in 1981–82 became the first

LEADING CURRIE CUP RUN-SCORERS (6000+ Runs)

Player	Mtchs	Inns	N.O.	Runs	H.S.	Av'ge	100s
R.G. Pollock	157	261	34	12409	233	54.66	34
E.J. Barlow	122	217	11	7881	212	38.25	20
B.A. Richards	79	140	15	7551	219	60.40	26
P.N. Kirsten	106	187	14	7178	204★	41.49	18
S.J. Cook	107	186	18	7168	201★	42.66	18
H.R. Fotheringham	110	179	16	6676	184	40.95	15
K.A. McKenzie	122	188	21	6076	188	36.38	12
C.P. Wilkins	114	207	8	6022	150	30.26	8

Barry Richards, top of the all-time averages in the Currie Cup.

Graeme Pollock, in a class of his own in South African cricket.

LEADING CURRIE CUP WICKET-TAKERS (300+ Wickets)

Player	Mtchs	Runs	Wkts	Av'ge	B/B	5 I	10 M
V.A.P. van der Bijl	109	9395	572	16.42	8–35	36	9
M.J. Procter	107	8690	461	18.85	9–71	26	10
A.J. Kourie	106	8345	378	22.07	8–113	21	3
G.S. Le Roux	74	6496	337	19.27	7–40	16	2
R.W. Hanley	82	6321	323	19.56	7–31	17	3
C.E.B. Rice	122	6137	320	19.17	7–62	8	1
D.L. Hobson	90	8661	319	27.15	9–64	18	5
E.J. Barlow	122	6881	317	21.70	7–24	10	1
J.E. Waddington	59	6896	317	21.75	9–105	32	8

and so far only bowler to take 500 Currie Cup wickets. The table places him more than 200 ahead of Alan Kourie, the leading current player and he appears to be nearly as unassailable as Pollock.

Vintcent Van der Bijl, still adding to his impressive total of Currie Cup wickets.

JAVED CHASES A PLACE IN PAKISTAN TOP THREE

Only three Pakistani batsmen have exceeded 25,000 runs in first-class cricket while the same three are also their country's leading first-class century scorers. The list is as follows:

LEADING PAKISTANI RUN-SCORERS

Player	Inns	No.	Runs	H.S.	Av'ge	100s
Zaheer Abbas	747	89	34289	274	52.11	107
Mushtaq Mohammad	843	104	31091	303★	42.07	72
Majid Khan	700	62	27444	241	43.01	73

Among current players only Javed Miandad appears to have any chance of approaching these figures in the foreseeable future, but at 23,990 runs and 63 centuries he still has some way to go, while his future in English cricket is somewhat doubtful.

Javed Miandad, still in pursuit of Zaheer.
Top Majid Khan, still safe in third place.

ONE MORE RECORD FOR AMISS?

These records were computed from the 1890 season, when the County Championship was officially recognized by the counties themselves, but even if earlier matches had been taken into account the tables would have been unchanged for both batting and bowling. Certainly the Press had been awarding a 'Champion County' accolade for many years before 1890, as their colleagues in the various Australian colonies had been doing before the institution of the Sheffield Shield, but I feel that Championship records which take into account performances only since the formalization of the competition have more relevance.

With regard to the county career records, the last batting record was established in 1979 when Glamorgan's Alan Jones overtook the legendary Emrys Davies; prior to that no county batting records had changed hands since 1959 when Don Kenyon took over the No.1 spot for Worcestershire from 'Doc'

Gibbons. No bowling record has been broken since 1975, when Fred Titmus took the lead for Middlesex from J.T. Hearne. Several records have stood for more than half a century and, frankly, most of them seem unbeatable. However, at the start of the 1987 season Warwickshire's Dennis Amiss required 1,129 runs to overtake W.G. Quaife; this was to be Amiss's last season so he will never have another chance. Another veteran, Keith Fletcher, needed 1,749 runs to take the Essex record but all the other batting records seem inviolate. One was disappointed to find Geoff Cook still more than 10,000 short of the Northants record while Harold Gimblett's distinctly beatable-looking Somerset record is also safe for the foreseeable future.

In bowling the situation is much worse. John Lever is 231 short of the Essex record – a target which must seem almost Everest-like to that admirable left-arm veteran. No other county has anyone anywhere near a position to challenge.

So, go to it Dennis Amiss. One final 'milestone' for you!

MOST RUNS FOR EACH COUNTY IN COUNTY CHAMPIONSHIP

County	Player	Inns	N.O.	Runs	Av'ge	Seasons
Derbys	D. Smith	682	57	19575	31.21	1927–52
Essex	P.A. Perrin	846	82	27703	36.26	1896–1928
Glamorgan	A. Jones	1000	63	30704	32.76	1957–83
Gloucs	W.R. Hammond	619	66	31344	56.67	1922–46
Hants	C.P. Mead	1117	157	46268	48.19	1906–36
Kent	F.E. Woolley	1121	62	43703	41.26	1906–38
Lancs	E. Tyldesley	782	87	31903	45.90	1909–36
Leics	L.G. Berry	968	46	27942	30.30	1924–51
Middlesex	E.H. Hendren	851	110	37418	50.49	1907–37
Northants	D. Brookes	820	63	26627	35.17	1934–59
Notts	G. Gunn	887	73	29522	36.26	1902–32
Somerset	H. Gimblett	568	29	19966	37.04	1935–54
Surrey	J.B. Hobbs	860	69	38707	48.93	1905–34
Sussex	J.G. Langridge	866	57	30340	37.50	1928–55
Warwicks	W.G. Quaife	1018	161	31469	36.71	1895–1928
Worcs	D. Kenyon	969	48	31375	34.06	1946–67
Yorks	H. Sutcliffe	721	74	32814	50.71	1919–39

MOST WICKETS FOR EACH COUNTY IN COUNTY CHAMPIONSHIP

County	Player	Runs	Wkts	Av'ge	Seasons
Derbys	H.L. Jackson	27144	1578	17.20	1947–63
Essex	M.S. Nichols	32131	1518	21.16	1924–39
Glamorgan	D.J. Shepherd	41978	2012	20.86	1950–72
Gloucs	C.W.L. Parker	58336	3022	19.30	1905–35
Hants	D. Shackleton	46070	2542	18.12	1948–69
Kent	A.P. Freeman	54543	3151	17.30	1914–36
Lancs	J.B. Statham	25537	1683	15.17	1950–68
Leics	W.E. Astill	46369	2029	22.85	1906–39
Middlesex	F.J. Titmus	46881	2170	21.60	1949–82
Northants	E.W. Clark	22463	1048	21.43	1922–47
Notts	T.G. Wass	30790	1517	20.29	1897–1920
Somerset	J.C. White	37184	2082	17.85	1909–37
Surrey	T. Richardson	27371	1531	17.87	1892–1904
Sussex	M.W. Tate	35415	2019	17.54	1912–37
Warwicks	W.E. Hollies	42826	2105	20.34	1932–57
Worcs	R.T.D. Perks	47931	2009	23.85	1930–55
Yorks	W. Rhodes	48911	3112	15.71	1898–1930

Dennis Amiss – yet another record within his grasp.